The Portuguese City of Braga during the Modern Era

Landscape and identity from the
late Middle Ages to the Enlightenment

Gustavo Portocarrero

BAR International Series 1928
2009

Published in 2016 by
BAR Publishing, Oxford

BAR International Series 1928

The Portuguese City of Braga during the Modern Era

ISBN 978 1 4073 0410 6

BAR Publishing is the trading name of British Archaeological Reports (Oxford) Ltd.
British Archaeological Reports was first incorporated in 1974 to publish the BAR
Series, International and British. In 1992 Hadrian Books Ltd became part of the BAR
group. This volume was originally published by Archaeopress in conjunction with
British Archaeological Reports (Oxford) Ltd / Hadrian Books Ltd, the Series principal
publisher, in 2009. This present volume is published by BAR Publishing, 2016.

Printed in England

BAR
PUBLISHING

BAR titles are available from:

	BAR Publishing
	122 Banbury Rd, Oxford, OX2 7BP, UK
EMAIL	info@barpublishing.com
PHONE	+44 (0)1865 310431
FAX	+44 (0)1865 316916
	www.barpublishing.com

ACKNOWLEDGEMENTS

This book is an adaptation of a PhD thesis defended at the University of Wales, Lampeter, in 2008. It would have not been possible, if not for the help and collaboration of a number of persons to whom I'd like to express here my thanks.

First of all, I would like to thank my supervisors, David Austin and Fernando António Baptista Pereira, for all their valuable support and guidance.

I would also also to thank the following persons for their informations on Braga's history: Eduardo Pires de Oliveira, Rui Maurício, Ana Maria Magalhães de Sousa Pereira, Luís Costa, Luís Fontes, Maria da Assunção Jácome de Vasconcelos and Henrique Barreto Nunes.

Finally, I would like to thank the following persons for having authorised me to research in private archives: Cónego Pio (Archive of Braga's See), Mário Moura (Archive of the Confraternity of S. Vicente), Alberto Quintas (Archive of the Confraternity of Santa Cruz) and Maria José Proença (Archive of the Confraternity of the Venerável Ordem Terceira de S. Francisco).

CONTENTS

1 – Introduction 1

2 – The study of Modern Era's Portuguese cities 3

3 – An alternative approach: landscape and identity 6

4 – Sources 9

5 – Braga in the late 15th century 12

6 – The New Braga (I) 18

7 – The New Braga (II) 27

8 – The Catholic Reformation 34

9 – A looming crisis 40

10 – An identity crisis 46

11 – A fragmented identity 51

12 – The New Jerusalem 59

13 – Conclusion 66

Bibliography 68

Figures 78

List of figures

Fig. 1 – Map of Portugal.

Fig. 2 – Braga c. 1500 (map adapted fromTeixeira and Valla 1999: 114).

Fig. 3 – Braga in 1530 (map adapted from Teixeira and Valla 1999: 115).

Fig. 4 – Braga in 1725 (map adapted from Teixeira and Valla 1999: 116).

Fig. 5 – Area of Medieval Braga (single line) superimposed on the area of Roman Braga (double line) (adapted from Bandeira 2000: 61).

Fig. 6 – Braga in an image of 1594 (source: Georg Braun, *Civitatis Orbis Terrarum*, volume V, fl. 3).

Fig. 7 – Medieval T/O map (source: St Isidorus, *Etymologiarum sive originum*, lib XX).

Fig. 8 – Braga in an image of c. 1694 (source: *Forum*, **15/16**, p. 23).

Fig. 9 – Braga in an image of c. 1757 (source: Biblioteca Nacional da Ajuda).

Fig. 10 – Section of R. Nova in the 1750 map. The Church of the Mercy House is on the lower left corner. (source: Mapa das Ruas de Braga).

Fig. 11 – The main façade of the Cathedral (author's collection).

Fig. 12 – A view of the main chapel of the Cathedral (author's collection).

Fig. 13 – Campo de Santiago: in the foreground the 1625 fountain, in the background the medieval tower (author's collection).

Fig. 14 – A view of the 15th century aisle of the Episcopal palace (author's collection).

Fig. 15 – Partial view of R. Direita in the 1750 map (source: Mapa das Ruas de Braga).

Fig. 16 – Some noble houses in R. S. João in the 1750 map (source: Mapa das Ruas de Braga).

Fig. 17 – The cross built by D. Diogo de Sousa in front of Gate S. Marcos (author's collection).

Fig. 18 – Church of S. Paulo (author's collection).

Fig. 19 – Decorated tiles of the early 17th century in the church of the convent of Salvador (source: author's collection).

Fig. 20 – The 1594 fountain that was built in Campo de Santana (author's collection).

Fig. 21 – A view of the square in front of the entrance of the Episcopal palace: in the front the 1723 fountain in the back the late 16th century colonnade (author's collection).

Fig. 22 – The obelisk that was in Campo da Vinha (author's collection).

Fig. 23 – The 1621 cross that was built in front of Gate Nova (author's collection).

Fig. 24 – The main façade of the church of Santa Cruz (author's collection).

Fig. 25 – The main façade of the church of S. Vítor (author's collection).

Fig. 26 – Decorated tiles from the church of S. Vítor (author's collection).

Fig. 27 – The main façade of church S. Vicente (author's collection).

Fig. 28 – The main façade of the church of the Oratory (author's collection).Fig. 29 – Houses in R. Souto (source: Mapa das Ruas de Braga).

Fig. 29 – Houses in R. Souto (source: Mapa das Ruas de Braga).

Fig. 30 – Church of S. Frutuoso (author's collection).

Fig. 31 – The arcade in the 1750 map (source: Mapa das Ruas de Braga).

Fig. 32 – The 1715 statue representing Braga that was on top of the arcade (author's collection).

Fig. 33 – Chapel of Nossa Senhora da Guadalupe (author's collection).

Fig. 34 – Image of the Sanctuary of the Good Jesus in an 18th century image (source: Luís Costa).

Fig. 35 – Pyramid-shape throne in the main altar of the church of S. Vítor (author's collection)

Fig. 36 – The sanctuary of Good Jesus from Campo de Santana (author's collection).

Abbreviations

IAN/TT - Instituto do Arquivo Nacional/Torre do Tombo

BNL - Biblioteca Nacional de Lisboa

BNA - Biblioteca Nacional da Ajuda

ADB - Arquivo Distrital de Braga

AMB - Arquivo Municipal de Braga

ASB - Arquivo da Sé de Braga

AISV - Arquivo da Irmandade de S. Vicente (Braga)

AISC - Arquivo da Irmandade de Santa Cruz (Braga)

AVOTSF - Arquivo da Venerável Ordem Terceira de S. Francisco (Braga)

1

Introduction

The construction of urban identities through the landscape during the Modern Era in Portugal, is an area of historical research which, so far, has been little explored. In this work, I will develop this theme with an emphasis on the city of Braga. This work also seeks to be an alternative to the empiricism that is, presently, common in the studies of the cities of that period. Empiricism is a philosophical theory that assumes that knowledge can be derived through careful observation and cataloguing of phenomena and extrapolating laws from these observations. Western empiricism was built on the idea of a mechanistic universe, something that was to a great degree influenced by Newton's theory that postulated that the world was a machine ruled by abstract laws that could be expressed in mathematical formulas, which, supposedly, were independent of historical circumstances and temporal variations (Taylor 2001: 79). In this way, there is "only one system of the world, and it is governed by immutable universal laws that make natural processes potentially transparent and predictable" (ibid.: 78). The most common image for this system is the clock, a mechanical device made of separate parts, that operate together at near equilibrium under laws that cannot be broken (ibid.: 79). While Newton's concern was primarily with the physical universe, his analysis was widely appropriated to interpret all aspects of society and culture (ibid.). Therefore the reasoning of empiricist historians regarding this vision of the world was that "insofar as human beings are part of such a world, they too are machines controlled by the laws that apply to all other physical bodies" (ibid.). In this way an empiricist history developed, consisting basically of two things: first, the determination of "facts"; second, the establishment of the laws that, supposedly, regulated human society.

There are, however, a number of problems with this perspective in what concerns historical research. One is that research tends to be more source-oriented rather than problem-oriented and it is not surprising that researchers found it extraordinarily difficult to determine when the time for synthesis had arrived (Tosh 2002: 139). Another problem, is that simply describing or placing evidence in its correct temporal sequence tells us nothing about "the relative importance of all these varied factors, or present a comprehensive account of how they interacted with each other" (ibid.: 177). Finally, due to its mechanicist character, it tends to give little value to human agency (Austin 1998: 164; Johnson 1999: 42, 43).

In this work, a more humanistic approach will, instead, be followed. Humanism, in the contemporary world, it is an attitude that attaches primary importance to human beings and to their faculties and actions in the world, as well as to their aspirations and well being. Therefore, the protest of contemporary humanism in relation to empiricism, is its reductionist tendency to construct systems of knowledge, which appear to determine the behaviour of human beings, with people being reduced to robots with little capacity for creative deliberation.

With regard to the structure of this book, it is organised in the following chapters. Chapter 2 is a critical overview of the study of cities as it is presently conducted in Portugal, which tends to follow an empiricist approach. In chapter 3, I delineate an alternative approach to the study of Modern Era cities in Portugal, with a focus on the concepts of identity and landscape. Finally, chapter 4 is a brief overview of the sources that were used in the research on Braga, with a particular focus on maps, documents and standing buildings.

The remaining chapters concern the study of the city of Braga. In chapter 5, there is an analysis of what the city's landscape looked like by the late 15th century and what can be inferred about its identity through it. Chapters 6 and 7 are about the radical changes that took place in the city's identity and landscape in the early 16th century, mainly through the impulse of Archbishop D. Diogo de Sousa. Due to the extent of these changes as well as the qualitative differences that it brought to Braga's space, I have chosen to divide this analysis in two chapters: 6 is about the space of the city proper and 7 is about the outskirts area. Chapter 8 is about the actions that took place in the middle of the 16th century under the initiative of the Church in order to consolidate Braga's catholic identity. Chapter 9 deals mostly with the actions of Fr. Agostinho da Cruz in the late 16th century in order to reaffirm Braga's primate status within the Hispanic Monarchy. Chapter 10 covers the years 1620-1670, a period of strong political and social turmoil, which caused a crisis of identity in Braga. In chapter 11, I argue that this crisis of identity was responsible in the late 17th century for a fragmentation of Braga's identity into smaller ones among its inhabitants. Finally, in chapter 12, I analyse the attempts by Archbishop D. Rodrigo Moura Teles in the early 18th century to create a common identity that again united Braga's inhabitants.

To finish this introduction, since most chapters of this book are about Braga, I think it is useful to provide some general information about its geography and history.

Braga is located in the centre of north-west Portugal (fig. 1), in a valley surrounded by hills, a landscape that is typical of this region. Descriptions of the area written during the Modern Era itself, describe it as being the most fertile and densely populated area of Portugal (Nogueira Silva and Hespanha 1993: 26, 27).

As far as we know at the moment, Braga was founded by the Romans in the late 1st century BC, in the area that lies today between the Cathedral and the River Deste to its south (Martins 2000: 4, 44-5). Its original name was *Bracara Augusta*, with the former being a reference to the people living in that area, the *Bracari*, while the latter is related to the Roman emperor responsible for its foundation, Augustus (ibid.: 3, 4). However, by the Modern Era, it was simply known by the diminutive Braga. The city had a considerable importance during the Roman period, being the capital city of the Roman province of Galicia, which then comprised all the north-western area of the Iberian peninsula (ibid.: 7).

With the German invasions in the 5th century, the city became the capital of the Suebian kingdom, whose borders roughly coincided with the north-western area of the Iberian Peninsula. After the Muslim invasion in the early 8th century, the city lost much of its importance and its population since it became a war zone. Only by the late 11th century when the border between the Christian and Muslim kingdoms was considerably to the south of Braga, was the city able to reach some stability. A new city developed around the area of the Cathedral, thus incorporating only the north-eastern part of the former Roman city in the medieval urban area (fig. 5), with the rest being abandoned (ibid.: 11). The medieval city occupied, therefore, a smaller area than the Roman one.

With the conversion of the Roman Empire to Christianity in the 4th century, Braga became head of an archdiocese, having obtained the status of primate of Hispania and the right to perform a specific rite (Bandeira 2000a: 59). Regarding the term "Hispania" it may be useful to note here that this was the name by which the Iberian Peninsula was then known. It is thus a largely geographical term. This must not be confused with the term "Spain", which derives from the former and refers to a political entity which resulted from the union of the kingdoms of Castile and Aragon in the late 15th century. Therefore, in this book, I am using the term "Hispania" when referring to the geographical entity and "Spain" when referring to the political entity.

This primate status was very prestigious to the city and it was something that it always attempted to keep. However, the city of Toledo also vied for it and there was always a dispute between them as to who had the superior claim; a dispute that still remains today. Needless to say, Portugal always supported Braga's pretensions, while Spain Toledo's ones. This rivalry between Braga and Toledo can be traced back to the Germanic period, when both cities were, respectively, capitals of the Suebian and Visigothic kingdoms, which were the two political entities of the peninsula competing for its full dominion.

The extent of Braga's archdiocese was considerable, covering most of Northern Portugal by the late 15th century (Mea 1998: 413-414). Only the area around the city of Porto, to the southwest, was outside it. In the middle of the 16th century, Braga lost control over the north-eastern area of its archdiocese, which became a new diocese centred in the city of Miranda do Douro (ibid.: 416). Nevertheless, Braga still retained a large hinterland, fertile and densely populated, factors that gave a considerable importance to this archdiocese.

Until the end of the Modern Era, Braga was also head of a temporal dominion of considerable dimensions in Northern Portugal over which it had a strong jurisdiction, thus having ample autonomy within Portugal, something that the Crown recurrently attempted to counter, albeit with little success (Bandeira 2000a: 80-82)

Finally, it is useful to notice that the city of Braga had one unique characteristic that distinguished it from many other Portuguese cities during the Modern Era: a clergyman, the archbishop, ruled it. The archbishops were helped by a Chapter – body of canons under control of the archbishops that assisted them and ruled the city when they were absent – as well as by a City Hall – over which the archbishops had a strong influence and whose members belonged to the secular aristocracy of the city. The strong presence of the Catholic Church in Braga gave it a key role in influencing the city's landscape and identity.

2

The study of Modern Era's Portuguese cities

There are several studies on Portuguese cities from this period[1], which, in my view, can be roughly divided in two approaches. One, influential within documentary history, privileges the study of structural spheres of urban life such as economy, society, administration and demography (e.g. Ribeiro da Silva 1994). Within any of these spheres, other themes can also be considered; for example, Fernando Castelo-Branco in his research on 17th century Lisbon (1990), when analysing the social milieu, divides it into official ceremonies, religious processions, bullfights, academies, etc. The problem of this approach is that it "compartmentalises human experience into boxes" (Tosh 2002: 35) being difficult to understand how all these elements interacted with each other.

The other approach is urbanism and it is exclusively concerned with the study of the physical space of cities, being mostly practised by archaeologists and, in particular, art historians. It is the character of this approach that I am now going to analyse in the remainder of this chapter.

In the last decades several studies on this field have been made either focusing on single cities (e.g. França 1962; Correia 1984; Ferreira Alves 1988; Câmara 1989; Carreira 1989; Murteira 1994; Alexandre Rodrigues 1995; Conceição, 1997; Ferrão Afonso 2000) or on general synthesis (e.g. Rossa 1995; Teixeira and Valla 1999). Let's, then, see what seems to me to be the main lines of these studies.

First of all, what do these studies mean by the word "urbanism"? The meaning of a word is not obvious: it results from an association with others. In the case of studies on urbanism, there is a noticeable and systematic association with the idea of order. Urbanism is represented as being about bringing order to the city. But, what sort of order is that? How does one recognise it? Here, enters another word: regularity. But, what is regularity? In these studies it is only one thing: a geometrical grid with straight lines perpendicular to each other. But, why should urbanism be organised along straight lines? Because they are the result of an "intellectual construction" (Teixeira and Valla 1999: 13; my translation), that is, they are rational. In order to make the meaning of these words more explicit they are usually articulated with others along binary oppositions: planning with organic, the latter meaning "the spontaneous aspects of a city" (Rossa 1995: 234; my translation), and, obviously, being spontaneous it is not rational: there isn't a pause for an intellectual construction. And, without the latter, there isn't a geometrical grid: the city becomes irregular, without order, chaotic.

While this association between grid and reason sounds "obvious" and "logical" for these researchers, it can be argued, however, that this is all common sense, that is, giving meaning to something using one's own experience as the only model (Johnson 1999: 6). This is because they are working within a framework developed by Enlightenment thinkers in the 18th century that "saw in the grid a figure of universal reason" (Taylor 2001: 30). Take, for example, the Swiss architect Le Corbusier to whom straight lines and right angles characterised human existence, the ability to follow a straight line being what distinguished humans from animals (ibid.: 26). Within this rationale, humans, in order to be considered as such and not as "primitives" or "beasts", must follow "the strict discipline of the grid through which the rule of reason is secured. As feelings and emotions are controlled, order is wrought from disorder" (ibid.: 27). Researchers on urbanism, by forgetting that they are working within an ideology and assuming the universality of these principles, end up assuming an ethnocentric view that devalues or excludes everything else deemed different from the grid. More, straight lines built before the Enlightenment are seen within an anachronistic viewpoint, as there is an implicit assumption that they are the result of reason bringing order to chaos. No straight lines, then no reason and no urbanism – only an organic chaos. With the geometry inherent in the grid, the city becomes therefore a machine (ibid.).

Researchers on Portuguese urbanism, usually consider four periods in the development of a "rational order" in the city of the Modern Era: the late Middle Ages (the condition before the Modern Era), the Renaissance (late 15th/16th centuries), the Baroque (17th and first half of the 18th centuries) and the Enlightenment (second half of the 18th century). So, for example, looking to the late Middle Ages city (e.g. Rossa 1995: 246-260; Teixeira and Valla 1999: 25-46) there is an identification and description of individual features such as the wall (built for defensive reasons and to delimit the space of the city's jurisdiction), the castle (the lordship focus), the city hall (the

---

[1] The word "city" is used in this book to designate the urban phenomena in general. Notice that during this period the most common word to designate urban areas in Portugal was "vila", being the word "city" used only for those "vilas" that were heads of a bishoprics.

administrative centre), the church (the religious centre), the types of houses (the residential areas), the yard (where the market took place), the pillory (where justice was applied), the hospitals, wells and fountains (the public utilities), and the areas where religious minorities lived. As to the road network connecting all these elements, if it was a city built after the 13th century it would usually have a "regular" form creating long rectangular blocks; if it was older, then it would have a more curvilinear form. Also, in all cities there was always one road (sometimes two) – the *rua direita* (straight road) – along which the most important urban buildings could usually be found. As it can be seen, with this sort of approach the purpose is to identify and describe within an empiricist framework the individual elements (religious, economic, military) and their connections that allow the city to *function* as a machine. One is dealing here with a de-humanising narrative that sees humans as robots orderly executing their activities (praying, shopping, working). This common sense approach based on present-day ideas ignores the possibility that those who inhabited these cities at that time could have seen them in different ways.

Not everything was well, however, in this city-machine and researchers point to the Renaissance as the beginning of an important effort to "rationalise" the city and provide "better" living conditions for their inhabitants (e.g. Câmara 1989: 33; Carreira 1989: 21; Rossa 1995: 260-266; Teixeira and Valla 1999: 83-120;). One of the most developed topics is the nature of the medieval "organic chaos" that existed along the roads: the upper floors of the houses projected over them, darkening them; shops on the ground floor extended onto them; roads themselves were narrow and curvilinear. According to scholars the main consequence of this was that it made traffic difficult. In order to solve the problem, in the Renaissance the façades of the houses were straightened. Thanks to these "rational" measures the city-machine, whose communication network was getting obstructed, could continue to work smoothly. It was also in this period that urban treatises, based on those of Classical Rome (especially Vitruvius), began to circulate. They favoured a city organised along a strict orthogonal grid with a central square where the main buildings could be found and with residential buildings of the same size and form. Despite the availability of such "rational" models, their application was not immediate, as it wasn't easy to change overnight the medieval fabric; the application of these treatises had, then, to be "pragmatic", according to circumstances (e.g. Rossa 1995: 263): a straight road here, a square there, a grid over there. Notice, however, that the use of the ideas of these treatises is seen only through their contribution to the formation of a "rational" city; that other motives could be at work is not considered.

As for the Baroque period, one looks here to a consolidation of the forms that emerged in the previous period (Correia 1989; Rossa 1995: 270, 292-296; Teixeira and Valla 1999: 149-214). Other changes are also observable at this period in the city form: there is a multiplication of churches and convents and several coastal and border cities were fortified with new walls built with bastions (something that the Renaissance treaties already suggested). While generic causes (the Catholic Reformation and wars with Spain) are mentioned for these changes, what matters in these works is to put them into a functional perspective: problems within the religious and defensive spheres were responsible for them. In this way the city-machine could continue to work.

An interesting exception to the empiricist and mechanistic character of the studies of this period are some iconological and sociological studies that deal with the attempts of some social groups to use some city spaces to stage ceremonies to affirm their power. Examples include the Crown's actions in Lisbon (Baptista Pereira 1994, Pimentel 2002), but also Lisbon's city officials' actions against the Crown (Kubler 1988: 110-133).

Finally comes the last period, the Enlightenment, when the city form finally assumes a strict grid-like character (França 1962; Correia 1984; Rossa 1995: 296-315; Teixeira and Valla 1999: 285-314). In this period, urbanism reaches its zenith. Reason prevailed over organic chaos.

All these researchers (except those working within a more iconologic and sociological approach) are working, as we have seen, within an Enlightenment ideology that promotes a mathematical view of reason, which reduces the world to a machine, visible in the figure of the grid. And within this ideology, history is nothing more than progress from an irrational to a rational world (Collingwood n/d: 129), exactly what the researchers on urbanism do when they organise the story of urbanism in neatly arranged periods stretching from a "chaotic" Middle Ages to a "rational" Enlightenment. Yet, what the researchers do is to select some features, "forgetting" or, at least, downplaying others. Notice, for example, that some of the features of the medieval city persisted throughout the Modern Era; Enlightenment urbanism only covers a handful of cities in Portugal, and so on.

A final problem with this sort of research is that there is confusion between the city and urbanism. The city is seen as having an essence valid for all time and space, with a "complex social organisation (…) [visible in the] specialisation of the roles and functions of its inhabitants and spaces" (Rossa 1995: 239; my translation). However, this is again the city-machine model and one that, ironically, reduces the city to a single dimension. More, this model treats the rural world as "simple" space, but this is an old ideology (cf. Cosgrove 1993): it is as complex as any space. Within urbanism studies, the character of each city is seen solely through the changes of its form, yet, as I have just argued, the periods identified by researchers are completely artificial. The complexity of each city is simply reduced to a comment on how well its form at a certain moment fits within the irrational-rational continuum. There are even a few empiricist attempts at determining a "law" to explain the character of Portuguese cities: they are the result of an articulation of planned and organic approaches (Teixeira and Valla 1999: 316). Yet, there is nothing special about this affirmation as the same happens in all European cities, as one can see in works on European urbanism (e.g. Burke 1975: 78, Goitia 1982: 119).

To conclude, in my view, urbanism studies are, at present, mostly empiricist narratives organised in such a way as to give an image of what a city is supposed to be within a framework influenced by Enlightenment ideas. How people constructed their urban identities through the landscape in the Modern Era is something that remains largely unexplored.

3

An alternative approach: landscape and identity

After reviewing the limitations of empiricism in the study of Portuguese cities of the Modern Era, it is now time to develop an alternative model centred on the concepts of landscape and identity.

With respect to landscape, it is important to notice that that this is "a singularly complex and difficult concept. The word has multiple meanings and its precise significance has shifted repeatedly" (Thomas 2001: 166). Within empiricism, the landscape is seen as geometric space where what matters is to identify and plot correctly all material findings in order to build a picture of what it looked like at a certain time (Tilley 1994: 9; Thomas 2001: 167). For example, the representations of the city of Braga in the 16th and 17th centuries are seen as "distorted" and with "little rigour" (Bandeira 1994: 26, 27; 2000a: 47) as they don't present the city's "real", i.e. geometric, physiognomy.

Yet, other approaches to landscape can also be considered. For example, Preucel and Hodder distinguish between four different approaches (1996: 32-33). The first is termed "landscape as environments", which "involve the reconstruction of specific environments. They deal with what was out there that people had to live in and adapt to" (ibid.: 32). Another way of saying this is that these studies deal with what is usually called "natural" phenomena.

A second approach is termed "landscape as system". These studies focus on the placement of sites within an overall pattern of site and off-site activities. This sort of approach is "well suited to studies of economics and social structure since there is generally some relationship between the ways in which sites are distributed and the economic and political systems within which they exist" (ibid.: 33).

The third approach is termed "landscape as power". Here, landscape is regarded as being "ideologically manipulated in relations of domination and resistance. There is an emphasis on contradictions and conflict that emerge in the cognised environment and are embedded in power relations" (ibid.). For example, conquest frequently involves the destruction of history though obliteration of the monuments of the vanquished, while resistance can be expressed in the destruction of symbols of domination (Knapp and Ashmore 1999: 19).

As for the fourth approach, termed "landscape as experience", the concern is "with how bodies experience the world around them" (Preucel and Hodder 1996: 33). It is the space of sensory experience (smell, hearing) and bodily movement (front/back, within reach/beyond reach). This approach is very recent, dating back to the 1990's with works such as those of Christopher Tilley (e.g. 1994).

On the other side, if one looks to how other authors order landscape approaches, one finds differences. For example, Richard Muir also considers as valid a "landscape as symbol" approach, where the focus is on the identification of the symbolic meanings and messages contained in the landscape (1999: 212). This approach, strongly influenced by iconology, can be divided into two variants. One of them, more recent and developed by cultural geographers, considers landscape as a "cultural image, a pictorial way of representing, structuring or symbolising surroundings" (Daniels and Cosgrove 1988: 1). As Cosgrove says in his influential work *The Palladian Landscape: geographical change and its cultural representation in sixteenth-century Italy*, landscape "represents a way in which certain classes have signified themselves and their world through their imagined relationship with nature, and through which they have underlined and communicated their own social role and that of others with respect to external nature" (1994: 15). So, in this variant, through the deployment of imagery, symbols tend to be used allusively and with ambiguity where they are subject to social negotiation within political strategies. The other variant concerns the use of symbolic structures (such as forms, colours, numbers) to interpret material culture. Unlike the other variant, this one is more specific and restricted to clear and closed formal interpretations. This is an older tradition, as it can be seen from works such as *Augustinus Mundus Symbolicus*, published in 1681 by Philippus and Erath Picinellus, which catalogued the received Catholic interpretation of symbols. In this book, the interpretation of symbols was made through the consultation of certain works such as those of Louis Réau (1955), George Ferguson (1966), Jean Chevalier and Alain Gheerbrant (1994) and Mircea Eliade (2000, 2002).

As can be seen, all these approaches have in common an idea of the "whole" though they diverge on the interpretation of what that is. This instability of meaning is quite useful if one assumes that there isn't a unique way to do research as in empiricism; therefore it is possible to articulate creatively these and other landscape approaches according to specific circumstances of research. Landscape offers thus an integrating framework for historical research, as a context which links dispersed human acts (Thomas 2001: 175). Such a framework also allows us to question ethnocentrisms, as it can accommodate activities that modern reason would tend to assign to separate categories. So, while contemporary Westerners tend to exclude spiritual matters both spatially and temporally, it is important to notice that in many cultures religious observances and other rituals are likely to fit into and inform the mundane pattern (ibid.). This observation is particularly relevant for the study of Modern Era Braga where a religious mentality, and not a mechanistic reason, was dominant. What this means is that in the study of Braga, attention must also be given to sacred geographies. The concept of sacred geography "encompasses those aspects of the landscape that are associated with religion, ritual, magic and the occult (…). A recurring theme in this sort of studies is landscape imagery and symbolism, whereby both natural and created features are examined in terms of their cosmological significance" (Parkes 2006: 3). This approach was pioneered by the works of Mircea Eliade (2002 [1957]) and here it is common to find concepts absent in empiricist analysis, such as *axis mundi*, cosmos or chaos, and which will be analyzed more thoroughly in the next chapters of the book. Much has been written about this by prehistorians and anthropologists, as well as cultural geographers (Coggins 1982; Townsend 1982; Carmichael et al 1994; Tilley 1994; Lahiri 1996; Parcero Oubina et al. 1998; Knapp and Ashmore 1999; Bradley 2000; Smith and Brookes 2001; Boivin 2004), but the innovating work on this theme in relation to towns and cities was Wheatley's *Pivot of the Four Quarters* on Chinese cities (1971). Studies on cities of other cultures can also be found, such as Insoll (2004) and Parkes (2006) on the Islamic city. However, it is interesting to notice that when it comes to Western cities, either in Portugal or in Europe (e.g. Russell 1972; Burke 1975: 78, Goitia 1982: 119; Schofield and Vince 2003), these elements are not usually taken into consideration and it is the mechanicist view of the city that predominates, something related to the contemporary Western vision of the world that divides it into a rational West and an irrational Other. One of the objectives of this book is, therefore, to introduce the study of sacred geography to Western cities of the Modern Era. Everything, thus, acts in, and is part of, landscape.

Some authors, however, question the commensurability of some of these approaches (e.g Preucel and Hodder 1996: 34); yet, it must be noticed that the concept of landscape as an integrated whole is not the same as a totality, where things are connected in only one way; wholes (or systems), like landscapes, are provisional, they are the result of specific circumstances, and, as such, a multiplicity of them can be constructed.

Landscape is better seen through the metaphor of a network, where a multiplicity of elements (nodes) interact at different scales (buildings, roads, neighbourhoods,

cities, regions, etc) influencing one upon another in a limitless and never-ending process. This quite contrasts with empiricism and its mechanical view of the world where what matters is to identify all the "nuts and bolts" of the machine and place them properly in order to know how it works.

If one accepts the idea that landscapes are relational and not fixed, then it follows that different persons and groups give meaning to the landscape in different ways. And here one enters into the domain of identity. The distinctive position of a person in relation to its landscape results from the simultaneous interplay of aspects such as gender, class, ethnicity, sexuality, age, cultural tradition and personal life history (Thomas 2001: 176). Therefore, the same location can be a different place for two different people, or it can simply not "exist" to one of them. It is all dependent on one's identity.

Identity is the pivotal concept that is going to be used in this book in order to give meaning to the changes observable in Braga's landscape throughout the Modern era.

Regarding the use of the concept of identity in this book I will closely follow the scheme provided by Kathryn Woodward (1997). Identity is about belonging: it marks the ways in which we are the same as others who share a certain position and the ways in which we are different from those who do not. It gives us, then, a location in the world and presents a link between us and the society in which we live. Laying claim to an identity is often defined by difference, by the marking of "us" and "them". Sameness and difference are marked both symbolically through representational systems and socially through the inclusion or exclusion of certain groups of people. Often, identity is seen through an essentialist lens, as if it was something fixed and unchanging. Sometimes these claims are based on Nature, such as kinship in some versions of ethnicity; in other cases they are based on a version of the past which is represented as an unchanging truth. In this book, however, identity is seen in a non-essentialist way: it is a social construction, a product of an intersection of different political and cultural discourses and particular histories, always changing in time and space. So, besides differences there is also a concern with common or shared characteristics and the circumstances of their construction. Moreover, each individual and group are part of multiple identities, which are not unified and sometimes contradict each other. This may force the marking of some differences in order to obscure others or a negotiation in order to allow them to be both equal and different.

Identity crosses with landscape as it needs a material context, that is, a space and a place, in order to be lived (Austin 1998: 168). For example, a family needs a house, a religious community needs a sacred place, etc.

Also relevant to the study of identity is the role of memory, since it helps to sustain identity. Landscape maps memory, fixing social and individual histories in space (Knapp and Ashmore 1999: 13). Since memory is more constructed than retrieved, landscape is used in order to affirm "mythic and moral principles for a society, reminders of triumphs and catastrophes in the social past" (ibid.). A good example of this complex relationship is Simon Schama's work on the appropriation of pre-modern elements of the landscape concerning the veneration of nature by contemporary society (1995).

As all humans living in Modern Era cities belonged to a multiplicity of social identities, the city then became "an arena in which individuals attempted to shape their personal fates within often rigid constraints of custom, law and social expectation. The tensions between individuals, groups and communal needs and aspirations lay at the heart of all social interactions in the early modern city" (Friedrichs 1995: 14, 15). How Braga's inhabitants shaped their urban identity throughout this period through landscape is, then, what is going to be analysed in chapters 5-12 of this book.

It is useful to notice that works on identities in Modern Era Portugal usually focus on a Portuguese identity (Bethencourt and Curto 1991; Nogueira Silva and Hespanha 1993) and not on the construction of identities in cities.

To finish this chapter, I'd like to make a couple of comments regarding the methodology followed in my research. From historical geography, I have taken the methodology of morphology as a way of revealing the sequence and purpose of urban development induced from the plans of cities. The first exponent of this technique in Europe was Conzen with his study of the medieval town of Alnwick (1960). He highlighted among other things the tendency for property boundaries to remain more or less intact and that city walls can leave a lasting imprint on the city plan. While interest in city plans is older and was much discussed before Conzen's seminal work, it was mostly focussed on the classification, taxonomy and hierarchy of urban plans in Europe (e.g. Fleure 1931, Smailes 1953), not fully understanding that these were the end result of undocumented processes which could be revealed by deeper analysis.

4

Sources

The purpose of this chapter is to present an overview of the material sources that were used in the research of this book. They can be divided into three groups: written documents, maps and built space. The chapter finishes with a brief survey of the kind of research that has been done on Braga.

Regarding the first group, I used documents from mostly three institutions: the Chapter, the City Hall and the Fraternities. Regarding the Chapter, the most important source is the notable *Índice dos Prazos do Cabido* (Index of the Rents of the Chapter). This document (henceforth referred to as *Index*) was made in the 1740's during a reorganisation of the c. 100 volumes of the *Prazos do Cabido* (Chapter's Registry) whose documentation goes as far back as the 15th century (Ferreira 1932: 275; Oliveira 1993: 28; Bandeira 2000a: 24, 25). The *Index* is divided into sections organised by roads and in each of it there is an indication of all the houses that the Chapter had there. The houses are ordered by numbers and in each of it a set of elements can be found. So, all rented contracts for each house are indicated in a chronological order with indication of the volume and page of *Prazos do Cabido* where the original contract is. This is very useful as it allows an easy consultation of the original contracts where a description of the house at that time can be found[2]; in this way it is easier to identify changes that were taking place in the structure of the house through time. Sociological elements such as the name of the tenant and his spouse and/or affiliation as well as their socio-economic status can also be found in this *Index*. This allows a better knowledge of both the types of house where members of different social groups lived and the changes in residential patterns through time. This *Index* is complemented with a map of the houses of the city, where those that belonged to the Chapter are indicated with the number with which they are registered in the *Index* (more, below, on this map). Taking into consideration that the Chapter was the main landlord in Braga (about half the houses in 1750 and not much far from that figure in previous periods) with houses throughout the entire city, it is easy to realise how useful this *Index* is in order to better understand social changes that took place in Braga during this period.

As for the City Hall, there is a wealth of documents that reveal several aspects of the city's civic life such as codes of law, minutes and letters exchanged with the archbishop and the Crown. The City Hall was the second largest landlord of Braga and the volumes with the descriptions of those houses constitute an important complement to those that belonged to the Chapter. Yet, unlike the houses of the latter, they were not organised in an *Index* and map, which makes their identification difficult.

Regarding the Fraternities, they were important social actors during most of this period; minutes and statutes of some of the most notable of them have been consulted in order to learn more about their role in the city.

Finally, one must also consider a number of texts that were left by people living during this period such as histories (e.g. Cunha 1634-35; Argote 1732) or diaries (e.g. Thadim 1764; Peixoto 1992 [1790-1808]). Other documentary sources exist in Braga, though my access to them was an indirect one, as it was based in material published by other researchers in their works.

With reference to maps, four of them representing Braga during this period are known. These maps are, within the Portuguese context, exceptional in their detail; only Lisbon is relatively closer in this respect. The earliest is from 1594 (fig. 6) and is usually known as Braun's map as it first appeared in the atlas of world cities (*Civitates Orbis Terrarum*) printed by this editor in the late 16th century. The map, however, seems to have been made by a Portuguese called Manoel Barbosa (Dias 1985). This map, made under the patronage of Archbishop Fr. Agostinho de Jesus, is the first known full representation of the city, presented from a bird's eye view.

The second map (fig. 8) is not dated on the document, but by taking into consideration some of the architectural features which are represented and whose date of construction is known, this has been assigned to somewhere between 1687 and 1694 (Oliveira 1994: 38). However, according to the Acts of the confraternity that administered the church of Santa Cruz, which is shown on the map, it was decided in 1693 to tear down the tower at the back of the church and substitute it with two new ones on the façade (AISC, *Livro Termos Santa Cruz* 1589-1701: 504). Since the map depicts a tower on the façade, c. 1694 seems a more appropriate date for this map.

This map is part of an album with a collection of 39 vistas of Portuguese cities of the 17th century, which

---

[2] Which, in the case of Braga, are quite detailed, covering elements such as measures, type of divisions, number and type of embrasures, type of stairs, type of trees in gardens.

belongs today to an anonymous private collector (Nunes 1994). Its owner, however, allowed the vista of Braga to be published in *Forum* magazine (ibid.). Like the former, the city is also represented from an oblique perspective. It is also important to notice that this map, unlike the others, is a representation of the city by an outsider.

The last two maps are dated from the mid-18th century and have a more accurate representation of space from a mathematical perspective than the previous two. One of them was made c.1757 (fig. 9), since the new building of the City Hall (finished in 1756) at the west side of Campo dos Touros is represented, while the chapel of Nossa Senhora da Torre (built in 1758) close to the Santiago Gate is not mentioned in the list of temples. It is signed by a well-known artist from Braga from that time, André Soares, and it was almost certainly made on the request of Archbishop D. José de Bragança. This map, unlike the one of 1594, was not made to be published, as it is quite large; instead, it was meant to be put on a wall of a room, though it is not known today where it was hanging as it was later moved to the library of Ajuda in Lisbon. Unfortunately, this map has now lost its upper corners; nonetheless, the vast majority of the city is still visible. Like the previous two maps, this one also has an oblique perspective.

Finally, the last and most notable map: the *Mapa das Ruas de Braga* (Map of the Roads of Braga). This map, drafted in 1750 by Priest Ricardo da Rocha under the guidance of the Chapter, is unique in Europe, since it represents the façades of almost all the roads of Braga (fig. 10, for an example). The detail of the houses is remarkable when compared with other maps of that period; moreover, several other architectural features that were on these roads are also present, such as fountains, crosses, walls, etc. The structure of the map is different from the others, as it is drawn road by road in strips of paper of varying dimensions according to the length of each road. The roads are represented with both sides in enfilade, though sometimes only one of those sides or even part of it is represented. The reason for this is that this map was mostly cadastral (Bandeira 2000a: 42, 45, 46). Thus, it is common to see that several houses are numbered, which means that they belonged to the Chapter: this map was then to be used in conjunction with the previously mentioned *Index* in order to identify those houses more easily. Therefore, if there were stretches of roads where the Chapter did not have houses, they were not usually (with few exceptions) represented. Nevertheless, most of the houses of the city at that time are represented here – 2310 in number (Oliveira 1993: 29) – and only a few hundred are missing. The front page of this map also has a partial view of Braga centred on Campo de Santana (today known as Av. Central) and Campo da Vinha (fig. 31), allowing the visualisation of some buildings that are not visible in the roads. Finally, despite the difference in detail, both the map of 1750 and the one of c. 1757 can be used to complement each other, as some of the roads and buildings that are missing on one are visible on the other.

Regarding the third main material source, the built space, there are dozens of buildings of this period still intact, particularly from the late 17th/18th centuries. They are usually churches and palaces of the aristocracy. More "common" houses are few as can be seen when comparing what remains today with what is represented in the 1750 map. Sometimes a window or a door is all that remains. The vast majority of the houses that can today be seen in Braga's historical centre are from the late 19th/early 20th centuries.

In relation to roads and squares, some of those that were inside the former city wall have been substantially enlarged in the 19th century, such as R. Maximinos, while others have been left intact, such as R. Souto and R. D. Gualdim. Those that were outside are mostly intact, allowing as such a better perception of the kind of space where people moved. While, as I mentioned before, most of the houses that border these public spaces are relatively recent, there is an area of Braga – Pç. Gavião (today known as Pç. Mouzinho de Albuquerque) – whose square and buildings are still mostly as they looked in the 18th century.

Something that, unfortunately, will be notably absent from this work are the results of archaeological excavations that have been taking place in Braga. The priority of these excavations have been the remains of the Roman city (Martins 2000) and, as a consequence, remains from more recent periods have simply been stored in the Museum D. Diogo de Sousa, without any possibility of access.

Another element related to built space and which has not been fully explored for the Modern Era are place-names. While there has been a bit more research for the Middle Ages, such as the existence of the guild organisation in roads (Feio 1982: 115), much more needs to be done in order to explore people's actions through the names they gave to places.

Finally, there is the research that has been done on the material history of Braga. The character of this research is very similar to what I have critiqued earlier for Portugal in general, i.e., empiricist works focusing usually on urbanism and architecture. As for interpretation, when it occurs, it is either too fragmented or too general, guided sometimes by a sort of "spirit of the time". For example, the construction of the sanctuary of Bom Jesus do Monte (Good Jesus of the Mount) in the 1720's is usually seen in the context of the Catholic Reformation (e.g. Massara 1988; Fernandes Pereira 1989) or the urbananist reforms undertaken by D. Diogo de Sousa in the early 16th century are interpreted as a result of the Renaissance (Bandeira 2000b: 24); more specific local circumstances are not taken in consideration.

Art historians and local historians are usually behind most of the research. The latter's works usually follow a sort of antiquarian perspective where "everything" of the city's past is registered. Among these researchers, names such as Senna Freitas (1890) Albano Belino (1895,

1900), Alberto Feio (e.g. 1954, 1984), Leonídio Abreu (e.g. 1983), Constantino Ribeiro Coelho (1992), Luís Costa (e.g. 1991, 1993, 1998) and Eduardo Pires Oliveira (e.g. 1993, 1994, 1999, 2001a, 2001b) are the most representative.

Among the works of art historians, Robert Smith, one of the first (and few) foreign academics to show interest in Braga, produced some now classic works (e.g. 1968, 1972, 1973). Other research works include those of António Matos Reis (1990, 1995) and Miguel Soromenho (1991) on early 18th century architecture; Manuel Rocha (1994, 1996) on 17th/ early 18th centuries' architecture and urbanism; Ana Sousa Pereira (n/d, 2000) on 17th/ early 18th centuries architecture, showing also a concern with more modest houses, something not very common among art historians; Rui Maurício (2000) on early 16th century urbanism and architecture, including also houses from different social groups; finally, the historical geographer Miguel Bandeira (2000a, 2000b) on early 16th century and 18th century urbanism. It is noticeable that most of these studies focus on the early 16th and early 18th centuries, which is due to the circumstance that these were periods of great construction activity. That is, research is not guided so much by questions about what it meant to live in the city of Braga, but rather to register its material dimension.

Though the main purpose of these and other studies is not so much interpretative but empiricist, they have contributed positively to a better knowledge of the forms, chronologies and artists/patrons of Braga's Modern Era.

5

Braga in the late 15th century

As I mentioned before, it was only during the 18th century that the idea of a mechanical universe as formulated by Newton began to spread, ending up being institutionalised in the 19th century. Before that, and during most of the period under study in this work, what predominated was a religious experience of the universe where space is not mechanistic and homogeneous but, instead, possesses ruptures, with portions of space qualitatively different from others (Eliade 2002: 35). Within this perspective there is an opposition between a sacred space – the only one that really exists – and a profane space – amorphous and without structure, surrounding the sacred space (ibid.).

The map of Braga of 1594 (the oldest known representation of the city) and the *Memorial das Obras que D. Diogo de Sousa mandou fazer*[3] (Memorial of the works ordered by D. Diogo de Sousa) (henceforth known as *Memorial*), written after the death of this archbishop in 1532 and which consists of a comparative description of the city in c. 1500 and the time of its writing, are good starting points in order to build an alternative view of the city's landscape that takes into consideration this sacred view of space.

The vision of Braga that can be seen in the 1594 map was substantially different in the late 15th century[4]. The built area and the public spaces beyond the city wall did not exist; instead, this area was littered with vineyards, kitchen-gardens and trees, plus a string of little churches and chapels – S. Pedro, S. Sebastião, S. Miguel, S. Vicente and S. Vítor. The wall marked the city limits. Inside the walled area, some of the buildings represented – the archbishop's palace façade turned to R. Souto, the City Hall and the church of S. Paulo - did not exist either. The same can also be said regarding some roads: Sousa, S. João and Misericórdia.

A building that already existed is visible on the map: the Cathedral. Its position in relation to the whole city is not casual: it is at its centre. This brings me clearly to sacred geography. Within a religious mentality, no world can be born in the "Chaos" of homogeneity and the relativity of the profane space (Eliade 2002: 36). In order to live in the world it is necessary to found it and, for that, an absolute "fixed point", a "Centre", is needed (ibid.). This Centre

has existential value for religious societies since nothing can be started or done without a primary orientation, that is, the discovery or projection of a fixed point that is the equivalent to the creation of the World (ibid.). For that to happen, a manifestation of the sacred that reveals such a Centre, usually taking the form of a mountain, is needed (ibid.). This sacred mountain, because it is the "highest" place of the world as it "touches" the sky, is where Heaven and Earth meet – it is an *axis mundi* (Eliade 2000: 26). Once this happens, the world around the "fixed point" becomes habitable for humans, which try to live as close as possible to what then becomes the "Centre of the World" (Eliade 2002: 36).

In the case of Braga in the late 15th century, the Cathedral, through its central position, clearly assumes the role of Centre of the World, which is not surprising taking into consideration that this was a city ruled by archbishops. However, it is not on top of a mountain: Braga's landscape is relatively flat, only rising a bit, closer to the gates of S. Sebastião and Santiago. Yet, in these cases a large temple or palace could assume the role of a mountain (Eliade 2000: 26), which allows one to understand better why the Cathedral was so large, imposing its volume over the houses that then existed (which didn't have more than one or two floors). In Portugal, however, it was more common to find a hill inside a city that assumed the role of the sacred mountain, such as, for example, the neighbouring city of Porto. In the case of Braga, the construction of the Cathedral in a flat area is probably due to reasons of historical continuity, as the place where it stands is perhaps where the first church dedicated to the Holy Mary (to whom the Cathedral was dedicated) in Braga was built. The construction of a new city in Braga in the late 11th and early 12th centuries coincided with a period when the Church gave a strong impetus to the cult of Mary, thus the choice of that place. Notice that archaeological research has indicated the existence of a Roman temple in that place (Fontes et al 1997/98), which, according to an inscription that can be seen today in one of the Cathedral's walls, may well have been dedicated to the goddess Isis, later Christianised as Mary.

Another aspect that reinforces the Cathedral's association with the symbolism of the Centre is the existence of two towers, one on each side of the main entrance. Within the Christian tradition the tower usually has two meanings: one (better known), is of vigilance and defence (Chevalier and Gheerbrant 1994: 649). It is useful to

---

[3] It can be found published in Rui Maurício (2000, vol. 2: 295-303).
[4] All places mentioned in the text can be found in schematic maps of Braga in figs. 2, 3 and 4.

notice that, in this case, the enemy was not someone with flesh and bone, but instead spiritual malign influences; after all, the roofs on top of the towers, as can be seen in the 1594 map, would make any attempt to defend the Cathedral quite cumbersome. The other meaning of the tower is spiritual, being associated with ascension (ibid.). That is, they were like stairs connecting Heaven and Earth (ibid.). The roofs might have been the same colour as can be found in other similar cases on several colour images of Portuguese and European cities from this time, that is, blue[5]. Blue is the colour of the sky, suggesting the idea of eternity, of immateriality and, as such, not of this world (Ferguson 1966: 151; Chevalier and Gheerbrant 1994.: 105). Again, we have here the symbolism of the *axis mundi*. And in the case of Braga's Cathedral, this was not any axis, it was a quite strong axis. After all, it had two towers. In Portugal, at this time, only cathedrals had two towers at their entrance; parochial churches only had one (when they had); other churches and chapels within a parish had none, though sometimes they could have one in the back area. A hierarchical arrangement of sacred places within a territory is easily discernible here.

With the Cathedral firmly established as the Centre, the World – the city of Braga – could be born and inhabited. However, this World did not extend indefinitely; it had limits. In this case, the wall surrounding the city marked those limits. The construction of city walls, in Portuguese studies, is usually explained in military terms, that is, as defence against external attacks, and as a way of marking the border between the urban and the rural space (e.g. Teixeira and Valla 1999: 29, 149). However, in my view, things are more complex than that. Let us examine the relationship of Braga's wall with the surrounding landscape.

If one looks again to the 1594 map it is possible to see beyond the outskirts of Braga a wood and a barren landscape. Yet, reading the books of the properties that belonged to the Chapter (who controlled a significant amount of the land around the Braga), one notices the existence of a myriad of farms (cf. ADB, *Prazos do Cabido*). So, why are they not represented in the map? It is important to note that this is not something unusual, as it is typical of 16ᵗʰ century images of cities not to represent anything beyond their limits. Here, I think it is important to call attention to J. B. Harley's position that maps are not value-free ("objective") images, but instead value-laden. In his words:

> Maps cease to be understood primarily as inert records of morphological landscapes or passive reflections of the world of objects, but are regarded as refracted images contributing to dialogue in a socially constructed world. We thus move the reading of maps away from the canons of traditional cartographic criticism with its string of binary oppositions between maps

that are 'true and false', 'accurate and inaccurate' (…). Both in the selectivity of their content and in their signs and styles of representation maps are a way of conceiving, articulating and structuring the human world which is biased towards, promoted by, and exerts influence upon, particular sets of social relationships (1988: 278).

Therefore, in this case, what one is seeing in the 1594 map is a representation of a landscape influenced by a religious mentality: there were farms there, but they were not part of the city; as such, unlike what would happen in a geometrical representation of space, they were not represented. While the map is from 1594, anyone, one hundred years before, would see the area beyond the city in the same way: a profane area that wasn't part of the sacred World to which the city belonged; an area full of deserts and dark woods, where wild beasts and sub-humans abound. The wall here marks not a separation between urban and rural worlds (a concept that did not exist then) but, instead, between order and chaos, the real and the illusion, the sacred and the profane[6].

This separation is even more marked in the morphology of the wall: a roughly circular one. The circle, being the only geometrical figure without any division is usually associated with perfection, unity, the astral cycles (sun, moon), eternity (Ferguson 1966: 153; Chevalier and Gheerbrant 1994: 202). It is, therefore, associated with the cosmic sky, the Heaven that humans attempt to emulate down on Earth.

Since the city of Braga was a Cosmos, all external attacks threatened to destroy it and transform it into Chaos. Here, one must consider the "Dragon". The Dragon is the emblematic figure of the amorphous, of everything that doesn't have a shape (Eliade 2002: 61), that is, of anything that does not belong to the World. Since the World (in this case, Braga) was founded through the imitation of the exemplary work of the divinity, those that attacked it were assimilated to the enemy of the divinity: demons and, above all, the devil, which rebels against the divine work – the Cosmos – and struggles to reduce it to a nothingness (ibid.: 60).

In these circumstances, human aggressors were just part of the Dragon and not the most threatening part of it, if one looks more carefully to the structure of the wall and its changes. According to medieval sources the wall was built in the 12ᵗʰ century (Feio 1984: 106), at about the same time as the Cathedral. Its first known description is from the early 15ᵗʰ century by a chronicler, Fernão Lopes, who informs us that Braga was not able to resist a Castilian attack in 1369, because the wall was too small

---

[5] For example, in Portugal, the image of the city of Évora known as "Ebora Colonia Romana", dated from 1501; in Europe, the well-known *Tres Riches Heures du Duc de Berry*.

[6] It is useful to notice that this analysis is only valid in what concerns the construction of a city identity. There were other dimensions in which both the inhabitants of Braga and the peasants in its outskirts shared a common identity, such as being subjects of the Portuguese Crown – in which the Other were subjects of other Crowns – or as part of the Christian Republic – in which the Other were members of other religions.

and there was only one tower (n/d: 91), the Homage Tower built in the early 14th century (Feio 1984: 107). After this attack the wall, the tower and the small castle around the tower were considerably reinforced in the 1370's (ibid.: 108). What this sequence of events shows is that at the time of the construction of the wall there wasn't a concern in making it high enough to defend the city from human attacks. Only after Braga was attacked was there a concern for strengthening the wall. This doesn't mean that the wall until then only fulfilled the role of delimiting the World that the construction of the Cathedral (the Centre) had made possible. It did also defend the city; the difference is that it was a metaphysical, a magical protection (Eliade 2002: 61, 62) since the circular shape of the wall was associated with the eternal, the sacred. In these circumstances, it is easy to understand the initial small height of the wall. This magical character is discernible, for example, in an episode that took place in 1570 in an epidemic, when the city's inhabitants made a ritual of circumambulation around the city wall (cf. Senna Freitas 1890, vol. 2: 71). The purpose of conducting these circular journeys is to imitate the astral cycles with the objective of assuring the harmony of the World (Chevalier and Gheerbrant 1994: 205), something direly needed as the city's existence was threatened by epidemics.

It is also important to note that in the 15th/16th centuries more towers were built along the wall, as can be seen on the 1594 map. It is interesting also to note that two of the towers were unfinished, an indication that they were being built opportunistically and not under some defensive urgency. Also, looking at the mid-18th century maps, it is possible to see that the towers don't have an internal back-face; only the three external faces were built. Recent archaeological work in the tower close to the Santiago Gate confirms this observation (Luís Fontes, pers. comm.). Now, this, from a military perspective is not very advisable as it weakens the towers' structure in case of attack. What one is seeing here, I argue, is just a utilisation of the symbolism associated with towers – strength and *axis mundi* (both, actually, closely related to each other) – in order to present to the chaotic world the image of a city close to the sacred and (because of that) capable of withstanding the attacks of the Dragon.

Though the wall and the towers had an important role as guardians of the threshold, there were also two others: the chapels of S. Miguel (St. Michael) and S. Sebastião (St. Sebastian).

St. Michael, the archangel, is the captain of the armies of God and the killer of dragons. The presence of a chapel dedicated to him was then a way of reinforcing symbolically the city's defences against the Dragon. According to mid-16th century documentation there was in this position a statue of Sr. Michael killing the devil (Soares 1986/7: 266), a common incarnation of the Dragon within Christianity. The location of the chapel in relation to the city is not accidental: it is right in front of the city gate (Maximinos) that leads straight to the Cathedral's entrance. The Cathedral, being the Centre of

the World was the most sacred place for Braga's inhabitants: if she fell to the Dragon then the World would become Chaos; the chapel's location would thus reinforce that sensitive area. If the Saint in the chapel did not succeed, then the Cathedral, as a last resort, could counter with the two towers at its entrance and with, in particular, the most powerful of all mediators to God: the Holy Mary, to whom the city was dedicated, and whose statue was on top of the door[7].

One of the most frightening aspects of the Dragon was the epidemic. Therefore, it is not surprising to find also a chapel dedicated to St. Sebastian[8] (the most powerful patron saint guarding against them) in the threshold area. Its location is not casual either. For a start, it is located on the route to Porto, the largest city and the major port in Northern Portugal. Under such circumstances, Porto, where people from several places intermingled was an ideal location for the transmission of epidemics, unlike more isolated places. The chapel was thus in the area where at least most of the epidemics would come from. The chapel's topographic location is also interesting: it was on raised ground. This would allow it to be a bit closer to the Heavens in order to be more effective. Around the chapel a large number of oaks are visible. Taking into consideration that the oak has a strong symbolism equivalent to that of the tower – strength and *axis mundi* (Chevalier and Gheerbrant 1994: 165) – their existence and abundance was simultaneously a way of protecting the chapel against the Dragon and making it more efficient against epidemics. The use of oaks in this role is something that sometimes can be found in descriptions of religious buildings. For example, the chapel of Sra. Lomba in the parish of Pinhanços, Seia, was between four big oaks (Santa Maria 1712: 533-535). The detail of the oaks is an indication that the chapel was not circular (perfect), but instead was built with four straight walls, which meant four dead angles in need of protection against malign spirits; hence the oaks. It is the same thing as positioning a tower in the dead angle of a castle.

Still within the Cosmos/Chaos topic, I would like to call attention to two more elements in the landscape that indicate the existence of such a dual vision of space by Braga's inhabitants. The first is the existence of a gallows outside the city (ADB, *Memorial*: fl. 333vl), possibly on the small elevation called Monte das Penas (Mount of Punishment)[9], according to local testimonies registered in the early 18th century (Argote 1732: 234) (fig. 2). This place is perfectly reasonable for a gallows if one looks to the contemporary *Livro das Fortalezas* (Book of

---

[7] As it can be seen in a sculpture of the Cathedral's façade in the chapel of S. Lourenço da Ordem, which was then about 1,5 km from Braga. The sculpture is dated from the 16th or 17th centuries, as the works ordered by D. Diogo de Sousa in the Cathedral in the early 16th century are visible; in the early 18th century, a new façade was built. More on these works in chapters 6 and 12.
[8] I could not find when this chapel and the one dedicated to St. Michael were built; they were certainly in existence by 1500 as the *Memorial* (fl. 333v) indicates works that took place on them.
[9] Where today stands the church of S. Pedro and which is a bit to the south of its previous location.

Fortresses), from Duarte d'Armas – a book with images of 55 cities and villages along the Portuguese/Castilian border –, where every time a gallows is represented (such as Alcoutim, Vilar Maior, Montalegre), it is on a high place outside (but near) the city. The purpose was dual: to intimidate through example and to leave the cursed soul, as the hanged did not have a right to a Christian bury, where it belonged – in Chaos.

The second element, relates to a common disease at this period: leprosy. There were two leper-hospitals just outside Braga: one, for men, in S. Lourenço da Ordem, while the other, for women, was close to the church of S. Vítor (Feio 1984: 90). This was a socially condemned disease, with a Church council in 1179 having ordered the separation of its victims from the remaining population, as they were seen as impure (Duby 1993: 138). Their place was, obviously, not the city-cosmos, but the Chaos.

This Cosmos/Chaos spatial division with a strong and well-demarcated threshold with its wall, towers and chapels, provides, I argue, clear indications of how Braga's inhabitants constructed a common identity. One is dealing here with an identity marked by difference, that is, the construction of an Other, associated with the Chaos. Towards this Other, Braga's inhabitants express simultaneously fear (as Chaos threatened their life) and scorn (as their city was created following a divine model, being as such "superior"). Yet, this sort of identity based on an Other is unstable as it is dependent on its existence in order to maintain a communality; if the Other disappears, so does the communality. Therefore, an alternative form of identity based on shared values is more enduring than the former. Was there also such an identity in Braga by 1500?

Taking into consideration that this was a society dominated by a religious world view, it is not surprising that "for all the many elements which bound together the men and women of the early modern city into a common civilisation, nothing was more central or enduring than their membership in the Christian church and their commitment to the Christian religion" (Friedrichs 1995: 6). But, how well was that Christianity lived in Braga's cosmic landscape?

Let me start with the Cathedral, the Centre of the World. It was a massive structure, made of stone and relatively closed to the outside, since it only had a few narrow openings (Maurício 2000: 33, 34), and was thus quite dark inside, being, as such, typical of the kind of religious building built in the 11th and 12th centuries in Northern Portugal (many of them still around) and throughout Europe (Duby 1993: 108). The symbolism of this set of elements – a closed, dark, subterranean space – is that of the cave, the archetype of the maternal uterus (Chevalier and Gheerbrant 1994: 177). The cave is associated with creation, with the beginning of life, having as such a "feminine" character, reinforced through the dedication of the Cathedral to the Holy Mary, herself resulting from the christianization of pagan goddesses of fertility in the

same manner that other gods were transformed as saints and angels (cf. Eliade 1989: 144). Considering also that this cave/temple is a micro-cosmos (Eliade 2002: 71), what image of the World does it transmit? For a start, its closed space reveals simultaneously protection and fear of the outside. It is also possible that there were in the Cathedral sculptures portraying beasts that inspired fear, something that was common in 11th-12th centuries' churches, both in Europe (Duby 1993: 182) and in Portugal (Rodrigues 1995: 307-312). The structure of the Cathedral thus reveals a world where fear is a constant and where human survival is threatened: it is this fear that keeps them united.

This fearful attitude is also visible in the relationship between Braga's inhabitants and the Blessed Mary/Mother Earth, to whom the Cathedral and, as such, the city, were dedicated. Her representations in Braga's seal in the Middle Ages show an enthroned Mary with a baby Jesus in her arms (Feio 1954: 8). She is, as such, glorious and mighty, but also distant and above humans. Her power over the mysteries of life makes her a ruler. The allegiance of Braga's inhabitants towards her is based on that and not necessarily on Christian love.

One of the most common forms by this time of demonstrating Christian love towards others was through works of charity, that is, by supporting hospitals to pilgrims and sick persons. There were some of these hospitals in Braga by then (Feio 1984: 84-91; Maurício 2000: 24, 95). Yet, these did not result from a communal or civic effort, but instead from isolated initiatives (ibid.; ibid.), which meant that the support to those who needed it was fragmented and limited to some groups. Again, it is possible to identify here some weakness in what concerns the existence of a strong Christian community.

Another problem that weakened the sense of community inside the city was the existence of a group of persons from a different religion: Jews. Small groups of Jews were a common sight in many Portuguese cities by this time. However, they did not live mixed with their Christian neighbours, but, instead, in particular neighbourhoods and roads, where they had their own sacred places (synagogues) – the Jewries. These differences between persons that lived inside the city but with different religions and sacred places, segregated from each other, meant that tensions existed between them, from which resulted a weakening of communal feeling. For example: the Jews until 1466 lived close to the Cathedral in R. Santa Maria, having then been forcefully moved to R. Santo António (Maurício 2000: 24). According to documentation, the reason for this change was that Jews were too close to the Cathedral (Oliveira 1993: 104), thus polluting it spiritually with their presence; R. Santo António was much farther away.

The analysis of roads and houses also reveals a weak community spirit. By this time, roads were narrow and irregular, as their space was successively encroached by the houses (Maurício 2000: 39), though when the city was built by the Romans it was organised around an orthogonal plan (Martins 2000: 13-15). Also, the existence of buildings whose upper floors protruded over the roads through balconies was common, which sometimes – when they belonged to the same family – were even connected with those in front of them (Maurício 2000: 39). What this set of elements means is that anyone walking in the city roads would do it within a dark environment, which is associated with the primordial darkness, that is, the Chaos (Réau 1955: 73; Ferguson 1966: 151; Chevalier and Gheerbrant 1994: 541).. This would have been something not very satisfactory in a city that claimed instead to be associated with the Cosmos, the creation. Actually, the situation was such, that the Cathedral – the main referent of the Christian population, as it was the Centre of the World – was only visible when one was very close to it (ADB, *Memorial*: fl. 329v).

What is interesting about this darkness of the roads is that it results from deliberate actions of the city inhabitants. It were individual families that perceived roads as being a chaotic space and therefore subjected to be occupied by the Cosmos of their houses. Obviously, these actions would make the roads even more chaotic.

The analysis of the houses' openings is also very revealing of their relationship with roads. In Braga, as elsewhere in Portugal, openings to the outside were few: doors were the only ones in many cases, though some narrow gaps and windows could also exist, though always in the upper floors (Conde 1993: 243; Maurício 2000: 45). While the archbishop's palace is the only house of this period that still stands in Braga, if one looks to other places where embrasures from this period are better conserved, such as Castelo de Vide, it seems that the most common sort of doors by then was arched. What is interesting about this, is its reference to divinity through its spherical shape: thus passing through this sort of door is equivalent to entering into a pure and sacred place (Chevalier and Gheerbrant 1994: 202). By then, the most common type was the so-called Gothic door which had a pointed arch with a triangular shape on its upper part; the symbolism is the same as the sphere since the triangle makes reference to the number three, the number of divinity (cf. Réau 1955: 67; Chevalier and Gheerbrant 1994: 657). Moreover, the shape of this door is the same of the almond and the mandorla. The archetype of these symbols is the female vulva, being in the Middle Ages connected with the purity of the Holy Mary (Ferguson 1966; 27, 148; Chevalier and Gheerbrant 1994.: 61, 435). To enter into a house is thus to enter into a pure world. What these characteristics reveal, I argue, is fear and distrust towards the outside, with the house closing upon itself with few and narrow embrasures lest the road-chaos should enter the house-cosmos. The arched door, symbolising a transition between a sacred and a profane space – house and road –, just reinforces this assumption.

So, within this reasoning, the irregularity that can be observed in the roads is not then, as traditional urban history argues, an organic or chaotic – in the sense of being non-orthogonal – urbanism, but instead the result

of a weak community spirit in which the space of the family – the house – has precedence over other spaces of the city.

And what about the archbishops? Should they not have been, in their role of lords of the city and God's officers on earth, be concerned in assuring a stronger sense of community? Looking again at the 1594 map, one notices a division of the city in two distinct halves: to the south there was an urbanised area where most people lived; the northern half, however, was mostly occupied by a large property that belonged to the archbishop, with his house (the tower and the adjacent building) at the middle of it. One is looking at an estate where archbishops isolate themselves from the rest of the population. This observation is reinforced by looking to the 15th century aisle (Oliveira 1999: 177) of the archbishops' palace (fig. 14): a massive building, closed upon itself, with battlements symbolically affirming its strength. The archbishops behaved like distant lords, isolated from the population in order to be above it (following the model provided by the enthroned Virgin in the Cathedral), as well as distrustful of its allegiance.

There were other reasons for the archbishops' attitude: the 15th century was a period when their authority over the city declined. Between 1402 and 1473, the city's civil administration was under the Crown's rule (Feio 1984: 91), with archbishops only retaining spiritual power. After this date, the archbishops regained civil power. However, during this period, Crown officials organised the establishment of noble families inside the city, something that until then was forbidden (Feio 1984: 89, 91), since the archbishops didn't want any competition. The problem was that one of those nobles, Fernão de Lima, was particularly powerful as he was the alcayde of the neighbouring city of Guimarães and was well connected through kinship with many of the region's noble families. He did not welcome the return of civil power to the archbishops (ibid.: 91). The result was a conflict between the supporters of both sides, with the archbishop's palace being occupied, the castle besieged, the population harassed and the archbishop himself being forced to flee to the neighbouring city of Porto (Cunha 1634-35, vol. 2: 252-255; Feio 1984: 91-97). This conflict ended up being resolved through royal intervention with the archbishop obtaining the control of the city and the noble family being forced to leave it (ibid.; ibid.). Yet, this was an episode that certainly weakened the archbishops' authority, giving to the city's inhabitants another good reason to see the area outside their houses as chaotic.

To sum up, going back to the question as to whether there was any strong and shared identity inside Braga, the answer is no: there was mostly fear and distrust. Though the (roughly) circular shape of the city-cosmos purported to symbolise harmony and unity, these conditions only existed in relation to the relationship with the outside, towards which the fear and distrust were even larger. Yet, though walls divide and seclude in an effort to impose order and control, the problem is that they are only part of a wider network (Taylor 2001: 23). In these circumstances, the more the connections with the outside existed, the greater were the chances of change. One of those connections were the archbishops (always coming from the outside) and one of them, D. Diogo de Sousa, was about to bring profound changes to the city.

6

The New Braga (I)

The arrival of D. Diogo de Sousa to Braga in 1505 marks the beginning of a long period of government – until 1532 – in which the Archbishop's actions would change profoundly the city's landscape, as well as its outskirts. In this and in the next chapter, it is my intention to understand his interventions in Braga's landscape in relation to the city's identity.

A good starting place to analyse the changes that took place at that time is the Cathedral, as it could be perceived, after all, as the Centre of the World. This building underwent substantial changes during this period, some of which are still visible, particularly the fine main chapel (fig. 12). This was completely rebuilt, using different design characteristics from what existed before. One of these new characteristics is the abundant use of vegetation motifs. This is quite interesting since until then, the Church, in order to detach people from a pagan Nature full of *manna,* a supernatural force supposedly existent in all things and which gives them life, developed an opposition between Nature and Grace (the state of being protected by the favour of God), with the former being considered as a source of problems (Lenoble 1990: 218). Nature was seen as a place of temptations that could corrupt the human soul through the weakness of the flesh, permeated by original sin (ibid.: 218, 219). Forests full of beasts were thus a common view of Nature, whose representation was, as I mentioned before in chapter 5, common inside 11th and 12th century churches.

After the 13th century this perception started to change gradually, with Nature being seen rather as a work of God, whose structure was independent of the human drama on Earth (ibid.: 219). It's not that the "evils" of the world had diminished; instead, Nature had no longer any responsibility for them (ibid.). The major reason behind this change was a theological one: human salvation started to be seen as being dependent on the fulfilment of good works in this world in order to transform it and make it a better place to live (Nemo 2005: 61-88). This led, among other things, to a greater interest in the study of nature in order to better know it and consequently of the ancient Greek science, in particular the works of Aristotle (ibid.). Here, Nature lost its *manna* – at least in the sub-lunar world, since planets and stars continued to be full of it – being seen in terms of matter and form with a certain finality, kept in balance by an "Idea of Good" (Lenoble 1990: 66-76). This view was accepted by the Church as it removed *manna* from Nature, thus allowing

it to be a creation of God for the good of humanity (ibid.: 219).

D. Diogo de Sousa was certainly influenced by these ideas when he rebuilt the main chapel, transforming it, though its abundant vegetation, from a cave into a garden. It is important to note that this was an agricultural society with a strong dependence on the fertility of the land and where there was an appetite for a sanctified Nature (Eliade 1989: 144-146). Actually, one only needs to note also that the ideal of Paradise, according to the Bible, was a garden: Eden (Genesis, 2, 8-9). In these circumstances, the previous attitude of the Church towards Nature was disturbing for the vast majority of the population, something that certainly caused problems to the authority of the Church. With these changes, the Archbishop attempted to bridge between the new views of the Church towards Nature and the older Pagan one, by presenting a "Christian Nature", as can be seen in the existence of Christian symbolism in natural elements such as rosettes, which symbolise the Virgin (Trens 1946: 184), and thistles, which symbolise the Passion of Christ (Ferguson 1966: 38). In this way, the world is no longer a place of fear, full of beasts trying to harm humans, but, instead, a place where it is worth living since it is now sanctified. Beasts are reduced to a few gargoyles whose role is to expel dirty rainwater though their mouths and to act as guardians of the threshold.

Another interesting change in the Cathedral was the placement of a statue of the Blessed Lady of the Milk at the back of the main chapel and turned to the street in order to be seen, breast feeding the baby Jesus (fig. 12). The Lady of the Milk is a symbol of Mary's zeal for her children (the Christians), who, through her milk, become adoptive brothers of Christ (Trens 1946: 457-480). Through this action, the Virgin now, I argue, becomes no longer a distant ruler but instead a Mother Earth within the ideal of womanhood in the Christian tradition: caring and tender[10].

---

[10] Two more notes regarding this statue: one, is that ladies from the nobility didn't breast feed their children by then, since that was seen as an activity typical of commoners, hiring as such maids for that (Lourenço Pereira 1998: 658). Yet, by that time, there was a movement that defended that breast feeding by biological mothers would make children more virtuous (ibid.). D. Diogo de Sousa, by patronising the construction of this statue, shows on what side he was. Another note, is that due to the strong identification between the Church and the Virgin, this statue was also a way of edifying the clergymen. Notice that the behaviour of many clergymen by then was not the ideal (Maurício 2000: 30). It is useful to notice that this statue was turned to R. S. Marcos,

Changes are also visible in the illumination of the Cathedral, particularly the presence in the main chapel of three large windows that allow abundant light inside. Additionally, according to the documents, windows were also opened in the walls of the nave (Maurício 2000: 33, 34). It is not known what they looked like since they were substituted by large windows in the beginning of the 18th century[11] (Oliveira 1996b: 240). Nonetheless, they were certainly wide enough to allow the passage of some light that illuminated the nave. In this way, the interior of the cathedral became a more illuminated space, particularly in the area of the main chapel where there was a strong concentration of light. Since the symbolism of light is associated with the divine and a pure and regenerated era (Chevalier and Gheerbrant 1994: 423) then, what this change in the Cathedral means, I argue, is that now the world is no longer a place of shadows where humans live in fear. One only needs to read the Bible to see how strong is the symbolism of light: "1. In the beginning God created the heavens and the earth. 2. The earth was without form, and void; and darkness was on the face of the deep. And the Spirit of God was hovering over the face of the waters. 3. Then God said, "Let there be light"; and there was light" (Genesis 1, 1-3). God is then light, a light on which all creatures participate and that unites them all (Duby 1993: 105).

The strong light that can be found in the main chapel results then from the circumstance that it was the most sacred place in the Cathedral and from which divine light emanated into the World. It is known that a limestone retable was also built at this time, though today, with the exception of an image of the Lady of Mercy, nothing remains, since it was destroyed in the late eighteenth century (Ferreira 1932: 367). Yet, according to a description from 1723-24 it is known that there was an image of the Lady of Mercy with the baby Jesus in her arms, another of the Lady of Assumption, as well as several images of apostles and archbishops of Braga (Figueiredo, ms. [1723-24]: fl. 30). So, taking into consideration that similar changes were also happening at that time in other Portuguese sees (Baptista Pereira 2001: 213), it would seem that Braga's retable was not much different from the others: a large structure narrating a number of evangelical episodes, one of them associated with the Lady of Assumption, since all cathedrals were dedicated to her. The use of these retables results then from attempts at normalisation of religious behaviour (ibid.: 72), something urgently needed (from the Archbishop's perspective) in a city where heterodox practices were by then common (Maurício 2000: 28), as a result of the preceding social environment. It is easy to imagine the strong impact that a brightening limestone retable filled with catechetic images would cause: it was God communicating with humans. God cared.

It is possible to recognise in the changes that took place at this time in the Cathedral, influences of cyclical ideas of time. These, so well studied by Mircea Eliade (1989, 2000, 2002), postulate that the Cosmos was created in a "beginning" by a divinity, from the outset sacred and perfect, serving as a model to the activities of human societies. Whenever humans feel there is chaos or decadence in their lives they try to return to the perfection of the beginning of the Cosmos. Obviously, the character of these points of origin varies according to the different circumstances of place. In the case of Braga, the return to a sanctified Nature and a generous Mother Earth was of paramount importance, due to the strong agricultural character of the society. As for the light, it plays with the well-known duality between light and shadow, Cosmos and Chaos, both succeeding each other in a cyclical way. Though Christianity had a linear conception of time with a beginning and an end of the world (since a circular notion of time would question the uniqueness of the coming of Christ to the Earth), it nonetheless accepted the theory of the cyclical undulation of time to explain the supposed periodical return of events during the duration of the world (Eliade 2000:157). It was, in fact, the idea that a new cycle was beginning that D. Diogo de Sousa tried to convey with the works in the Cathedral. A new cosmic era and therefore a new city, or more correctly, a *renewed* city, had begun.

This idea was reinforced with the placement of seven statues on top of the Cathedral's narthex (fig. 11). These statues represent S. Michael in the middle, flanked by St. Peter and St. Paul, which are in their turn flanked by the four saint archbishops of Braga (two on each side), S. Pedro de Rates, S. Martinho, S. Frutuoso and S. Geraldo (Maurício 2000: 87). St. Michael is defending the Cathedral from attacks of the Dragon. S. Peter and S. Paul are the two most important apostles, being connected with the beginnings of the Church. S. Peter was the first bishop while S. Paul was the apostle of the heathens. Regarding the four archbishops: S. Pedro de Rates was the first; S. Martinho and S. Frutuoso were from the Germanic period, with the former converting the Suebians and the latter creating a network of monasteries to convert the pagan rural areas; as for S. Geraldo, he restored the Cathedral in the late 11th century.

There is an interesting play of associations here, which suggests that the placement of these statues by D. Diogo de Sousa was anything but casual. For a start, there is a strong reference to the figure of the bishop and the apostolic succession through S. Peter to the four from Braga. As they are all connected with the beginnings of the Church in Rome and Braga, their presence now indicates that those "perfect" early times are back. These bishops, as well as S. Paul, through their association to S. Michael also contribute to defend the Cathedral from attacks of the "Dragon". The association of the bishops to the figure of St. Paul is also important, as they are also seen as contributing to the spread of the Christian faith among the heathens.

---

which was mostly inhabited by nobles and clergymen, something that would make the messages more explicit to these audiences.

[11] Themselves removed in an architectural intervention in the 1930's that sought to transform parts of the Cathedral into its "original" form.

The form of the statues is also very revealing. Sculptures at the front door of 11th-12th centuries churches were always rigid and hieratic (Rodrigues 1995: 268). Now, like the statue of the Blessed Lady of the Milk, they present a more human shape and a more benign body language raising their hands to the faithful and establishing eye contact with them. The dreaded majestic figures from before are put aside in the name of a renewed Christianity.

Another interesting aspect about these statues is their number – seven –, something that I also do not think is casual. The number seven, within the Christian tradition, has a rich symbolism, being the number of perfection since it results from the addition of the numbers three and four, Heaven and Earth (Ferguson 1966: 154; Chevalier and Gheerbrant 1994: 603, 604). The number seven is also associated with the conclusion of the world and the fulfilment of time (Chevalier and Gheerbrant 1994: 604). This is related to the episode of Genesis in which God rests on the seventh day in order to restore the divine forces through the contemplation of the finished work (ibid.). In this way, humans are invited to rest also on the seventh day (Sunday) in order to turn to God and rest on Him in order to reach perfection (ibid.). A pact is thus established between God and Humanity through the number seven (ibid.), and the characters represented in the seven statues of Braga's Cathedral are the guarantors of such a pact.

With these statues and the messages they convey, D. Diogo de Sousa is then, in my view, attempting a reaffirmation of the role and prestige of the office of the archbishop, which was seriously damaged in the eyes of many of Braga's inhabitants before his arrival. This is then done on one side by reclaiming an antique and illustrious genealogy, and on the other by assuming a more paternal and patriarchal role by spreading the faith and protecting the faithful. In other words, the "good shepherd" that takes care of his "sheep".

These attempts of D. Diogo de Sousa in seeking a closer relationship with the city's inhabitants are also visible in changes that he undertook in the archbishops' palace, where a new façade along R. Souto was built (ADB, *Memorial*: fl. 330). Whereas, before, the palace was isolated from the other houses, now, with this extension (visible in the map of 1594), it is not only closer but is integrated with other houses. The archbishop no longer keeps the distance; though a shepherd, he lives among the flock.

To sum up, what these changes reveal is a conscious attempt by D. Diogo de Sousa to strengthen the city's Christian identity by reference to a set of elements – a sanctified Nature, the light of God and a paternal and patriarchal archbishop – that would unite the inhabitants in a more positive way, since they were not based on what was predominant until then – fear.

This reaffirmation of a Christian identity in order to bridge the differences among several of the city's groups

was also facilitated by an event that took place in 1497: the expulsion of Jews from Portugal. The relationship between Jews and Christians in Portugal had considerably deteriorated after 1492, when the former were expelled from Granada after the Spanish conquest, with many heading towards Portugal, threatening, with this sudden influx, the delicate balances that existed between both communities (Dias 1998: 48, 49). In 1497, the Portuguese Crown also decided, on its turn, to expel the Jews. Yet, because the human and economic capital of the Jews was considerable, the Crown, in order not to lose it, allowed many Jews to convert to Christianity continuing, as such, to live in Portugal (ibid.). The same also happened in Braga, since some of the Jews that lived there continued to do so, although, due to the forceful conversion, their Christian faith was not very strong, as inquisitorial visits, such as the one of 1558, quickly found (Mea 1990: 70). Despite the permanence of a crypto-Judaism in Braga, the open tension that existed between both communities disappeared since now, officially, everyone inside the city was a Christian. It is interesting to notice that after this date, according to information in the *Index*, the Jewry was renamed R. S. António (St. Anthony), with some of its houses, including the former synagogue (house 12; cf. vol. I: fl. 376), being occupied by Christian clerics (vol. I: fl. 361-386). The intention of these actions is obvious: to cleanse spiritually the space and erase the memory of the Jewish presence.

In order to emphasise the character of the Cathedral as Centre of the World and, consequently, as a model for human actions inside the city, D. Diogo de Sousa undertook some changes around the building. Until then, as I mentioned in the previous chapter, the area around the Cathedral was full of buildings, making it hardly visible. The Archbishop ordered the enlargement of a small square in front of the Cathedral (*Memorial*: fl. 329) into the large square that can still be seen today – the Praça do Pão (Square of Bread). The width of this square is the same as the Cathedral's façade, which means that now the latter is highly visible from a distance. The R. Maximinos, which connects this square with one of the city's gates, was also remodelled (ibid.: fl. 329v) in order to allow a better view of the Cathedral. A similar change also happened at the back of the building with the removal of several houses and yards and the construction of a new road (ibid.: fl. 329v) – S. Marcos[12] – whose width is the same as the main chapel. With these actions, D. Diogo de Sousa isolates a considerable area around the Cathedral, making its presence more visible and more imposing, just like a sacred mountain.

The reordering of the square in front of the Cathedral also reinforced the central role of the latter in other ways, as it was on the southern side of the square that the City Hall was rebuilt, whose previous building, which was too close to the Cathedral, was destroyed in order to give more space to the new square (ibid.: fl. 329, 329v). The City Hall was of paramount importance in the civic life of the city due to its administrative functions, being also

---

[12] Known as S. João in the 18th century maps.

there that bread, the major staple of this society, was sold (ibid.: fl. 329v), thus the name of the square. The association of these two buildings in this square put, due to the Cathedral's larger size, the City Hall (and the aldermen, who were of noble status) in a subservient position to the Cathedral. In this way, the Archbishop, due to his strong association with the Cathedral (particularly after the recent changes), affirms himself as the sole ruler of Braga uniting his and the city's destinies.

The centrality of the Cathedral was further emphasised through a reordering of the main axes of the city that also took place at this time. The crucial element was the construction of a new road – R. Sousa[13] (in homage to D. Diogo de Sousa) – between a new gate[14] opened in the city wall and R. Souto (ibid.: fl. 329), both connecting near the Cathedral. The union of both roads allowed the formation of a continuous and almost rectilinear axis that crossed the whole of the city in an east-west direction, dividing it into two halves. This axis is clearly visible in the 1594 map, with the Cathedral standing at its middle and connected to it through a small square adjacent to the cloister[15]. Another axis is also visible in the same map, though this time in a north-south direction, constituted by R. Santa Maria[16], between the Cathedral and the Santiago Gate. This road, which was until then one of the main axes of the city due to its access to the Santiago Gate and the market in Campo de Santiago (Oliveira 1993: 104), divided the southern half of the city into two smaller halves.

From this reorganisation, two major axes thus resulted forming a T-shape, with the Cathedral in the middle. Obviously, from a geometric perspective of space, this T shape is not very regular, as one can see in the c. 1757 map. Yet, what matters is how people gave meaning to the space and, from the perspective of those that lived in the 16th century, the disposition of these axes did consciously form a T, as it can be seen in the 1594 map. What is interesting about this spatial reorganisation is the imitation of the forms of a T/O map.

T/O maps were the most common sort of cartographic representation of the world created during the Middle Ages, having a solid footing in the Iberian Peninsula, as they were first made by St. Isidore of Seville in the 7th century (Boorstin 1987: 104). In the territory of what constitutes Portugal today, the oldest surviving example of such a map can be found in an Apocalypse made in the monastery of Lorvão in the 12th century. In these maps, all habitable land was represented as a circle bounded by the Ocean – the O – and internally divided by a body of water with a T shape (ibid.) (fig. 7). Above the T there was the continent of Asia; below and to the left of the vertical there was Europe; whereas to the right was Africa

(ibid.). The bar splitting Europe from Africa was the Mediterranean Sea; the horizontal bar separating these continents from Asia were the rivers Danube and Nile, which were thought to run on a single alignment (ibid.). At the centre of the map, there was a representation of Jerusalem, the most sacred place on Earth within the Christian tradition, the "navel of the world", as the latin version of the Bible calls it (ibid.). An argument that could be put against this interpretation is that the American continent, known since 1492 after the voyage of Christopher Columbus, is absent. Yet, it must be noted that most members of the European elites of this period showed little concern with the geographical discoveries that were taking place throughout the globe (Delumeau 1994: 129). They were mostly concerned with a better knowledge of classical writers and, as a result of that, until the mid-16th century, it was still widely believed that the world had three parts (ibid.). It is also useful to notice that Christopher Columbus, who died in 1506 (that is, one year after D. Diogo de Sousa started his urban reforms), never realised that he had discovered another continent. So, as can be seen, even for those participating in voyages of exploration, it still took some years to realise that a new continent had been found. As such, it is not surprising that the American continent is not represented in Braga.

From a geometrical perspective of space, T/O maps are a caricature of the world, yet, their purpose was an ecumenical one, that is, they were intended to show the habitable world (Boorstin 1987: 104). In the context of early 16th century Braga, what one is seeing is the transposition of this world view to the plan of the habited city. Since within a religious mentality, the only thing that is "real" and worth following as a model is the sacred world, then humans attempt to translate it into Earthly form (Eliade 2000: 20-26; 2002: 45). In the case of Braga, the micro-cosmos of the city, through the conscious decisions of D. Diogo de Sousa, was then imitating the ideal model of the macro-cosmos. Another important aspect of this version of the Cosmos is that its main axis – the T – formed a cross, more precisely a Tau cross (a cross without head). One only needs to remember the importance of the symbolism of the cross within Christianity: it was on a cross that Jesus Christ died to redeem humanity from its sins. In this way, the Christian character of the city is being affirmed. On the other side, within the language of symbols, the cross connects the original centre, from which life emanates, to the totality of the Cosmos, having as such a key intermediary role (Chevalier and Gheerbrant 1994: 245). Taking into consideration that in T/O maps the T results from the conjunction of water currents, I argue that roads assume symbolically the role of rivers through which divine energy flows to the city. As for the "ocean sea" surrounding the World, though also made of water, it is not flowing from an original centre. As such, it is just an undifferentiated mass, an infinity of possibilities that do not materialise: in other words, it is the Chaos beyond the Cosmos. As for Braga's Cathedral, replicating Jerusalem through its central position in the T/O that the city now

---

[13] Sometimes also referred in documentation as R. Nova (New Road).
[14] Called Porta Nova (New Gate). Until then, there were five gates in Braga: Maximinos, S. Francisco, Souto, S. Marcos and Santiago (cf. Feio 1984: 106, 107).
[15] This square is visible in the c. 1757 map and it is still there today.
[16] The continuation of this axis to the north of the Cathedral is from the 1565 and will be analysed in chapter 8.

assumes and participating in all its symbolism, reaffirms its role as the Centre of the World.

While roads could be the means through which life emanates, in Braga's case there was the problem, as it was seen in the previous chapter, that their narrowness and irregularity made them quite dark – an environment more appropriate for symbolising Chaos. This aspect obviously contradicted the idea of roads as "divine rivers" and, so, it is not surprising that an intensive rearrangement on the city's roads took place during this period. These rearrangements assumed two forms: either building new roads (such as R. Sousa or R. S. Marcos) or regularising as much as possible the façades of the buildings along existing roads (such as R. Maximinos or R. Souto) (Maurício 2000: 39). In both cases, the result was the same: wider and straighter roads. As a consequence of these changes the roads became much lighter. But this light was not just any light: it was God's light spiritually illuminating Braga's inhabitants; a light that reached all parts of the city, uniting everyone in a common Christian identity. Moreover, thanks to these changes in the roads and to the intentional convergence of the city's road network on the Cathedral, this building became more visible at a distance down the line of the roads, supporting the perception that light radiated from it, reaffirming itself as Centre of the World. In this way, roads, through their umbilical connection to the Cathedral, became extensions of it and, thus, more spiritual and enlightened spaces.

With the transformation of roads from dark to light, civic authorities made a significant effort in the following decades to keep that spiritual status. For example, in a set of civic laws compiled in 1551, it is mentioned that it is forbidden to throw filthy things onto the roads (AMB, *Livro das Vereações*: fl. 63v), as well as onto the walls, towers and gates of the city (ibid.: fl. 103) and onto the area around the castle (ibid.: fl. 82). While to present-day observers this may sound more related to public hygiene, it is important to note that only in the 19th century was it discovered that bacteria transmitted diseases, from which resulted the association between filth and disease (Douglas 1991: 50). Until then, filth was seen as impure in the sense of something that is not in its proper place (ibid.). This presupposes the existence of an ordained set of relationships and their subversion (ibid.). In Braga's case, I argue that organic filth in the roads and the smell it caused was seen as impure because they did not have a spiritual character.

There are more examples of this policy to keep the city clean in a religious (not hygienic) sense. For example, a law of 1577 only allowed blacksmiths to unload coal onto the roads as long as they were cleaned afterwards (AMB, *Livro das Vereações*: fl. 165v). More, it was strictly forbidden to unload coal in the city's squares and near crosses (ibid.: fl. 150v). These actions are understandable if one also considers that the dark colour of coal can be associated with Chaos: its permanence in public spaces would question their purity. Another example was the construction of a slaughterhouse with a porch in R. Sousa during the period of D. Diogo de Sousa (ADB, *Memorial*:

fl. 329). It is interesting to notice that two small houses were also built close by, which were intended for the persons responsible for the cleaning of that space (ibid.). Considering that pollution through blood was a common notion (Douglas 1991: 78) and that the slaughter-house was in one of the main axes of the city, it is not surprising that its blood was regularly cleaned in order to keep the spiritual status of the road.

In my view, there was also another reason for making roads, particularly the main axes of the city, wider and straighter: their transformation in "royal roads". These are the direct routes, in contrast to the tortuous ones, that lead to the centre of the kingdom (Chevalier and Gheerbrant 1994: 307). Within Christianity, royal roads signify Christ – "I am the road" (John 14, 6); "I am the king" (John 19, 21) – that is, the absence of anything that can distract the soul and divert its attention (ibid.). Therefore, it is not surprising that in the *Memorial* the existence of tortuous roads is condemned and their transformation is praised (fl. 329v). With the transformation of the city's main axes in royal roads, the latter not only emphasise the Cathedral as the Centre of the World (or the "capital of the kingdom"), but they also become staging points for important ceremonies of the city's religious and civic life, such as processions and archbishops' entrances[17] (cf. Basto 1627: 12v; Rodrigues 1627: 16).

The changes that can be observed in the city's roads during this period are usually seen by other researchers as a functional means of facilitating traffic (e.g. Bandeira 2000b: 33; Maurício 2000: 40). However, I don't find this enough. On the one side, it fails to take into consideration the religious mentality of this society, opting instead for a mechanist approach that sees the city as a machine with problems of circulation, whose resolution is attempted, so that the city does not "malfunction". Indeed, there are some elements that contradict this functionalist explanation. For example, during the 16th century some of the houses of the elite had external stairs that extended onto the roads. A couple of them are seen in the axis of the R. Sousa/R. Souto in the 1594 map. The church of the Mercy House built in 1562 in R. Sousa also had similar external stairs (fig. 10). Some documents also indicate this scenario for other houses (e.g. ADB, *Prazos do Cabido,* tome 51: fl. 3; tome 78: fl. 3). These stairs obviously inhibited the flow of traffic nearby. Also, some of the roads rearranged as this time, such as R. S. Marcos, were predominately inhabited by aristocrats and bureaucrats (cf. Bandeira 2000b: 52-54). This means that these roads did not have heavy traffic associated with business and craft, invalidating any claim that the construction of larger and straighter roads was solely to facilitate the movement of traffic.

---

[17] It is interesting to notice that archaeological excavations in the Roman City of Braga have revealed that the average width of the roads was 3 metres; yet, one of the roads leading to the forum was 7.5 metres (Martins 2000: 14). What this means is that there was also at that period at least one royal road, in this case leading to the forum, which was the equivalent of the Centre of the World.

This effort of transforming the city space into a Christian space was not limited only to the Cathedral and the roads: houses were also part of it. One of the most notable changes that takes place by this time in Braga's houses is that almost all of them were whitewashed (Maurício 2000: 107). Until then, several houses were mostly made of wood, with their frames visible from the outside (ibid.: 100). Henceforth, the external walls were fully plastered and whitewashed. Only in some houses belonging to some aristocrats was this practice not adopted (for reasons which will be analysed later in this chapter); instead, they were made of squared stone (e.g. ADB, *Prazos do Cabido,* tome 52: fl. 88; tome 56: fl. 25), presenting façades similar to the one that can still be seen in the 15th century section of the archbishop's palace (fig. 14). Considering that white is usually associated with purity and divinity, as well as with light (Réau 1955: 72; Ferguson 1966: 152; Chevalier and Gheerbrant 1994: 129-130), it is easy to understand, following what has been said, the intentions behind the whiteness of the houses: they, too, were Christian places. In this way, the covering of the city with a mantle of white further helped to unify its inhabitants into a common Christian identity. Also, as white reflects light, houses also helped to enlighten the roads even more, further emphasising the Christian character of the latter.

The construction of a common Christian identity also influenced the houses' layout in other ways. One of the most important concerns the relationship between their openings and the roads. Starting with windows, whereas before they were few and narrow, if not simply non-existent, now there is a multiplication of their numbers. The descriptions of houses that can be read in the *Prazos do Cabido* reveal the existence of at least one window in the ground floor and another in another floor, with the creation of two or three windows in the first as well as in the second floor being common[18]. The form of these windows is also considerably different, being systematically large and square. That is something that can be read in the descriptions of the houses, where references to squared windows are constant. Some of these windows are also still around in the city and are easily recognisable since they have chamfered edges, a technique that was very common during the 16th century and part of the 17th. This window format (with or without chamfer) would become the norm in Braga's houses throughout the Modern Era as it can be seen in the 1750 map, where almost all the windows are square and large (fig. 15).

The result of this multiplication of large windows is that the previous closure of houses towards roads disappears, since now with all these openings there is a strong connection between both spaces. Roads become visible from inside houses and, as such, events taking place in roads influence the lives of those inside houses. The opposite also occurs: the interior of the houses becomes more visible from the outside, influencing it. The

squarish shape of the windows also points towards this connection between inside/outside. It is useful to notice that the square is the symbol of the Earth as well as the symbol of the created universe in opposition to Chaos, since its four sides, not being dynamic, symbolise the idea of stability (Réau 1955: 67; Ferguson 1966: 153; Chevalier and Gheerbrant 1994: 548-550). On the other hand, the square maintains a close relationship with the circle, since they symbolise two fundamental aspects of God: divine unity (circle) and manifestation (square) (ibid.: 550). When the square is inserted in a circle, the Earth is dependent on Heaven (ibid.). Within these circumstances, a squared window may symbolise a terrestrial receptivity to what comes from Heaven (ibid.: 382).

Taking into consideration that roads were sacred, since they were extensions of the Cathedral, Heaven is then entering inside the houses through their squared and multiple windows. The same also applies to rectangular doors (the rectangle results from two or more squares put together), which become quite common by this time, as one can read in the documents from *Prazos do Cabido*, and which would become the norm in Braga as can be seen in the 1750 map.

I argue that what these changes in the openings as well as in the whiteness of walls mean is that the previous sacred/profane division that existed until then between houses and roads is diluted: they all now share a common sacred space. The light of God enters inside houses bringing its previous secret and dark interior into public and Christian eyes. Families no longer live closed upon themselves in fear inside the small sacred space of the house, but instead, turn outwards towards a new Christian space that preaches a more positive view of life on Earth.

These changes had consequences for the internal organisation of houses. According to the descriptions in *Prazos do Cabido*, the existence in the upper floor of houses of a hall turned to the road became the norm by the 16th century. Until then, the hall only existed in elite houses (Vieira da Silva 2002: 21), while "common" houses lacked one (Conde 1997: 245-248). The hall had a ceremonial role, being connected with certain solemnities as well as some festive events (Veiga de Oliveira and Galhano 2000: 40). In this way, by the 16th century, through the public character of the hall and the existence of one or more large windows, the road entered into the house; but the house also extended into the road.

A clear demonstration of this for example, is the small chapel that existed inside the tower of Maximinos, which was visible from the road of the same name since, as I mentioned in the previous chapter, the towers didn't have an interior face towards the city. According to documents, the inhabitants of that road, from the windows of their own houses, could take part in masses being held in the chapel (Abreu 1983: 6). This situation was only possible because there wasn't a discontinuity between the hall and the road: they were both sacred spaces. Indeed, in the early 17th century some of the

---

[18] It's rare the existence of a third floor and when it occurs is usually an attic.

people that were taking part on the masses weren't doing it in a respectful way (the documents are not very specific on this point) and so the archbishop only allowed the masses to continue if the altar was covered (ibid.). In other words, because there was a connection between both spaces, the more profane behaviour from the halls would affect the spirituality of the road.

The appearance at this time, as already mentioned, of external stairs in some houses of the elite connecting the road with the hall, is another indication of this dilution of distinct spaces. Until then noble houses only had internal stairs since they were closed to the outside (Vieira da Silva 2002: 33, 158). The existence of these external stairs, accessible to anyone, means then less suspicion towards the outside, since they were connecting spaces with a similar meaning.

The ground floor of the houses, where the commercial and craft activity of the city took place, was also affected by the changes in the openings. While being a more informal area than the hall, the relationship established with the roads was similar to what was happening with the upper floors. It is useful to notice that, by then, "skilled work was honourable and expected to be public, visible and open to scrutiny. In many towns it was expected that the shutters of the shop front would remain open so that members of the public could watch the master and his journeyman as they worked" (Friedrichs 1995: 160). In this way, the previous darkness of that space was avoided as was the possibility that a less ethical approach towards work could disturb the life of the Christian community.

Although the areas of the house turned to the road – hall and shop – underwent major changes by becoming public spaces, the same did not happen in the areas turned to the back – bedroom and kitchen - which remained private. It was in the kitchen that most of the social life of the family took place (Veiga de Oliveira and Galhano 2000: 111). The changes that houses underwent in the areas turned to the road were not meant to transform the totality of the house in a public space but, instead, to add to a previously private space a public sphere in order to integrate the family into a wider city identity.

While the area of the houses turned to the back remained private, that doesn't mean that there weren't substantial changes there, more precisely in their back yards. These yards were then a common feature, being normal for the houses' owners to use that space for cultivation and to install some ancillary buildings such as baking houses, horse stables and haylofts (Maurício 2000: 116, 117), something to be expected given that this is a strongly agricultural society. As I mentioned before in this chapter, after the 13th century Nature ceased to be demonised being instead seen as a work of God. A consequence of this was that in the 14th and 15th centuries gardens started to appear in the back yard of houses, alongside its previous elements. Gardens are symbols of Paradise (Chevalier and Gheerbrant 1994: 382) and their introduction in houses is thus an attempt of their dwellers

to be closer to God through the sense experience of Nature. Gardens by then copied Islamic models in which the use of fruit trees with strong odours such as orange and lemon-trees was predominant (Carita and Cardoso 1987: 26). The use of fruit trees is perfectly understandable, if one takes in consideration that fruits are symbols of abundance (Chevalier and Gheerbrant 1994: 340), which is, after all, the ideal of any agricultural society, where the threat of hunger is constant.

In the case of Braga, the oldest reference I found for gardens is from 1393/94 and refers to two orchards in the house of one of the canons (*Tombo do Cabido*, vol. 2: fl. 69). But it would only be in the 16th century that the use of gardens in the back yards would become common, as can be read in the *Prazos do Cabido*, and so graphically illustrated in the c.1757 map. The changes that had taken place by then at the Cathedral towards a greater promotion of Nature certainly played an important role in the development of gardens. The size of gardens was variable: most houses had only one or two trees, whereas in some of the elite the number was considerable. For example, in the house of the Coimbra family there were 60 orange trees (Maurício 2000: 130). D. Diogo de Sousa built a quadrangular garden (symbolising an ordered space) inside the new aisle of his palace (visible in the 1594 map), subdivided into 4 quarters, each with four orange-trees (ADB, *Memorial*: fls. 330, 330v). Oranges were by then the most popular fruit. This is understandable if it is taken in consideration its symbolism: its circular form is associated with eternity, while its colour can be associated with the sun. And the sun is one of the emblems of Christ (Réau 1955: 69; Chevalier and Gheerbrant 1994: 611).

So, as it can be seen, in this new city, private spaces are only acceptable as long as they are also Christian: not necessarily a Christianity based on public rituals as happened in the houses' interior spaces turned to the roads, but instead a more individual and inward experience of God.

Though, as I've been arguing, transforming Braga's identity into a Christian one was of paramount importance for D. Diogo de Sousa, it is interesting to notice that the analysis of the houses also reveals another dimension in identity politics: transforming the city into a noble one.

The idea that Braga was noble is something that can be found already in the Middle Ages by reference to the meanings of its city walls. One of these was their nobility, due to their association with dissuasion and force (Sousa 1993: 545). One can also add that their towers contributed to that noble character, since by being closer to Heaven they legitimated the superiority of those living inside the city. In this way, it was being affirmed to the exterior that the city and, therefore, its inhabitants, were noble. Yet, there was the internal contradiction that only some of the houses of the city were noble.

Noble houses in the Middle Ages were those that besides the ground floor also had an upper floor (Vieira da Silva 2002: 121). This first floor expressively transmits the idea of height, of being above mortals (ibid.: 24), which is understandable as it is closer to Heaven. The problem in Braga was that by c. 1500 there was a significant number of houses with only a ground floor (Maurício 2000: 45). In practice, what this meant was that some families were nobler than others were. Even more problematic was that farmhouses outside the city by this time only had a ground floor, as it can be read in the numerous descriptions from the *Prazos do Cabido*. This certainly caused internal tensions in Braga, since what was being implied was that those who did not live in houses with an upper floor were at the level of peasants, or more correctly, of those sub-humans that lived in the Chaos outside the sacred space of the city. In other words, they were lesser humans because of their lower houses. That this caused tensions and that the existence of the city wall was not enough to diffuse them is visible after the arrival of D. Diogo de Sousa when the building of houses with upper floors became common, as the *Prazos do Cabido* describes. Other documentation from this time reveals a notable enthusiasm by the Archbishop in his promotion of several housing projects designed to raise the quality of the building stock (Maurício 2000: 101). This concern by the Archbishop to give the city a noble character and make all its inhabitants part of this identity can be seen as the result of his "good shepherd" policy. It also raised the prestige of the city in the outside world as well as his own, since he was the lord of Braga. Almost no houses with solely a ground floor remained. After the 16th century, I have only found a couple of houses with solely a ground floor in R. Verde (a secondary road) and even so they were not for living but instead to support gardening activity (ADB, *Index*, vol. 1: fl. 407).

Height was not the only means of ennobling houses: material also counted. The city wall is once again revealing: the material from which it was built was stone, as can be still be seen in some surviving areas such as the Santiago Tower (fig. 13). Symbolically, the stone is associated with hardness and permanence, giving the idea of remaining unchanged (Eliade 2002:164). Within religious mentalities this absolute character of the stone reveals by analogy the absolute of the sacred (ibid.). So, a stone wall, more than defending the city more effectively against an external attack, affirms the sacred character of the city. Yet, as happened with height, there was also the internal contradiction in the Middle Ages that only the houses of the members of the elite were made of stone, such as the archbishops' palace, whereas those of the majority of the population were mostly made of perishable materials such as wood. Again, there are similarities between these latter houses and those of peasants. Though the descriptions from *Prazos do Cabido* don't mention the type of material in which peasants' buildings were made, and here the lack of archaeological excavations is a further hindrance, there are however some graphic sources from this period with representations of farmhouses. One of the most notable is

a book of hours from the 1520's (*Livro de Horas de D. Manuel*) and here one can see that the most used materials were wood and earth.

In the early 16th century there is a distinctive use of stone in the city's new houses (Maurício 2000: 104), and one can see here, again, a concern by D. Diogo de Sousa to defuse tensions and create common identities. Notice that the rental contracts made by then by the Chapter and the City Hall systematically impose the use of certain materials in the construction or reconstruction of houses (ibid.: 101, 103, 104). However, this does not mean that now all houses were fully made of stone. Instead, it is in relation to some architectural elements, such as corners and openings, that the use of stones becomes visible (ibid.: 105). As for the house walls, though it is noticeable by the early 16th century that there was a more common use of more resistant materials, such as brick and even stone of varying qualities, they were plastered and whitened (ibid.: 104, 107), for reasons already explained. Nevertheless, now all houses could show stone in their façade referencing and claiming, as such, a nobler status.

That height and material were important in order to express status is further emphasised by the fact that during the 17th century it becomes common (but not systematic) to read in the descriptions of farmhouses in *Prazos do Cabido* that they started being made of stone having also an upper floor. Also common is the appearance of a tiled roof, something that was only common until then in cities or in high ranking building in rural areas. Until then, peasants' houses roofs were usually made of thatch. In other words, peasants were not very satisfied for being seen as sub-humans by local lords and city-dwellers and started emulating their houses in order to affirm equality. The introduction during the 16th century of maize (after the discovery of America) as a major staple (Magalhães 1993a: 258), certainly played a part in these changes due to its high productivity and the growing demand of cities. The financial revenue of these activities allowed many peasants to substantially change their houses. It is useful to notice that the stables adjoining these houses continued to be built with wood and covered with thatch – the material of animals.

Though D. Diogo de Sousa gave a strong push towards a betterment of the visual social status of several inhabitants of the city, it is useful to remember that this was still a society based on social orders, with the clergymen and nobles on top and commoners below. How were these differences kept as the changes in the material form of the city were instigated?

In some cases it was through the large size of the houses. Already in the Middle Ages, aristocratic families had houses of large dimensions, being something that also occurred in Braga (ibid.: 44), with the archbishop's house occupying a prominent place. It is important to notice that in these societies the grandeur of a family was dependent on the number of servants it had (Carita and Cardoso 1987: 78). So, the larger the house, the more servants it had, the more powerful it was. Big houses continued to exist throughout the Modern Era, often occupying the corners of roads (as it can be seen the 1750 map), having in this way their façade extending along two roads, giving as such the illusion of being even larger.

Another important element of distinction was the existence of a tower (fig. 16). Noble families of ancient lineage had the right of having a tower adjacent to their house in order to symbolise their status (Vieira da Silva 2002: 62, 68). There is here an obvious association with the prestige of the symbolism of the tower. However, it is interesting to notice that those sectors of the elite that didn't have the means of acquiring a large house or the right of having a tower, circumvented those limitations by adding a second upper floor to their houses in order to emulate towers[19]. For example, the axis of R. Sousa /R. Souto was by then mostly inhabited by members of the elite, with many of the houses having two upper floors (Maurício 2000: 50, 54). One can also add to this example the prestige that resulted in living on one of the royal roads of Braga. It is also useful to notice that some wealthy commoners also mimicked these actions (e.g. ADB, *Prazos do Cabido,* tome 56: fl. 76; tome 57: fl. 34), as they aspired to a higher status.

Another form of affirming a difference was through the use of external stairs connecting directly the road with the houses' hall in the upper floor. Stairs symbolically connect Heaven and Earth (Chevalier and Gheerbrant 1994: 289-292) and, as it was seen before, the upper floor had a more Christian and noble character than the ground floor, which was always seen as a working area[20] and, as such, closer to the body than to the soul. Reading the descriptions from *Prazos do Cabido* or looking to the 1750 map, one can easily notice that most of the houses had their doors on the ground floor, which means that in order to gain access to the upper floor, people would have to enter the ground floor first. So, some of the members of the elite, including D. Diogo de Sousa himself (ADB, *Memorial*: fl. 330), by building external stairs were avoiding that stigma by going straight from the road to the hall. It is useful to notice that this division already existed in the Middle Ages, since there were houses with two entrances, that is, one to each floor (e.g *Tombo do Cabido*, vol. 1: fls. 119v, 120), and was something that persisted in the Modern Era in some houses. Yet, since in the 16th century the road ceased to be seen as Chaos, it became safer to have external stairs connecting to the upper floor. In this way, the members of the elite that followed this layout could show in a theatrical way to the audience of the city that they did not frequent "lower" places.

One last form of distinction that can be observed in some aristocratic houses was the persistence of a façade fully made of square or rectangular stone. This geometrical form stands, as I mentioned before, for a stable and organised world. Though other houses also incorporated the figure of the square through their overall form and their corners and openings, in this case, the multiplicity of squared stones added more prestige to their owners. The lack of white plaster on the walls of these houses does not mean, however, that the families living there did not identify with the new Christian identity of the city, since these houses present several windows and did not protrude into the roads (except in the specific case of external stairs).

So, on one side, by providing a better social status to the non-elite groups of Braga vis-à-vis the peasants that lived in the vicinities, and on the other, by making sure that those changes didn't affect the existing social order, D. Diogo de Sousa was able to carry out a profound program that reconstructed the social identities of the city, to the point of being possible to talk of a new city (in the cosmological sense of renewal). This point is important because if there weren't a wide social consensus regarding these changes, many of them would have not been possible. Yet, it wasn't only the in-wall area city within its walls that underwent major changes by this time; the same also happened in Braga's outskirts.

---

[19] I even found a description of a house with two upper floors, where it is commented that because of its second floor "it goes up like a *tower*" (*Prazos do Cabido*, tome 66: fl. 203v; my translation and my emphasis).
[20] It is useful to notice that all houses in this period were organised along this scheme. Even when a building was divided by half, the division was made vertically (e.g. ADB, *Index*, vol. 1: fl. 119) and not horizontally, as it happens today.

7

The New Braga (II)

As I mentioned in chapter 5, by the time of the arrival of D. Diogo de Sousa in Braga, the area around the city was dotted with farms. Yet, by the time he died in 1532, this area was completely different, being filled with roads, large public spaces and several buildings, as can be seen on the 1594 map. It is the character of these changes in the outskirts and its relationship to Braga's new identity that is going to be analysed in this chapter.

The first issue that needs to be considered is that these changes took place in an area which was seen, as I have argued before, as Chaos. Even the then recent revaluing of Nature did not change the status of this area since the "Nature" that was valued was the one that followed the sanctified model of the garden. The cultivated fields around Braga where the odour of muck was stronger than the smell of orange certainly did not fit that model. So, within societies with a religious approach to space how can Chaos be transformed into a space where humans can live? The answer? By transforming Chaos into Cosmos through the imitation of the rituals of creation (Eliade 2000: 24, 25).

Looking carefully at the 1594 map, it is possible to see a set of roads and large public areas organised in a circular way around the city walls. Assuming that the symbolism of the circle is connected with totality, with Cosmos, then what is happening through this spatial organisation is the incorporation of this area into the order of the Cosmos. The city and its outskirts now share a communality: they are both part of the Cosmos; Chaos receded in the outskirts area though still continuing beyond it, as can be seen in the 1594 map.

Transforming the outskirts according to the symbolism of the circle was not the only ritual of creation taking place in these changes. It was also necessary to give a character to this newly created Cosmos and since Braga's primary identity was Christian, it is not surprising to find this area dotted with crosses, chapels and churches. This process was similar to what was happening at the same time with the Portuguese explorers that were finding other islands and continents which were not Christian and therefore part of the Chaos. As Mircea Eliade says when referring to these explorers, every time they reached one of these lands they would reclaim it in the name of Christ by putting a cross there (ibid.: 25). The placing of a cross was the equivalent of a "consecration" of the land, of a "new born" (ibid.). The same thing was also happening in the outskirts of Braga.

These crosses and buildings, found in crossroads or in the middle of open spaces, acted then as local *axes mundi* spreading divine energy to the area around them (there are also other aspects related with them which are going to be seen shortly). These sacred places were either newly built or resulted from the incorporation of existing ones.

In the first example, there are the chapel of Santana and the church of Nossa Senhora a Branca in Campo de Santana (ADB, *Memorial*: fl. 331), and the church of Espírito Santo in the hospital of S. Marcos (Figueiredo, ms. [1723-24]: fl. 69). As for crosses, six were built near the city's gates and another close to the leper-hospital (ADB, *Memorial*: fls. 331v-332v). Looking at their sole survivor, the one near the gate of S. Marcos[21] (fig. 17), and reading an old description of the one near the Souto Gate (AMB, *Tombo da Câmara* 1737: fl. 97), it is clear that their form and iconography reflect the symbolism of the *axis mundi*. At the base was a square pedestal, and on the top was a circular globe with a cross and in the middle a column with eight sides connecting both. The numerological symbolism of eight is related to the mediation between the square and the circle, that is, Earth and Heaven (Réau 1955: 68; Chevalier and Gheerbrant 1994: 483).

With regard to those sacred places that already existed, there are the churches of S. Vicente (to the northeast), S. Vítor (to the east) and S. Pedro (to the southwest), besides the chapels of S. Miguel and S. Sebastião[22]. As for the other crosses visible in the 1594 map, only the one near the church of Nossa Senhora a Branca can be identified with any certainty as being there already (ADB, *Memorial*: fl 331). With the exception of the one to the southeast, built shortly after 1570 (Araújo 2003: 27-29), I

---

[21] This cross is today in the garden behind the old archbishop's palace (Araújo 2003: 22). As for the other crosses, those near the gates of Santiago and Nova were removed in the early 17th century (v. chapter 10), whereas those near the gates of Maximinos and S. Francisco, where removed somewhere before 1737, since they are not referred in the *Tombo da Câmara* from that year. Though there are descriptions from 1737 of the other two crosses, in the case of the one close to the leper-hospital it is not known if its form was still the same since it was rebuilt shortly before (AMB, *Tombo da Câmara* 1737: fl. 94v). It is very likely that some of the removed crosses simply changed places. For example, in 1737 there was a cross with the coat of arms of D. Diogo de Sousa in R. S. Vicente (ibid.: fl. 98), an area in the Northeast corner of the 1594 map and where no cross is visible then. This scenario obviously assumes that the 1594 map represents all the crosses that existed by then.

[22] The chapel of N.ª Sr.ª do Amparo, visible in the eastern side of Campo da Vinha in the 1594 map, was built after 1532 (Oliveira 1999: 71).

don't know when the others were made, though they were probably of medieval origin since they were on existing regional roads that connected Braga with other places.

The outer limits of the outskirts of Braga were well demarcated. As can be seen in several places of the 1594 map, where roads end and Chaos begins there is usually a church, a chapel or a cross marking that boundary. They simultaneously announce the limits of the sacred Cosmos and defend it against the forces of Chaos. However, in some places this role was fulfilled by the river – called Deste[23] – that is seen crossing the 1594 map from the east to the southwest. Rivers, due to the flow of water, are associated with fluidity of forms, which means that by crossing a river one becomes something different (Chevalier and Gheerbrant 1994: 569, 570). Developing this idea, rivers can be construed as separating two domains: the world of the living and the world of the dead (ibid.). This is what can be seen in the southern stretch of the 1594 map, where the river separates the city (to the north) from the Chaos (to the south). Actually, it is interesting to notice that a new gallows was built to the south of the river (ADB, *Memorial*: fl. 333v). This change of location is quite logical if one considers that the area between the river and the city (where the previous gallows stood), by becoming part of the Cosmos, was no longer a place for cursed souls. The *Memorial* mentions that the new gallows was built on a hill, probably Mount Picoto, whose isolation and conical shape easily attract the attention. The new location of the gallows was also visible from a distance, keeping therefore its intimidation message for potential criminals. There is a further curious detail: unlike the previous gallows, the new one had a wall around it (ibid.) in order to keep the cursed souls locked inside.

To sum up, the saturation of religious symbols throughout the outskirts of the city, making them a constant presence to anyone walking in this area, and the circular motion of the human bodies throughout its circular road network, would create the sensation of being in a Christian Cosmos.

The formation of these outskirts is interpreted by other researchers as an extension of the medieval city, which was until then confined to the in-wall area (e.g. Bandeira 2000a: 127; Maurício 2000: 33, 89, 94). In other words, there is no difference between both areas, which are seen as being part of a single whole: the city. Their only difference is simply their spatial relationship: the older area becomes the centre, whereas the most recent becomes the periphery. Another distinction is simply to call the older area in-wall and the other out-wall. This view simply assumes that any mass of houses is part of a single whole, sharing as such the same qualities. There is, as it can be seen, an emphasis in quantitative analysis, something typical in empiricist approaches. Yet, this is

not my view. While both areas share the same Cosmos, I don't agree that both can be seen as a single city. Therefore, I am going to argue here that there were profound qualitative differences between both areas, which tell a different story regarding what a city meant at that time.

There are some incongruities between both areas, which seriously question the idea of continuity between them. One of them is the wall. Taking into consideration that its prime role was to mark the limits of the city, then I question why it didn't undergo any changes. Assuming the existence of continuity between both areas, the wall should have been dismantled and rebuilt around the limits of the peripherical areas. An alternative would be to envisage the wall being similarly dismantled, but instead of building a new one, the symbols separating the periphery from the Chaos beyond would have been enough to mark the limits of the new city. Yet the old wall remained, separating both the new and the old urban areas.

Another anomaly is the placing of crosses near all the gates in the wall. As I mentioned in chapter 5, one of the roles of the wall was to protect the community from the attacks of the Dragon. Considering that gates were the weakest points in a wall, the placement of crosses in front of them was a form of symbolic reinforcement against those attacks[24]. Yet, if both areas are the same, shouldn't religious symbols of protection be placed solely at the outer limits of the whole urban area? Why then add extra protection to the original area within the walls? If one assumes the existence of continuity between the areas inside and outside the wall, this action doesn't make any sense. Unless, of course, both areas were qualitatively different.

The analysis of the houses found in both areas is here very revealing. Starting with the similarities, they both share tiled roofs, walls with whitewashed plaster, quadrangular and rectangular openings and are well lit, unlike the dark houses of the peasants that are always represented with only a single door. So far, nothing unexpected since both areas share the same Christian Cosmos. What is interesting is the difference regarding the existence of upper floors. While in the area within the wall, practically all houses have one or two upper floors, in the area outside the wall it is common to find, from the reading of *Prazos do Cabido*, houses with only a ground floor. Actually, this situation still persisted in 1750, as can be seen on the map of the city for that year, where about a quarter of the houses represented in the area outside the wall only have a ground floor[25] (Oliveira

---

[23] Sometimes also known as Aleste, as it can be read in the scroll at the right side of the 1594 map. In both cases the meaning of the name is the same, referring to the geographical point – East – from which the river flows in relation to the position of the city.

---

[24] There isn't here a contradiction regarding what has been said before about these crosses since, if the intention was solely to consecrate an area, there wouldn't be a need of putting them in front of the gates; another place in the vicinity would be enough. Only the cross close to the S. Francisco Gate is a bit dislocated in order to also sanctify Campo da Vinha. These crosses have therefore a dual role.

[25] Eduardo Pires de Oliveira suggests that many of these houses were used to support agricultural activity and not for living (1993: 32). Not always, since it is common to find descriptions mentioning the existence

1993: 32). Yet, as I argued before, it is noticeable that in the early 16th century a notable effort was made to prevent the existence of houses with only a ground floor in the space of the city. So, why is this fully executed in the area within the wall, whereas in the outside area there is more tolerance permitting the persistence of houses with only a ground floor? If both areas were seen as city, then the existence of a substantial number of houses without upper floors would put in question the attempts of building an urban identity which claimed to be noble.

There are also some interesting anomalies in the new public spaces in the area outside the wall. One is their names: they are all known as Campos (Fields). A contrast can be seen when one compares these with the names given to the public spaces in the area inside the wall: Praças (Squares). By giving the name "Campos" these areas are associated with terrain where agriculture is practised, something that was not supposed to happen in the public areas of a city, where they would have been dedicated to the celebration of community events. This concept is further reinforced by the existence, in some of these Campos (Vinha, Santana and S. Sebastião), of trees, while in the inner area there are none in the public spaces. Though there was at this time a valuing of Nature, what is predominant in the public spaces of the inner area is light, which is closer to God. Nature is to be found only in the private spaces of the houses.

Another anomaly in the public spaces of the city is their shape. While in the inner area the public spaces built by that time, such as Praça do Pão or those at the northern entrance of the Cathedral and in the main entrance of the Archbishop's palace, were square or rectangular, the shape of those built in the outer area was irregular, that is, non-geometric. The square, as I mentioned in the previous chapter, is the symbol of the Earth, of a stable and ordered world. That is visible, for example, in the rectangular blocks of medieval cities; in the squared cloisters of monasteries and cathedrals; in the squared or rectangular plans of houses or the yard around which some of them were organised. So, as it can be seen, there is a profound difference in the organisation of public spaces in the areas inside and outside the walls that question the existence of conceptual continuity between them. While the former presents a stable character (to which can be added the cross shape of its main axis, which is closely related with the symbolism of the square, since it also stabilises a space), the latter presents a more fluid character, closer to that of the Chaos.

A final anomaly is that the descriptions from *Prazos do Cabido* clearly state that the inner area is "the city", whereas the outer area is "the outskirts". If they were all the same, why not simply apply the term "city" to the outskirts?

I think this set of anomalies is sufficient to question the thesis that the outer area was an extension of the city of Braga, sharing the same attributes as the inner. The city of Braga continued to be delimited by the medieval wall. While both areas were part of the same Christian Cosmos, sharing attributes such as being inside a circle or having whitewashed houses, there were other aspects where they strongly contrasted. Yet, the outer area was not Chaos, since it had some of the attributes of the city. So, if it was neither city nor Chaos, what was it then?

My answer is that it was a middle landscape. Middle landscapes, also known as Gardens, are an old ideology, already existing in the Classical world (Cosgrove 1993). They are part of a mythical narrative in which the social landscape

> is rendered spatially through a concentric, cosmic pattern of (…) three mythic landscapes, each representing a progressively greater intervention by human design and labour in the forms and patterns of (…) [Earth's] surface. At the centre of this mythic geography is the city, [then] its immediate environs gardened and cultivated, grading finally into untouched wilderness (ibid.: 293).

In this tripartite archetypal landscape, the City is the realm of culture and political power, with its landscape "divorced from organic life, a world of stone, columns and monuments, of words, of texts (…) [with its pattern] modelled on the pure intellectual geometry of the heavens" (ibid.: 296). As for the middle landscape or Garden, it is an area of cultivated and lovingly controlled Nature, being as such less touched by human intervention and closer to the idea of Paradise (ibid.: 291, 296). It is the landscape of "domestic economy, of the loving family and the private life of citizens" (ibid.: 296). Its middle position also makes it "the locus for a yearning nostalgia, a place of fleeting youthful wonder balanced between childhood innocence and cynical age" (ibid.: 297); one only needs to remember the first days of Adam and Eve in the Eden. As for the wilderness, the furthest removed from the City and civil life (ibid.), it shares the characteristics of the Chaos[26].

This rearrangement of Braga's landscape with the addition of a Garden, gives, therefore, some explanation for these anomalies. However, one question needs to be asked: why was D. Diogo de Sousa adapting Braga's landscape to this model? Or, to be more specific, what was his agenda? In order to answer this, I think it is useful to make an analogy between the City/Garden and the Christian duality of the soul/body. With the changing view towards Nature, mentioned in the previous chapter, this duality was no longer seen in terms of an opposition. Thus, what the Archbishop is basically doing is "cleaning the house". In other words, the mixtures and heterodoxies that existed in Braga before his arrival were being

---

of a kitchen and a sleeping room, which shows that there were people living there.

[26] From here on, the word "City", with a capital "C" will only be used when mentioning the space of Braga with such quality. The words "city" with a minor "c" as well as "Braga" will be used for the set City/Garden.

separated and put in "their" places. Therefore, those elements more connected with the "soul", that is what was seen as the higher dimensions of human life and which was analysed in the previous chapter, were in the City, whereas those more connected with the "body" were in its outskirts. Actually, this is exactly the same thing that was done, albeit on a micro-level, on every house with their division into public and private spheres (v. chapter 6).

But, what does this "putting in order the body of the Braga" mean? In the Classical sense of the word, the Garden was a place where humans nurtured and complemented the processes of Nature. Yet, in the case of Braga, this can't be taken literally since only some trees are visible in its public spaces. What, then, is this "body", in the context of early 16th century Braga?

The analysis of the relationship between the social status of the inhabitants and their spatial distribution is very revealing. Starting with the City, according to the *Index*, about 54% of the rents were paid by clergymen and nobles, 14% by bureaucrats and merchants (the higher strata of the common people) and the remaining 31% by craftsmen (Bandeira 2000b: 53). These numbers are a bit relative since they don't take into consideration some houses that didn't belong to the Chapter. Nevertheless, they clearly point to the fact that most of the population living by then in the City belonged to the higher social strata. This is a complete inversion of the typical pattern of medieval cities, in which craftsmen were the majority. This shows that the growth of the population that happened at this time through the opening of new roads resulted mostly from the immigration of elite members. Also, several of the ruined houses that existed by then inside the City were acquired and rebuilt by the elites (Maurício 2000: 100). There was also some acquisition by the elites of existing houses. An example is R. Souto, which by the late 15th century was socially mixed and in the 16th was mostly inhabited by members of the higher strata (ibid.: 47, 54). It is interesting to notice that D. Diogo de Sousa didn't forbid noble families from entering Braga, although they were all from lesser families, since no big names are found living in Braga. The reason is obvious, if one remembers the events of the 1470's: the Archbishop was not interested in any challengers. As for the craftsmen, though many were probably descendants of others that already lived there, there was also strong craftsmen immigration to Braga. Where were these people? The answer is easy: in the Garden. Reading the *Index*, almost all those mentioned living in this area belonged to this social group.

A division between both areas according to social status is clearly visible here. So, the City –centre of power and closer to the heavens – is mostly inhabited by the social elites. These were particularly concentrated in roads such as Sousa, Souto, Santa Maria, S. Marcos (Bandeira 2000b: 53), which were the main axes of the City; the common people was, it is clear, mostly concentrated on secondary roads. As for the Garden, where humans complement Nature through their physical work, it

becomes the most appropriate setting for the activities of the craftsmen. These were not being rejected, since they were part of the Christian Cosmos and their activity was essential for the good health of its material dimension; they were simply being shown, through spatial divisions, what their role within Braga's society was.

This division according to status and social role was not the only thing that resulted from this City/Garden dichotomy. The analysis of the public spaces outside the walls is also revealing. Starting with the large one to the north – Campo da Vinha (Vineyard) –, this area is the result of a transformation of an existing vineyard (thus its name) into a space dedicated to resting, talking and relaxed walks (Oliveira 1999: 71). There is here influence from the Roman Virgil with its defence of the simple pleasures of places outside the cities, places devoted to idle conversation where people could rest from the artificiality of city life (cf. Duby 1993: 264). In the case of Campo da Vinha, it is possible to see the existence of trees in this area on the map of 1594, something that would make it resemble a garden. Basically, what one has here is the community equivalent of the private gardens that could be found by then in the back yards of the houses.

Another large public space can be seen to the East of the City, beyond the Souto Gate: Campo de Santana (Saint Ann). This space, I argue, was the great meeting point between those living in the Cosmos of Braga and those living outside it. Since the latter didn't share the same "soul" with Braga, the appropriate meeting place, lest there should be any spiritual pollution, was obviously a more material one: the Garden. A number of structures can be found in this public space[27] through which that contact was made.

For a start, this area became the major commercial centre of Braga, since it was here that many itinerant traders from elsewhere would go to sell their articles. According to the *Memorial*, in order to boost this activity, the Archbishop ordered the construction of some structures near the Souto Gate to support the activities of these merchants: a place to sleep in, stables for the animals and a portico for trading (fl. 331v). Similar structures were also built near the Nova Gate (fl. 333), although this area didn't have the same dimensions and complexity as Campo de Santana. Notice that in both cases, these structures were outside the walls, since these traders were not from Braga. Finally, because the strong commercial activity generated here would attract people from several places, anyone, that for whatever reason needed to enter into the City, would do it directly to the axis of the R. Sousa and R. Souto, the most important and impressive royal road of Braga.

All this commercial activity attracted several sorts of people about whom the Church had doubts regarding their religiosity. There were merchants, more concerned

---

[27] Except the fountain, which was built in the late 16th century (v. chapter 9).

in getting rich whatever it cost; artists and actors, with a reputation for being libertine; thieves and prostitutes (Minois 2004: 205). With such bad examples so close to the City, the Archbishop couldn't just stand idle. According to the *Tombo da Câmara*, the cross in front of the Souto Gate and, as such, close to the commercial area, had two statues on top of it: one, representing Christ on the cross, while the other was a representation of the Blessed Mary in a *Pietá*-like posture (fl. 97). It is interesting to notice that the cross that was near the S. João Gate, a non-commercial area, did not have any statue on top of it. Therefore, there seems to have been, in putting these statues near the Souto Gate (and perhaps also near the Nova Gate), a conscious intention by the Archbishop to catechize the persons that would go there, through the image of Christ suffering on the cross in order to convince those that doubted the virtues of his sacrifice. As for the statue of the Blessed Mary, it was created with the female half of the population in mind: depicting, as it did, the suffering of the mother for the death of her son.

Another structure that was built at the same time near the Souto Gate, in substitution of an older one that existed inside the city, was the pillory (ADB, *Memorial*: fl. 331v). This was basically a post (visible in the 1594 map) where criminals were punished and displayed to the public. These punishments were always public in order to show that Justice worked and to intimidate potential criminals. Its construction in this area resulted, in my view, from two circumstances: one, was that with the City acquiring by then a "soul" character, activities that involved physical punishment were not appropriate for this area. Therefore, their place should be in the area of the Cosmos of Braga where there was more proximity with the physical world: the Garden. The other, was that Campo de Santana, being the public space outside the wall where there was more movement of people, either from Braga or beyond, was, as such, the most convenient place to place the pillory. Its proximity to the commercial area made it clearly visible for everybody, particularly for those more problematic individuals who didn't repent when they saw the statues of Christ and Mary. Its position near the door would also make it visible to anyone passing from the City into this area.

Overshadowing this area close to the Souto Gate there was the huge mass of the castle built in the 14th century. Since Braga was the lordship of an archbishop, its Centre was the Cathedral and not, as happened in several cities, the castle. This doesn't mean that the archbishops were willing to be without a castle: quite the opposite. While castles could serve as a refuge in dangerous times, as happened in the 1470's, more often they were strong affirmations of the power of their lords and this one, with its walls and towers made of stone, certainly conveyed an idea of strength. So, D. Diogo de Sousa, by making sure that the castle was integrated into this public space, was affirming his authority to a large audience. Its closeness to the structures that supported the commercial and judicial activities made its presence even more imposing. In order to make it more impressive, the castle walls,

which until then were made of rough uncoursed stone, were rebuilt with dressed ashlar (ibid.: fl. 331v). In this way, the prestige of the symbolism of the square was associated with the castle (whose towers were already square).

The most notable structure on the Campo de Santana was the chapel of Saint Anna in the middle of it. This building had eight sides and was surrounded by twelve inscribed columns (set in a circular fashion, as can be seen in the 1594 map) dating from the Roman period, which had been collected from the Roman ruins of the ancient Bracara Augusta or other places in the vicinities of Braga (ADB, *Memorial*: fl. 331). Some Roman stones with inscriptions were also inserted in the walls of the chapel (ibid.). These explicit references to the Roman past of the city show that the purpose of this structure was not solely to make the surrounding space sacred. What, then, was D. Diogo de Sousa's intention in constructing this chapel?

A starting point for answering this question is the Roman columns themselves. It is useful to notice first that the Roman columns were just an assortment of different types (military and celebratory) selected regardless of their context (Cunha 1634-35: 11-20).

The element of that past that is significant here is the letters. Letters or, more abstractly the Word, are all powerful in the Christian tradition. They have creative power (it was through the Word that God created the World) and it is God's medium of communication with humanity (the Bible) (Chevalier and Gheerbrant 1994: 501, 502). In the specific case of Braga, the letters in the columns are not just any letters: they are Roman letters that go back to the "perfect" days of the Roman Imperium under which both Braga and Christianity were born and had their first established existence. There is, therefore, an attempt to legitimate Braga's power and prestige through reference to an illustrious and antique past.

The next point is the number of columns – twelve –, which is not casual. Twelve is the number of election, of the people of God, of the Church (Ferguson 1966: 154; Chevalier and Gheerbrant 1994: 272). When Jesus chose twelve disciples he proclaimed, in the name of God, the intention to choose a new people (Chevalier and Gheerbrant 1994: 272). The circular disposition of these columns also affirms through the symbolism of the circle that there are no differences between this people: they are all one in God. Taking into consideration that this is Braga, it is God's local people – the Church of Braga – that is being represented here. The columns, which were whitewashed (Argote 1732: 244), sharing therefore the symbolism of white, and had an *axis mundi* character, show the strong and pure foundations of the Church of Braga.

The "perfect" days of the beginnings have, therefore, returned, with the chapel of Santana, in the middle of the circle, acting as guarantor of that. Notice also that the chapel has a central plan and eight sides, a form commonly found in baptisteries where the sacrament of baptism was performed in some Paleo-Christian religious buildings. In this way, there is again a clear reference to origins, with the chapel acting as a mediator, not only between Heaven and Earth, but also, in this case, between Old and New Braga, with the Roman inscribed stones inserted in its walls reinforcing that connection.

It is very probable that D. Diogo de Sousa was inspired to use remnants from the Classical world following the two visits he made to Rome in 1493 and 1505, where he certainly observed how the Roman past was being used by the popes to create a new Rome. He is then emulating Rome and putting Braga at the same level.

The reference to the Roman past was not the only thing in which the Archbishop emulated Rome. The last public building in Campo de Santana – the church of Nossa Senhora a Branca (Blessed Lady in White), at its eastern end – refers to the episode when the Virgin appeared in the heat of the Summer on the Esquiline Hill in Rome, whitening it with snow, showing her desire that a church dedicated to her should be built there (Carvalho da Costa 1706, vol. I: 155). The church that was built there in Rome, *Santa Maria Maggiore*, is considered to be the first Christian church dedicated to the Blessed Mary. The cult of Mary became of paramount importance during the Middle Ages since, being simultaneously mother and wife of God, was humanity's main intercessor with God (Duby 1993: 155, 156). Actually the importance of Mary was such that the Church strongly identified with her; the Church was Mary's body (ibid.: 156). The Church, therefore, becomes the wife in whom God is made flesh through Jesus; through Mary, humanity unites with God (ibid.). This identification between Mary and the Church ends up by celebrating the sovereignty of the Roman Catholic Church (ibid.). Taking into consideration the importance of this cult among Catholics, it is more understandable why D. Diogo de Sousa ordered the construction of this church. By evoking the episode of the appearance of the Virgin on the Esquiline Hill, the antiquity of her cult in Braga was also being affirmed. In this way, Braga, proclaimed itself as a major player in Christian religious history, at the same level as Rome, something which was obviously a matter of prestige for the city.

These last two buildings allow to understand better why this public space was called Campo de Santana. S. Ann was the mother of Mary and grandmother of Christ, the two most emblematic figures of Catholicism. She is therefore strongly associated with the origins of Catholicism, with the primordial birth. In the case of this Campo, her name is being borrowed in order to emphasise the messages that are being communicated about the prestigious origins of Braga.

But towards what audience was this complex program in Campo de Santana directed? Certainly towards those outside Braga. However, there weren't people from all over the world going frequently to Braga. Were there any specific groups in mind when this program was

organised? One way to answer this question is to see from where the roads that lead to this Campo come from: northeast, east and southeast. The first two were part of regional roads that crossed northern Portugal in an east-west direction, corresponding as such with the territory that belonged to the archdiocese of Braga. Notice that Braga was close to the coast, so these roads would connect most of the places under its jurisdiction. As for the other road, it leads to Guimarães, the largest city of the archdiocese. The Church of Braga had frequent quarrels with the Chapter of Guimarães because the latter considered itself to be outside Braga's jurisdiction and under the direct authority of Rome, something that the Church of Braga did not accept (Soares 1983: 6; 1997: 63). So, in my view, these were the two main audiences of this program: the population of the archdiocese in general and Guimarães in particular. Notice that there is no similar program on the road to the southwest, which leads to Porto, the largest city in Northern Portugal, and beyond it, to the capital of the Kingdom, Lisbon. The Archbishop was, therefore, more concerned in reaffirming the authority of the Church of Braga over its territory after a period of weakness[28].

The last public space outside the wall I will talk about is Campo dos Remédios (Medicines), to the southeast of the City, in front of the S. Marcos Gate. It was here that a large hospital dedicated to S. Marcos (S. Mark) was built (ADB, *Memorial*: fl. 32). It seems that the name of this area relates to the previous existence here of a small medieval chapel allegedly containing the tomb of S. John Mark, a Christian bishop and martyr, who performed a range of miracles curing the physical infirmities of those who sought his protection (Figueiredo, ms. [1723-24]: fl. 69v). Thus, this public space, unlike the others in the Garden, was dedicated to the cure of physical diseases, though, like the others, it was related to what was perceived as a material dimension of life. One interesting characteristic of this hospital is that it wasn't just another hospital to add to those that already existed. Quite the opposite: D. Diogo de Sousa incorporated within this one hospital all the others that had existed in Braga until then (ADB, *Memorial*: fl. 32) – in other words, he created a central hospital. In this way, the division of care that had existed before was put aside in favour of a unified hospital that served everyone living in the city as well as pilgrims looking for shelter.

The administration of this hospital was initially given to the City Hall, although in 1559 it passed to the Mercy House (Oliveira 1999: 169). This institution appeared initially in Lisbon in 1498 and its model was quickly copied by other Portuguese cities (Almeida 1993: 186-189), reaching Braga around 1513, being initially installed in a chapel of the Cathedral's cloister[29] (Oliveira

---

[28] Still within this topic of affirmation towards other cities of the territory, it is useful to notice that Braga's city hall had two upper floors, whereas the city halls of other major cities of this territory, such as Guimarães and Viana do Castelo (whose buildings are still intact), only had one upper floor.

[29] Today known as *Misericórdia Velha* (Old Mercy House) (Oliveira 1999: 119).

1999: 119).The main purpose of this institution was the practice of works of mercy (Almeida 1993: 186). These were fourteen: seven spiritual and seven physical (notice the reference to the number seven, the perfect number, through which humanity unites with God). Regarding the former, they were: teach the simple, give advice to those who ask for it, punish charitably those who commit faults, console the disconsolate, forgive the offenders, suffer injuries with patience and beg to God for the living and the dead (ibid.). Regarding the latter: redeem the captives and visit the imprisoned, cure the sick, cover the naked, feed the famished, give drinks to the thirsty, shelter the pilgrims and poor and bury the dead (ibid.). In other words, Mercy Houses were committed to the practise of the Christian virtue of Charity towards the poorer elements of society. The introduction of this institution, therefore, enabled the uniformity and standardisation of these practices throughout Portugal (ibid.: 185).

Regarding its membership there should always be members from the aristocracy and the common people represented, half from each side. This apparent equality hides the fact that the head had always to be a member of the elite (ibid.: 187), which meant that in practice these institutions were controlled by the elite. In Braga's case, the archbishops always had a say in the administration of the Mercy House (e.g. Costa 1993: 74; Oliveira 1999: 171). Nevertheless, the association of an equal number of members from the elite and (the higher strata of) the common people, and the help given to the poorer members of the society, made this institution a guarantor of equilibrium and social order (Almeida 1993: 193).

This latter observation can be further developed in the case of Braga by taking into consideration the name given to the church built in the new hospital: the Holy Ghost. This reference to the Holy Ghost is very interesting since it points to the works of the Cistercian monk Joachim de Flore. He defended in the late 12th century a theory in which humanity's history was a linear progress towards an era of peace, rest and contemplation: the Age of the Holy Ghost (Minois 2000: 222-225). He considered that humans were meanwhile living in another era – the Age of the New Testament or of the Son -, which started with the arrival of Christ. The period before this – the Age of the Old Testament or of the Father – was the first of human history (ibid). This theory was certainly not well regarded by the Church, who, despite also having a linear notion of time, considered that the present era was the last before the end of the world and that no further change was possible (ibid.: 226, 227). Unfortunately for the Church, the many discontents throughout Europe with the Feudal order, adopted this scheme in the belief that another era was possible, an era with a new religion, free, spiritual and without hierarchies (ibid.: 270-274). Rebellions and religious ferment became constant after the late 14th century, particularly in Central Europe (ibid.). In the case of Braga (and Portugal), while it was in the interest of the elite to keep the present social order, there was also the risk of its violent subversion. So, in the early 16th century, there seems to be a compromise

between those two positions: the era of the Holy Ghost had indeed arrived, as the hospital's church name indicated, yet, instead of equality, there was the Christian virtue of Charity. This was a charity that was meant to be genuine and not cynical; thus the careful organisation of the Mercy Houses. Yet, in the end, the existing social order with its inequalities continued. Actually, one only has to notice that the hospital was built on, and took its name from, the tomb of a bishop. Again, there is here a reification of the figure of the archbishop, but this time as healer of physical diseases.

It is interesting to notice that while in the programs of the Cathedral and the Campo de Santana there is an emphasis in circular time with a return to the perfection of the beginnings, here, there is, instead, a progressive linear time that ends in an era of plenitude. In other words, for different dimensions of the Archbishop's activity, either there is a return to a Classic Golden Age, or a projection of the future into a fraternal Age of the Holy Ghost.

This emphasis on charity also brought changes regarding the location of the leper-hospitals. The older ones were abandoned and a new one was built (ADB, *Memorial*: fl. 332), unsurprisingly called S. Lázaro (Lazarus), in the space of the Garden, close to the hospital. The lepers were, therefore, given more dignity, although it is useful to notice that they remained outside the spiritual area of Braga. It is possible to see in this attitude towards lepers the influence of the Franciscan Order, who defended them and was the champion of the practice of charity among Catholics. Actually, this Order had also been installed by then in the vicinities of Braga, with the Archbishop supporting the construction of a Franciscan monastery about 1,5 km to the northwest, in the church of S. Frutuoso (ibid.: fl. 332v), as well as a nearby house to support pilgrims (ibid.: 333v, 334v).

To conclude, as has been seen throughout this and the previous chapter, there was a profound redefinition of the character of Braga's space and its identity at the beginning of the 16th century under the leadership of D. Diogo de Sousa, whose actions were much more complex than previous analysis has suggested. Yet, if the Archbishop was expecting that this new city would mark the (re-)emergence of an era of plenitude and the end of history then he was wrong, as his successors would quickly find out.

8

The Catholic Reformation

Despite D. Diogo de Sousa's best efforts to build (in his perspective) the ideal city, Braga was part of a complex network, which meant that interaction with other elements would make that stability temporary. As such, by the 1540's, it started to become evident to the city's elite that a set of circumstances was threatening Braga's Christian, or more precisely Catholic, identity. So, in the following decades a number of measures were taken by the archbishops, helped by the Chapter and the City Hall, in order to reaffirm such identity. Those measures can be seen as being part of a wider reform movement that was happening at the same time throughout Catholic Europe and which was later known as the Counter-Reformation, but which may be more accurately called the Catholic Reformation, since there was a full reorganisation of Catholic life and not solely theological differences with Protestants (Tourault 1998: 215).

In the case of Braga, the circumstances of this were the following: the Protestant Reformation, crypto-Judaism and a persistent paganism.

Starting with the first of these, the Protestant movement started in 1517 under the initiative of Martin Luther in Germany. The doctrine of this monk can be basically summarised under three headings: one, is that salvation is obtained solely by faith, with the practice of good actions being useless (Tourault 1998: 206). The second is that all Christians are equal through baptism, something that makes them all priests and, as such, part of the ecclesiastical order (ibid.). As for the third point, there is a refutation of the spiritual authority of the pope and the Church, with it being possible for any Christian to read and understand the true meaning of the Bible (ibid.). These theses were obviously unacceptable for the Catholic Church. This wasn't the first time that the Church's official doctrine was questioned since this was constant throughout the Middle Ages (ibid.: 86-90, 152-156, 193-196). Yet, either through dialogue or through force, all those previous challenges had been eventually resolved, with the Church maintaining its predominant position throughout Europe. However, this time things would be different: Protestant ideas spread quickly and by the 1540's most of Northern Europe was separated from the spiritual authority of the Church. This would plunge most of the continent into religious wars for more than a century until 1648, when Europeans grudgingly accepted this division under the terms of the Treaty of Westphalia.

Next, with reference to crypto-Judaism, it is useful to remember that Jews in Portugal were forcibly converted to Christianity in 1497 (v. chapter 6). Yet, because this conversion was not sincere many kept the old ways, despite the Crown giving them a period of adaptation of twenty years (Magalhães 1993b: 475-477; Mea 1998:435). As the Christian population started to notice that many Jews were only Christian in name, some conflict emerged (ibid.; ibid.). This also happened in Braga, since in an inquisitorial visit in 1558, 23 Jews were arrested (Mea 1990: 70). On the other hand, some Jews took advantage of their new Christian status to fill places in the secular and ecclesiastical administration, entering into direct competition with the "Old" Christians, something that became less and less acceptable to the latter (Cordeiro Pereira 1998: 334-336; Magalhães 1993b: 476-477). So, either through passive resistance or, paradoxically, through a (too) successful integration, by the 1540's, the Jewish problem resurfaced, with "Old" Christians considering their existence as a threat to Portugal's Christian identity.

While in the case of Protestantism the concern was with controlling the flux of ideas and reaffirming the Catholic dogmas and in the case of crypto-Judaism the elimination of a minority group, in relation to the persistence of pagan practices the problems facing the elite were much more complex. This is because the majority of the population one way or the other practised them.

In the specific case of Braga, the persistence of pagan practices resulted mostly from two circumstances: one was that most of the large numbers of persons that moved to Braga in the 16th century came from rural areas where heterodox practices were more common. The other was the weaker status of the female half of the population, who was marginalised within the hierarchy of the Church (Soares 1997: 396-401). In these circumstances, it is not surprising to find women actively engaged in marginal activities such as witchcraft and pacts with the devil in order to find solutions for problems that were not satisfactorily resolved within the confines of the Church, in particular emotional problems (Araújo 1990: 118; Mea 1990: 73; Soares 1997: 396-401).

An example of this activity in Braga is described in the inquisitorial visits of 1558, when a woman, during a night, made a pact with the devil, which was represented by a statue inside the chapel of S. Miguel (Araújo 1990: 115). In order for this pact to be effective she should not bow to the saint and should not look to the cross (ibid.). What I find interesting in this example is the existence of a subversion of the original meaning of the statue, which was to represent the defeat of the devil by St. Michael. By focusing her attention solely on the representation of the devil, this woman is giving it a new meaning. In other words, meanings change according to circumstances. This sort of heterodox behaviour was probably common throughout Braga by then. Yet, for the Church, this subversion was problematic since the compromise achieved in the early 16th century between Grace and Nature (v. chapter 6) was not going according to plan.

In order to counter all these threats and reaffirm the city's Catholic identity, Braga's elites took a number of measures.

One of the most notable and effective instruments at the service of the Catholic Reformation was the Inquisition (e.g. Mea 1998: 432-441). This was a religious tribunal created with the objective of repressing the heresies and reincorporating into the Church those sheep that had gone astray. After a false start in the 1530's, it started to function regularly after 1547. Its *modus operandi* was usually though inquisitorial visits to suspicious places where, through sermons, local residents were invited to spontaneously denounce their own faults and those of others in order to be absolved.

A similar process of inquiry into the habits of their inhabitants was conducted by the archbishops or their delegates during systematic visits to the city or other places of the archdiocese (Soares 1997: 433), as in the parish of Santiago in 1562 (ibid. 1986/87). This more vigilant role of the archbishops towards their flock was one of the decisions of the Council of Trent (1546-1563), where a more careful definition of Catholic dogmas also took place (Tourault 1998: 219).

Another important decision of this Council was the creation of seminaries in order to inculcate devotion and the spirit of religion in those teenagers desiring to be priests (ibid.: 220, 221). It was assumed that the younger they started in this life, the less the possibilities of becoming attracted to the pleasures of the world (ibid.). After all, the bishops needed to be supported by efficient clergymen if they wanted the Catholic Reformation to be successful. The archbishops of Braga didn't waste time in implementing this measure and already, in 1571, the first seminary in the Iberian Peninsula began to be built on the southern side of Campo da Vinha (Oliveira 1999: 73). On the map of 1594 the large mass of the seminary, called S. Pedro (S. Peter), is already visible. In my view, its construction in this area was not casual. As I mentioned in the previous chapter, this became the quietest area of the city, a place favourable to meditation. These qualities made this area the most appropriate place to educate young men desiring to be priests.

There were also by the mid-16th century major changes in the Portuguese educational system, with the pedagogy in colleges (pre-universities) and universities being delivered by the Jesuit order (Mendes 1993: 406). The purpose was to guarantee that the teaching was in accordance with Catholic dogma (ibid.). In Braga a small college of humanities had been working since 1531, teaching Latin, grammar and rhetoric (Maurício 2000: 29). It was believed by then that since Latin was the vehicle of all learning, either Classical or Christian, the student should be able to speak it correctly in order to facilitate the practice of a Christian life (Delumeau 1994: 84). As elsewhere in Portugal, the direction of this college, called S. Paulo (St. Paul), was given in 1560 to the Jesuits (Oliveira 1999: 135). Besides teaching, the Jesuits were also interested in a closer contact with Braga's inhabitants through confessions and sermons (ibid.: 137). So, in order to support these activities, a new church, also called S. Paulo, was built between 1567 and 1590 (ibid.: 135-137), being already visible in the 1594 map[30].

It was also in the mid-16th century, more precisely between 1544 and 1549 (ADB, S. José 1759: 12), that the first female convent in Braga was built. This is the building with a porch and tower, whose façade occupies most of the northern side of Campo dos Remédios on the 1594 map. The initiative came from the assistant bishop Fr. André de Torquemada, who even provided a house he had in that area, having also bought and demolished others that were adjacent, in order to build the convent (ibid.: 11). According to a 1699 copy of the original foundation document for this convent, there were three reasons behind its construction: the presence of a convent ennobled and magnified the city; Christ was honoured by it; and the population was comforted and edified with the example of the virtuous persons who lived in the convent (BNA, 54-VIII-24, n. 72). The first two reasons are closely connected: Braga's identity had a strong Christian and noble character and, as such, the institution of a convent, whose members were closer to a higher spiritual condition, was a way of reinforcing and reaffirming through its material presence the city's identity. The third reason is more important to the issue of the Catholic Reformation. As I mentioned earlier, women were quite active in the practice of heterodox activities in Braga. This convent would, in this context, be a way of educating the women of Braga in the practice of Christian virtues and, simultaneously, abandoning more heterodox behaviour. The presence of a bishop in the institution of this convent and its placement under the jurisdiction of the archbishops (ADB, S. José 1759: 13) are indications of the importance that this convent had for the lords of the city.

The location of this convent was well chosen. Notice that it is in Campo dos Remédios, an area reserved to the healing of physical infirmities. In this case, the convent would also cure another infirmity, more precisely those related with heterodox practices. Actually, the name of

---

[37] The two rectangular windows that are visible in the façade are not original. Their model suggests a mid-18th century addition; notice that they are already visible in the c. 1757 map.

the convent is very suggestive: Nossa Senhora dos Remédios, Piedade e Madre de Deus (Our Lady of Medicines, Piety and Mother of God) (ibid.: 12). Medicines against heterodoxy, presumably. That is why the bishop took so much trouble in giving his own property as well as acquiring others in the vicinity instead of looking for more readily accessible space elsewhere, of which there was then a lot in the city outskirts.

There was also a fourth reason behind this construction, which is not mentioned in the foundation document. By that time, there were a considerable number of noble families living in Braga, something that was not normal in the Middle Ages. Taking into consideration that in many noble families it was usually the first-born male that inherited the goods of the family, this meant that most of the women were forced to live in convents (Monteiro 1993: 282). Looking to the genealogies of several families of Braga, it is common to find two or three sisters in each generation going together to the same convent (Afonso 1954, 1962, 1968, 1969, 1970, 1975). In this way, they would be company for each other and would still remain close to their relatives living outside the convent. As for the archbishops, they would in this way get a steady supply of nuns for the convent. However, there was the problem that many of these women were not nuns by conviction, having been forced rather into that state. Therefore, many of them were not the most appropriate choices to serve as models of Christian virtues to the women of Braga, something that would become more and more evident later (v. chapter 10).

In order to promote a more rigorous discipline and deeper spiritual commitment among the faithful, the clergy throughout Catholic Europe also encouraged the formation of new confraternities whose members were expected to join solely as an expression of religious devotion (Friedrichs 1995: 80). Braga was also part of this movement, with all sorts of confraternities popping up after the mid-16th century. Those dedicated to the Passion of Christ were very popular, whose members, through the memory of the suffering of Christ on the cross, sought to have a more humble and virtuous life (Marques 1993). Also popular were the confraternities of the souls, whose members, through masses and prayers, sought to speed the transference to Heaven of the souls suffering in Purgatory due to their sins. The largest in Braga was the one dedicated to S. Vincent, having been founded in 1588 (AISV, *Livro Termos S. Vicente* 1594-1609: 3) and with a strong following among the members of the common people. There were even confraternities that intermeshed closely with certain crafts, such as the one dedicated to S. Crispim and S. Crispiniano, founded in 1629, and whose members were shoemakers charged with the task of looking out for the spiritual good of each other (ADB, *Estatutos S. Crispim e S. Crispiniano* 1731: 3, 4v).

A network of confraternities compassing several aspects of social life is thus created, to enable individuals to absorb more fully a Christian way of life. It became common, therefore, for individuals to be part of several confraternities.

One of the most complex buildings built in the mid-16th century Braga was the new church of the Mercy House, to the north of the Cathedral's cloister and where the roads of Sousa and Souto meet. It was in 1554 that this fellowship decided, with the approval of the archbishop, to build this church (Senna Freitas 1890, vol. II: 174), and construction started in 1562, being finished a few years later (Oliveira 1999: 119, 121). Taking into account the fact that the church we can see today has major 18th century modifications, it is useful to take a look at its oldest known graphic representation on the 1750 map (fig. 10), in order to have a better idea of what it looked like, although we must exclude the statues flanking the main door, which date from 1735 (ibid.: 121). Here, one can see a stairway connecting this entrance with the road, which, due to the symbolism of connecting Heaven and Earth, is a way of giving more emphasis to the sacredness of this church. As for the building itself, it was large, following the lines of Classical architecture, such as the arched door and the Corinthian columns (still visible today). The use of Classical lines became possible after the 1540's thanks to the publishing of several architectural treatises with numerous representations of Classical orders (Moreira 1995a: 350). The publication of these treatises was part of the wider European movement of recovering the Classical past, which is usually known by historians as the Renaissance. In Portugal, the works of the Italian Sebastiano Serlio became very popular and were considered to be representing the "true" model of the Classical (ibid.: 351). Notice however that, these Classical forms were not much different from those that preceded since both followed the same structural archetypes, which means that the symbolism was also much the same. Thus, the arched door would still be easily identified as an entrance to a more sacred dimension and the columns as a representation of the *axis mundi*.

The resulting church was an imposing building that would be impossible for anyone passing there to ignore, and considering that this was the main axis of the city, it means that practically everyone was familiar with it. However, why would those who built it wanted to create such an impact?

It is useful to remember what I have said previously about the Protestant critique of the Catholic practice of good actions as a way to ensure salvation. In Portugal, the practice of charity was organised around the Mercy Houses, and it is perhaps not surprising that a new church had been built by then. The Mercy House is thus leaving the discrete space of the Cathedral's cloister and through a more visible public presence was reaffirming the importance of the practice of charity as essential to guarantee salvation.

It is also interesting to note that in 1565 the City Hall decided to open, within the city and right in front of this church, a new road called R. Nova da Misericórdia (New

Road of the Mercy House) (Arquivo Municipal 1976: 749). This is the road that can be seen on the 1594 map meeting at a 90° angle the middle of the primary axis of the R. Sousa and R. Souto, thus cutting the upper half of the city into two halves and passing through a new gate in the northern part of the wall, called S. António (S. Anthony). Both the location and the name of this road leave few doubts that the church of the Mercy House was the main reason behind its construction. This road allowed a new line of vision right to the front of the church, focussing, as such, all the attention on it and making its presence fully felt.

However, a more careful analysis reveals an even more complex motivation behind the construction of the church and the road. As I mentioned in chapter 6, the City was organised around a cosmological cartographic scheme with a T axis that divided it in three parts that corresponded to the three continents then known (Asia, Africa and Europe). With the opening of the R. Nova da Misericórdia, the vertical bar of the T was extended further north. The adding of an extension to this T didn't change the symbolism of the cross that was associated with it and which has already been analysed in chapter 6. The big change with this addition was that instead of three continents represented, there were now four. This fourth continent was obviously America, which was already well known by this time. It is interesting to look to the northwest sector of the City in the 1594 map and see how was this new continent represented (Asia was now reduced to the northeast sector[31]). The most notable feature of this sector, taking up most of its area, is a large open space called Campo do Arcebispo (Field of the Archbishop) (ibid.). This was a somewhat irregular area, without any roads, buildings and gardens; an area closer to the conditions of the Chaos and, as such, completely different from the rest of the city. This obviously raises the question of why this area should have such a central role in representing the American continent. This can be better answered by reading the descriptions that were being written at that time about Brazil, the area of America with which the Portuguese were most familiar. Initially, it was seen as an Eden-like land peopled with innocent people but, as contacts became more regular, it was increasingly seen as a wilderness peopled with humans more akin to beasts and without religion (Pires 1991; Markl 1995: 420-423). It is, as it can be seen, a landscape that is far from the European model of society. Therefore, it is not surprising that in Braga, the American continent is represented by a relatively disorganised plan and open space, a place yet to be filled and made complete by Christian, civilised ordering.

This "actualisation" of the Cosmos, with the church of the Mercy House at the centre of it, undoubtedly

reinforced the idea of the importance of charity within the cosmic order of things. This does not mean that this church was a substitute for the Cathedral as the Centre of the World since, it is useful to remember, the former was umbilically connected to the latter. Rather, their close association and the circumstance that the Mercy House was built along Classical lines, also allowed to the Cathedral to affirm more visibly, through architecture, the Roman past of the city. This, until then, was mostly done through the Word, that is, inscriptions (as in the Campo de Santana) or humanist studies and writings. The circulation of architectural treatises after the 1540's allowed Classical architecture to be used in the service of the present.

One of the most important actions taken by the Church after the mid-16th century was the elimination from the sacred sphere of the multiple animist elements, which had been inherited from the old naturalist beliefs (Minois 2004: 222). For the Church, Nature was a work of God created for the good of humankind, not an object of devotion as happens in pagan practices. Though there was a sustained effort to desacralize the natural world, this does not mean that it was demonised again as it used to be throughout most of the Middle Ages. Instead, what is happening now is an attempt to give an even more transcendent character to the divine, to separate it even more from the world (ibid.). So, I am finishing this chapter focusing on how this effort of a more clear separation between the sacred and the profane affected religious practices in Braga. Although some of the initiatives I have previously mentioned were also part of this effort, I am concentrating here on how the Church and the civic authorities of Braga intervened on more concrete aspects related to the lived-in practice of the sacred.

One of the areas of intervention was in the uncontrolled exuberance of festive holidays. This was something that Catholic leaders found distasteful and tried to reshape, by stripping them of their unpredictable and uncontrolled elements and encouraging a greater focus on their devotional content (Friedrichs 1995: 252). I will give three examples from Braga.

The first is bullfights. These were very popular among the population and there was always one on the most important festivals (e.g. Arquivo Municipal 1971-1972, 1973). Yet, in 1562 some things started to change: the City Hall decided that bullfights could no longer take place along the city's roads, as it used to be, but instead should be confined to the Campo do Arcebispo (ibid. 1975: 378). The reason given for this change was that bullfights hindered pilgrims (ibid.). This was, therefore, a first attempt at separation between the spiritual activity of pilgrimage and the profane (in the eyes of the civic authorities) activity of bullfighting. The Campo do Arcebispo, being a large open space where there wasn't any tradition of religious festivities seemed a more appropriate place for bullfights. With this transfer of the bullfights, this area, by 1567, was already known as Campo dos Touros (Field of Bulls) (ibid.: 1979: 506).

---

[31] As a side note, it is interesting to notice that the Episcopal palace continued to be placed in the area of the city that represented Asia. This continent, within the medieval cosmology was considered the most important one (thus its placement above the other two), being here that the Garden of Eden supposedly was (Boorstin 1987: 105). Not surprisingly, it is where the archbishops' gardens, which were the largest in the city, were concentrated.

Even this separation, however, was not enough for the civic authorities and in 1568 it was determined that no more bullfights should be allowed in Campo dos Touros (ibid. 1980: 964). No explanation is advanced for this prohibition in the City Hall's Acts, but one can assume that the physical violence involved wasn't considered appropriate in a city that had reclaimed a spiritual status.

The second example is the festivities of St. John. Their main event was the hunting of a black pig in the area to the south of river Deste, close to Mount Picoto (Coelho 1992: 236). This black pig was just one of the manifestations of the Dragon. The pig, symbolically, is seen as the most impure of the animals, greedy and voracious, eating up everything that it finds (Ferguson 1966: 20; Chevalier and Gheerbrant 1994: 537). The black colour, connected with Chaos, only adds to the negative symbolism of this animal. However, in 1614, the civic authorities prohibited the hunt and the killing of the pig, declaring that it was not decent in a festival where the flag of the Virgin was present for such activities to take place (Coelho 1992: 238). Again, one can see here an attempt to give a more pure and transcendent character to religious festivals. Nonetheless, this decision was not well received by everyone and there is record of some resistance taking place, such as in 1638 when two men were fined for killing a pig (ibid.: 247).

Prohibitions, however, were not the only way of fighting paganism; another way was by example, in other words, by showing people alternative practices that should be emulated instead. This was a more effective strategy since it was based on a sincere adherence to moral ideals, and my third example, processions, demonstrates this strategy.

Among the several confraternities founded after the mid-16th century was the Arquiconfraria do Cordão (Archconfraternity of the Cordon), whose members sought to emulate the austerity of the Franciscan Order. This was particularly notable in the processions organised by their members who should avoid the dances and other "profane" festivities that were common in processions organised by other confraternities (AVOTSF, *Estatutos Arquiconfraria Cordão* 1615: 6). In this way, this archconfraternity was promoting a more solemn form of public procession, which wouldn't go unnoticed by others because of the contrast and which would thus eventually induce them to reconsider some of their 'sinful' actions.

Another area of intervention in the delimitation of the sacred and the profane was the suppression or, at least, containment of those material elements that could be used in the service of more pagan practices.

Among those material elements were the boulders situated in the public spaces of Braga's Garden. Between 1569 and 1572, the City Hall ordered the breaking of the boulders that existed near the crosses in the middle of R. Chãos, in front of church Nossa Senhora a Branca and in front of the leper-hospital of S. Lázaro (Arquivo Municipal 1982: 565; 1983: 551; 1984: 419). According

to the Acts, the reason given for this destruction was the damage they caused (ibid.: 1982: 565). Yet, it is not specified what kind of "damage" that was. Within the functionalist mentality that is prevalent today, one could assume that this was related to making the flow of traffic easier. Yet, if this was the reason, then it sounds more like an excuse, since it is known that there were crosses near those boulders as well as other boulders on the northern side of Campo de Santana (cf. AMB, *Livro Actas Câmara* Cx. 21, lv. 42, fl. 18), which certainly bothered the traffic, and yet they were not destroyed. So, what was so specific about these boulders?

As I discussed in the previous chapter, stones were associated with permanence and, by analogy, with the absolute and the sacred. On the other hand, we should notice that all the destroyed boulders were at crossroads, something that would give them the status of Centre. This role, from the viewpoint of Braga's elite, ought to have belonged solely to the Christian symbols in those areas. Indeed, the very destruction of these boulders suggests that they were seen as sacred by a significant segment of the population to the detriment of the nearby crosses. This might also explain the conservation of the boulders in Campo de Santana: by not being at a crossroads they didn't have any importance

Boulders had by then a long story of hierophany, that is, the manifestation of the sacred (Eliade 2002), which helps to explain why they were so popular. For example, in an early 18th century compilation of manifestations of the Virgin in Portugal, many of them were depicted as taking place among boulders[32] (Santa Maria 1707). Actually, anyone who today visits small villages in rocky areas can still hear a lot of stories associated with certain rock formations, while chapels or crosses in the vicinity are simply ignored. The destruction of boulders occurred only in extreme cases because it was more common to Christianise them by adding Christian symbols. That they were destroyed in Braga, suggests that the local elite believed that the other approach was not working effectively.

The material elements of a number of churches also came under scrutiny due their potential misuse and misrepresentation for pagan purposes. If we look at the two churches built in Braga in the second half of the 16th century – Mercy House (fig. 10) and S. Paulo (fig. 18) – and compare them with the early 16th century main chapel of the Cathedral, one can notice other differences than those we can simply attribute to their Classical lines. One such difference is the complete absence of gargoyles in the new buildings. These beasts, which already occupied a marginal position in the Cathedral, were no longer to be found in churches after the mid-16th century. The only images that are visible in churches after this

---

[32] Usually in the presence of little shepherds, which is understandable if one takes in consideration that children represent the human condition before sin (Chevalier and Gheerbrant 1994: 240), whereas shepherds are the chosen of God (ibid.: 506). The last such manifestation in Portugal (for those who believe it) was in Fátima in 1917.

date are human ones. This is understandable if one remembers that, in the Christian perspective, only humans are made in the image of God; since churches were the House of God, only images most closely related to that condition were to be allowed there. So, any images that made reference to elements closer to the Chaos and that could be used and reinterpreted by segments of the population for other means were eradicated. As for the function of gargoyles in ejecting dirty rainwater and their role as guardians of the threshold, they started to be substituted after this date in Portuguese churches with small-sculpted cannons; in this way, it was avoided the use of images with beastly looks connected with Chaos.

The representation of Nature in churches was also affected. Whereas in the Cathedral's main chapel there is an explosion of natural motifs, the contrast is almost shocking when one looks to the other two churches. In the church of S. Paulo, the façade is completely plain, while in the Mercy House it is noticeable some curtailment with only some spirals, which symbolise the cosmic forces of life (Chevalier and Gheerbrant 1994: 303-305), being represented. In both cases, in order to emphasise the spiritual character of the churches, the representation of Nature is severely curtailed allowing geometrical forms, which have a more "pure" character, to be more prominent. The differences between both churches result from the background of their promoters: in S. Paulo, the strongly intellectual and radical Jesuit Society; in the Mercy House, secular laymen. Notice that this kind of architecture with considerable plain façades became quite common in Portugal after the mid-16th century (Kubler 1988; Moreira 1995b), probably for similar motives (Horta Correia 1986: 95).

Changes are also visible inside the churches. After the mid-16th century it became common to cover the churches' walls with patterns of green or blue lozenges (Meco 1986: 131, 198, 199). Again, there is here a use of geometrical figures as a substitute for natural images. However, notice that these new patterns still kept a connection, albeit a very abstract one, with Mother Earth. After all, the lozenge is a form associated with female fertility (Chevalier and Gheerbrant 1994: 416) and the green colour that lozenges sometimes have (the colour of Nature) also points to that connection. Yet, it is useful to notice that the blue colour that other lozenges have points to an attempt to give Mother Earth a more celestial character, due to the symbolism of that colour. The choosing of the colours was therefore dependent on how radical were the promoters.

The use of lozenges doesn't mean that the representation of Nature inside churches ceased after the mid-16th century. A considerable number of churches still continued to represent images of Nature in their walls including, for example, the church of S. Paulo in Braga. An early 17th century description, mentions that the church's frieze was painted with two orders of large jars with green plants and flowers (Basto 1627: 53). The change in intent is clear, however, when one looks to the forms that the vegetation started to assume. While S.

Paulo's paintings are no longer visible today, there are still several churches extant from this period with decorated tiles decorated with similar motifs (cf. Simões 1971 for a listingsuch as the chapel of the former convent of Salvador in Braga (fig. 19). If we closely examine them we can see that the forms are not as realistic as the ones from the early 16th century, but are, instead, much more abstract. In this way, there was less danger that some persons would see them as objects of devotion full of spiritual value, or *manna*.

Also common is a mixture of these motifs, with vegetation around lozenges (fig. 19), where the vegetation is disciplined and subject to the strict forms of the lozenge.

Finally, spatial variation in the location of these motifs can also be found, such as blue lozenges in the most sacred areas of the church (the main chapel and the baptistery) and abstract vegetation in the nave.

With these changes inside the churches, it was expected that the devotion of the faithful would become exclusively focused on the retable behind the altar and its concentration of images of the saints. These had become the only realistic images inside the churches.

In conclusion, this reform movement was a sustained effort that would continue for the next decades and through a combination of repressive and educational measures, some with a more specific application and others with a wider one, achieved a considerable success. The spreading of Protestant ideas in Portugal and, consequently, the risk of a religious war, was avoided. Crypto-Judaism was broken, either through the killing of its practitioners or through their exile; those that remained were eventually absorbed into mainstream Christianity. In the case of persistent pagan practices, the success was more mixed. The problem here was that for most people the sacred was lived through Nature. The Church, by trying to transform the sacred into an intellectual and interior devotion without any connection with the material world, made the contact of the human spirit with the sacred much more problematic for most people (Minois 2004: 104, 222, 411). On the other side, the Church made this act of separation more difficult by retaining an ambiguous position on some miracles, such as the Eucharist (in which bread and wine are transformed into the body and blood of Christ), something that left the spirits of the faithful confused and prone to the continuation of some heterodox practices (ibid.: 411). Finally, the enforcement of this strict division was dependent on a vigilant and repressive clergy. In its weakness or absence there was the risk of the return of some heterodox practices. That was something that would take place periodically in Braga, such as the return of bullfights in the late 16th century (v. chapter 9) or the churches built by confraternities in the late 17th century (v. chapter 11), obliging the clergy to readapt some of its actions to the changing circumstances.

9

A looming crisis

In 1580, Portugal was shaken by a political earthquake when Philip II of Spain became king of Portugal. In relation to Braga, this turn of events was catastrophic. As if all the troubles and difficulties discussed in the previous chapter were not enough now there was a new political situation that threatened Braga's status as the see of the primate of all Hispania. As I mentioned in the Introduction, since the Middle Ages there was strong rivalry between Braga and Toledo with each city reclaiming this primate status. Before 1580, the position of both contenders was considerably reinforced by the existence of two independent kingdoms in the Iberian Peninsula, with each of them defending the positions of their own city. The events of 1580, in which this region became politically unified, this time under an Hispanic Monarchy, obviously emphasised the dispute between Braga and Toledo. Yet, Philip II, wishing to conquer the "hearts and minds" of the Portuguese didn't force a decision on that subject; rather, he preserved Portugal's autonomy as an independent kingdom, with the only difference being that Portugal and Spain shared the same king (Magalhães 1993c: 566). Nonetheless, it was widely believed that it was only a question of time until a decision came about the primacy and nobody had illusions that the winner would not be Braga, since Philip II made Madrid and not Lisbon the capital of this new shared monarchy. So, implicitly, there already appeared to be some predisposition to support Toledo's pretensions. Losing such status, would also be very damaging for the archbishop of Braga since much of his prestige and authority came from his title of primate.

That a significant proportion of Braga's population was not satisfied with this threatened turn of events is clear when reading the Acts of the City Hall. After an official acclamation of Philip II in early September, by the end of that month there are reports of constant civil agitation in the city, during which some people were killed (Arquivo Municipal 1970: 304, 309). The situation was so serious that by the end of October the city was under the military occupation of Spanish troops (ibid.: 310, 311). After that the situation got calmer, at least on the surface (ibid.: 312).

In the end, however, and despite the fears, officially Braga still kept its primate status, and so there was still scope for reaffirming it in the context of the new Hispanic Monarchy. That was something that Fr. Agostinho da Cruz, archbishop of Braga during a long period, between 1589 and 1609, attempted to do through the patronage of an important number of works, as I intend to show in this chapter.

One of his first works was the construction of a fountain on the western side of Campo de Santana in 1594 (Oliveira 2001a: 216). This fountain can already be seen on the map of Braga of that same year, though the form that is visible does not correspond to what was actually built[33]. This fountain is still intact today, being outside the Nova Gate (fig. 20). Its form is considerably different from Braga's previous public fountains, whose constructions date from the period of D. Diogo de Sousa (cf. ADB, *Memorial*). Some of these fountains are visible on the map of 1750, such as in R. Cónegas (n. 58) and in Nossa Senhora a Branca (n. 42). The form these earlier fountains present is of a tank with a wall topped by battlements and a niche with a statue of the Virgin in the middle. Water, as I mentioned in chapter 5, is the symbol most strongly associated with the beginning of life. Therefore, it is not surprising to find a statue of the Virgin and battlements in a protective role. Indeed, it is very likely that, once again, D. Diogo de Sousa was emulating Rome with the construction of several fountains. It is also worth noting that papal Rome itself had, in the 15th century, decided to emulate ancient Rome by reconstructing one of its glories: the water supply system which fed the public fountains (Schama 1995: 286).

There are clear differences in form between these early 16th century fountains and the one built in 1594. While the others are relatively discrete and compact, the later one has large dimensions. It has a high central axis, with spirals and foliage sculptures arranged up it and from whose top the water flows. Along this axis there are three cups, whose diameter is increasingly smaller as they approach the top, allowing the water to create a cascade effect. On the top of the fountain there are some sculpted Hermes, the coats of arms of Portugal and those of the Archbishop as well as an armillary sphere, which is crowned by a cross with two arms. In order to give meaning to the differences in form, an iconological and spatial analysis of this fountain is needed.

First of all, the large dimension of this fountain, its water effects and its placement right in the middle of the western side of Campo de Santana, means that there was an intention to make it visible to a large audience. After

---

[33] Though in the maps of c. 1694 and c. 1757 its form is correctly depicted.

all, it mustn't be forgotten that this was the most important meeting point between the inhabitants of Braga and outsiders (v. chapter 7). Actually, very often, the fountain, or Well of Life, marked, within Christian iconography, the gathering place of the nations (ibid.: 287), being as such a key place of public sociability and, therefore, prone to be used to transmit messages to a wider audience. But, what messages was this fountain transmitting?

First of all, it is important to notice that the central axis shares the symbolism of the *axis mundi*. In this case, it seems to be inspired by the old archetype of the Tree of Life. In this interpretation it is significant that along with the existence of sculpted foliage there is also the treetop effect that the water makes when flowing from the upper part of the column to the lower tank. Notice that in Christian iconography the Tree of Life was commonly represented with a river flowing from its roots and feeding the Well of Life (ibid.). The theme of the tree of life was well known in Northern Portugal, with oaks being commonly associated with sacred revelations (cf. Santa Maria 1707). Another characteristic of the *axis mundi*, the support of the totality of the Cosmos, is also represented here. The cups have a spherical form, the shape of Cosmos, and there are three of them which may be taken as a reference to the three levels of the Cosmos: Heaven, Earth and the subterranean world or Hell. In order to further emphasise the idea of a living Cosmos in perpetual regeneration, associated with the Tree of Life, some more symbolic elements were added to this fountain. One is, obviously, the water, symbol of the beginning of life, which in this fountain is in constant regeneration. The other is the cup, associated with the medieval Grail, where the blood of Christ was gathered, and which is the drink of immortality (cf. Chevalier and Gheerbrant 1994: 627).

The purpose of this complex iconographic program is better understood if one looks at the highest part of the fountain, above the upper cup. Here it is possible to see the two-armed cross, which is directly associated with archbishoprics (Ferguson 1966: 165; Chevalier and Gheerbrant 1994.: 246), thus symbolising Braga itself. As for the armillary sphere, since the early 16th century it had been the symbol of the Portuguese Crown, being associated with Portugal's imperial expansion throughout the globe following the arrival of Vasco da Gama's expedition to India in 1498. This association between Braga and the Portuguese Crown is also visible in the two coats of arms, which stand side by side. So, in my view, what is being affirmed here is the predominance of the primate status of Braga and its archbishops at least within the realm of the Portuguese kingdom. This status, in the political events of the 1580's faltered, as we have seen, but now, with all the rich symbolism of regeneration of the Tree of Life, combined with the water and the cup, its sacredness and permanency were being reaffirmed. The placement of this fountain in the most frequented public space of Braga is an indication of how important it was for the Archbishop to publicise this message.

The fountain was also used to transmit other messages, namely the six Hermes figures in the upper part of the fountain. Hermes was the Classical god of travel and commerce. Considering that this was the main commercial area of Braga, I think their presence here is not casual and they were symbolising the merchants and their activities. Actually, this connection is further reinforced when one looks to the façade of the church of Mercy House in the neighbouring city of Viana, which was ruled by a merchant oligarchy, and whose colonnade contained a number of Hermes statues. In a class perspective also we can consider that the cross in the fountain symbolises the clergy and the armillary sphere the nobility that ruled Portugal. With the Hermes figures then standing for those that labour, one can then find on the column all three social orders represented. What was the purpose of this scheme? Here, it is useful to notice that the Jews were not the only ones whose social elevation was being blocked by the traditional elite since the same was also happening, in particular after the 1560's, to the urban artisans (Mea 1998: 334), that is, merchants and craftsmen. So, the deliberate and conscious placing of these symbols along the line of an *axis mundi* and its precise location in the main commercial space of Braga would be a way of legitimating and communicating to the viewer the place of each social order within the cosmological scheme. This affirmation of a world dominated by the aristocracy was thus part of a process of marginalizing the merchant classes and their activities

It is interesting to notice that a similar use of fountains for propaganda reasons can also be found in Rome in the second quarter of the 17th century, in the context of rivalries between local aristocratic families in their ambitions for the papacy, when a number of them were built in Rome's public spaces, such as the famous Fountain of the Four Rivers in *Piazza Navona* by Bernini (cf. Schama 1995: 289-306).

It was also in 1594 that the first known visual representation of Braga was made: the so-called Braun map (fig. 6). This map is commonly used by researchers (e.g. Oliveira 1999; Bandeira 2000a, 2000b; Maurício 2000; Sousa Pereira 2000) as a way of retrieving data about Braga, due to its elaborate depiction of buildings (with an emphasis on the most important), the road network, the configuration of property blocks, the city wall, gardens, crosses, fountains, place names, etc. Yet, there is also awareness that many of the elements displayed here are not properly represented since the map doesn't follow a strict geometric representation of space (e.g. Bandeira 2000a: 47). Therefore, this map is usually seen as having mostly an iconographic character (for display) and not so much a functional one (ibid.). The problem of this distinction between objective and subjective or functional and artistic is that it is, as I have discussed before in chapter 5 quoting J. B. Harley, a hollow one, since maps are always value-laden images, since they are in the end influenced by a number of specific circumstances, which are anything but "neutral" or "merely aesthetic". So, what were the purposes behind the drawing of this particular map? What can its analysis tell us about it?

For a start, it is useful to notice that this map appeared in the well-known atlas of world cities printed by Braun. This indicates the audience to whom it was directed: the European elite, the only group who could afford it. Another indication that points to this audience is that the inscriptions are all in Latin, the international language of the elite. What image of Braga is being shown here? Looking to the upper left corner, one can see the coat-of-arms and titles of the Archbishop (under whose patronage the map was made) and where he reasserts the title of Primate of Hispania. So there it is: international propaganda. And the city, of course, must present an image that is in accordance with the high titles that the Archbishop reaffirms.

The choosing of the city name used on the map – *Nova Bracarae Augusta* – was not casual: as I mentioned before, the concept of "new", within circular notions of time, is what is closer to the perfection of the beginning, and thus more "authentic". It is a city in all is grandeur that is being represented here, or more precisely, an idealised city. And in order to be more effective, this map presents something that is common to all maps made for political purposes: deliberate distortion (cf. Harley 1988: 287).

So, at the centre of the map, concentrating all the attention, is a disproportionate image of the Cathedral, in order to emphasise its role as Centre of World. To allow space on the map for the central position of the Cathedral, the area between the southern part of the city wall and the river was actually larger than shown, having been severely squeezed in the cartography. Moving outwards from the Cathedral, is the cross pattern already analysed and which wasn't as geometric as the map makes it appear. The wall around the City was also less circular than depicted. Yet, these are all the forms of an ideal city and that's how Braga was intended by its creator and patron to be perceived, and this is how we should view it as well.

Besides the Cathedral, some other buildings are also emphasised by size or, at least, by being given a label naming them. These comprise all religious buildings, as well as crosses. Thus the potential audience is being shown how Christian Braga was. Moreover, the urge to represent as many religious buildings as possible was such, that in the northern part of Campo da Vinha there is a letter "b", which is explained in the key on the lower left corner of the map as a convent of nuns that was going to be built there[34]. This was due to its transfer from Vitorino das Donas under the pretext that it was isolated in a rural area (the Chaos) (Senna Freitas 1890, vol. II: 257). Also emphasised in this way were some secular buildings essential to civic life such as the City Hall, the

college, the hospital, the pillory and fountains. As for residential buildings, which constitute the mass of the houses, they are mere stereotypes, since they were not contributing to the grandeur of the city; they are there just to fill space. One only needs to look to their form and number. For example, according to the *Index* and the 1750 map, there were some houses with adjacent towers in R. S. Marcos (fig. 16); yet, none are shown on the 1594 map. Again, the number of houses that the same sources indicate to have existed on the R. Sousa/R. Souto axis is greater than those that can be counted on the 1594 map. Except for a couple of houses with external stairs visible on this axis and a couple of others on the north side of Campo da Vinha, the only house that is carefully drawn, and perhaps more accurately depicted, is the episcopal palace, in order to leave no doubts as to who was the lord of the city.

In order to emphasise this renewal of Braga's Christian character, it is interesting to notice that some elements that might have been associated with a pagan past were inserted on the map to make the contrast more notable. These elements are the small wood and the cave between the word MERIDIES, both of which are on the lower part of the map. Notice that they are in the area of the map associated with Chaos, an indication that they were acting as its representatives. In relation to the wood, named on the map *Sylva primatialis*, as I mentioned in chapter 5, woods, alongside deserts, were used to represent Chaos and, in the case of Braga, there was already a millenary history of condemnation of woods as places of pagan activities, which were seen as demonic, as one can read in the *De Correctione Rusticorum* from S. Martinho de Dume[35]. The wood was also being depicted in the map as living place of hares (four are visible), with an inscription mentioning that they are abundant there. The hare is connected with the old cults of Mother Earth, to the symbolism of water, vegetation, and of perpetual renewal of life, with the prolific character of these animals having a key role in that association (Ferguson 1966: 20; Chevalier and Gheerbrant 1994: 402). Unsurprisingly, in less animist religions such as Christianity, the hare is condemned, their prolific character being attributed to wantonness and lust (Chevalier e Gheerbrant 1994: 403). So, the wood on the map with the hare, water and vegetation, symbolises old pagan practices. Its position in the lower part of the map and, therefore, in a position inferior to that occupied by the city, is a way of symbolising the defeat of pagan practices by Christian Braga.

The same can also be said about the cave. This cave is not a feature in the real landscape since there are no caves around the city. In my view, this cave is actually a representation of a megalithic monument, a dolmen, and, if I am right, this is the oldest known iconographic representation of such a monument in Portugal. These are

---

[34] The capital letters that can be seen spread throughout the map refer to the German translation, which in the original map can be found in its back.

[35] This 6th century text can be red in its original Latin with a modern Portuguese translation in the journal Bracara Augusta, vol. II, pp. 223-239.

common in the Portuguese landscape and there are several of them still visible in the north-west of the country. While today, in many cases, only the internal structure of the monument with its large stones is the only thing remaining, originally they were covered by a cairn of earth and gravel. This is what is visible on the map as well as its entrance. These monuments were already by then an old headache for the Church since local populations usually associated sacred events and rituals with many of them. With the Catholic Reform there was a significant effort by the Church to control this phenomenon, with several approaches being followed, such as building chapels nearby; adapting them to become chapels (e.g. S. Brissos); destroying them and transferring the prehistoric remains of the "saint" venerated there to the local church (Oliveira et al. 1997). There is no record of a megalith near Braga but, whether it existed or not, I consider its presence on the map as a way of marking a contrast with the Cathedral. Note that the megalith is called *Antrum Reginae* (Cave of the Queen) and that it is aligned with the Cathedral. That name makes a clear reference to the symbolism of the cave and the old cults of Mother Earth. A contrast can be construed with the Christian Mother Earth who is venerated in the Cathedral, the Holy Mary, with the superior and central position of the latter symbolising the victory over paganism.

This map also celebrates the antiquity of Braga through reference to a number of Roman remains spread throughout the city. So, the roads leading to the northeast, southeast, southwest and the road indicated with the letter "d" (to the north) are mentioned as being of Roman origin. The previously discussed Roman columns around the chapel of Santana, marked with the letter "f", are also indicated. In Campo da Vinha, the letter "c" refers to a Roman cemetery found in that area. The last two references to the Roman past are in the area of the chapel of S. Sebastião. Two labels can be found on the map there: the one below the chapel refers to an arch that was still standing at the time. As for the other, it mentions that this was the area where the Roman forum was, which is confirmed by recent archaeological work. I don't know what sources were used in the sixteenth century for this identification, though it may be connected with a stone that was once to be found there with the Roman name of the city inscribed on it (v. chapter 10 for more on this stone).

Another public work patronised by the Archbishop was a new slaughterhouse (Cunha 1634-35: 411). This building appears on the c. 1757 map between the Nova and Maximinos Gates in the city wall. Its previous position was on R. Souto and its transfer is understandable if one considers that, though the building was cleaned at the end of each day, its polluted association with animal blood and its smell would have been quite striking. So, the Archbishop, by removing it to the part of Braga more connected with the material dimension of life attempted to purify the City (the in-wall area) and give it a more sacred character.

One of the most important changes that took place in the city landscape at this time was in Campo dos Touros. This area again became a space dedicated to bullfights (Cunha 1634-35: 411), but it is noticeable that there weren't any changes in terms of permanent structures; this whole area remained as it was before. There were, of course, platforms for the spectators, but they were all temporary, used only when there were events in that area. What actually changed with the reintroduction of these festivities in this area was its character. To understand this we must first ask why the Archbishop decided to revoke the decision taken in 1568 to forbid bullfights in Braga? A good starting point to answer this question is reading the descriptions of the festivities that took place in this area some years later, in 1627, when a new archbishop, D. Rodrigo da Cunha, arrived in Braga (Basto 1627; Rodrigues 1627).

After solemnities and processions in the Cathedral and in the major axis of the city, there were days of festivities in Campo dos Touros. There were bullfights here (ibid.: 29-30; ibid.: 29-30), as also happened in ordinary religious festivals after the processions, however, since this was a special occasion – i.e. the arrival of a new archbishop – there were also other events. There was a simulated battle between two companies of soldiers under the leadership of Braga's nobility (ibid.: 15v-18; ibid.: 20-22) and another mock battle between two groups of horsemen drawn from the same nobility, one dressed in Hispanic clothes and the other in Moorish dress (ibid.: 23v, 24; ibid.: 23-27).

These ceremonies were not "mere" festivities, since they had a cosmic and symbolic meaning. Ceremonies such as this, which involve fights between two groups of combatants, represent the duality of the transition from Chaos to Cosmos, with the group symbolising the latter defeating the former (Eliade 2002: 89). The same can also be said about bullfights. The bull, here, is a symbol of Chaos and primitive force, from whose death life would emanate through its blood (Chevalier and Gheerbrant 1994: 650). In the context of this set of performances the ritual of fighting and killing the bull can be understood. Frutuoso Basto, who was a good observer, mentions that bullfights were the most popular festivities among the common people and that the more violent the bull the more they liked (1627: 23v, 24, 29).

These elements allow us to make a first outline of the reasons behind the reversal of policy regarding bullfights as well as the other festivities that involved a degree (even if somewhat simulated) of physical violence. In all of these the members of the nobility occupied a central role. This was also true of the bullfights. Until then, they were not much different from what can still be observed today in small villages in Portugal where any man can participate (cf. Veiga de Oliveira 1984: 263-272). By contrast, the reactivation of Campo dos Touros meant that only men from the nobility could participate in these activities; men of the common people thus became simply spectators. What was until then a communal activity thus became one restricted only to the nobility. In other words, these festivities, where the cosmic drama was recreated, allow the nobility to play the role of the civilising hero who enabled the perpetuation of the Cosmos. They seem to have had some success in convincing their audience about that. Fighting such an indomitable animal as the bull was not an easy thing and, as I mentioned before, these fights were popular. Also in the simulated combats, the choreography was so well done that everybody was in suspense (Basto 1627: 18). What then was the political purpose of the monopoly of these activities by the nobility?

Nobles, by putting themselves at the centre of the stage and the common people as spectators, the former "proved" through their actions to the latter the "essential" role they had in the resolution of the cosmic drama. In this way they linked the perpetuation of the social order with the perpetuation of the Cosmos. As for the commoners, all that was left for them was to applaud the nobility for their actions.

Yet, attempting to keep social peace through a reaffirmation of the traditional social order, was not the only reason behind the Archbishop's decision to reinstate bullfights and similar activities in Braga. An interesting detail mentioned by both chroniclers of the 1627 festivities is that in the aisle of the episcopal palace turned to Campo dos Touros there was a window through which the archbishops participated in the ceremonies (Basto 1627: 16, 16v; Rodrigues 1627: 23). From that position the archbishops presided over the festivities that were taking place below them; they were the patrons offering these festivities to the expectant spectators waiting for the beginning. Moreover, while the bullfights that took place here in the 1560's were a mere expedient, now the Archbishop was offering the whole of this area to the city for the sole purpose of these festivities. There is here, through this patronage, with the scenario (aisle and window) and with the careful choreographed actions of the archbishops, a theatricality of power that instigates a sort of cult of personality in the figure of the archbishop. With the charismatic power that resulted from this, the archbishops were in a position to compensate for some of the weakness that resulted from their unresolved primate status. It is because of this weakness that the Archbishop (and the city elite) decided to take advantage of violent festivities that in other circumstances he would condemn. As for the common folk, they had bullfights back, albeit in a very different form and with different implications for the city's social life.

There is still one more aspect about these festivities that I want to explore: why were they taking place in the area of Braga that is supposed to have a more spiritual character? Shouldn't they have taken place rather in the outskirts of the city, in the Garden? Not necessarily. There were, in my view, good reasons for the Archbishop's decision to opt for this area. First of all, by taking place inside the City these festivities acquired a more solemn character. Secondly, it is useful to notice that in the micro-cosmos of the city, they took place in the area that corresponded

to the American continent, which, as I mentioned in the previous chapter, was associated with the beginning of the Cosmos, not having yet reached full maturity. Thus, this was an appropriate place for the celebration of violent festivities that recreated the cosmic drama. Thirdly, by confining this sort of festivities to this area, it separated them from the more religious ones that took place in other public spaces of the city such as the R Nova, R. Souto, R. Maximinos and the Praça do Pão. This, again, shows the care taken in separating profane from religious activities. Finally, it allowed the Archbishop to make effective use of the aisle of his palace for this theatre of power.

There were also other changes in the episcopal palace at that time, besides the opening of the aisle window. On R. Souto, the western aisle of the entrance of the palace was transformed into an open colonnade with a ground-floor gallery behind (fig. 21) on top of which the Archbishop had a new room made for himself (Cunha 1634-35: 411). This colonnade has 14 columns, that is, twice seven (the perfect number); repetitions are a way of multiplying the symbolic value of an image (Chevalier and Gheerbrant 1994: 270). So there is here a use of the *axis mundi* symbolism of the column and the number 7 in association with the Archbishop's room in order to further his prestige. On the post-1594 maps, particularly the 1750 one, a window is depicted with a balcony following Classical lines (perhaps similar to the other one, whose form is not known) connecting this room with the axis of R. Sousa/R. Souto and which is known to have been used by archbishops for overlooking the processions that passed that way (cf. Veríssimo Serrão 1958: 25). As happened on Campo dos Touros, this was a way of presiding over the ceremonies, this time religious, that passed along this important axis of the city. Along with his intervention on this place, it is possible that Fr. Agostinho da Cruz was also responsible for two other structures that are shown here on the c. 1694 map: a fountain and a double stair at the entrance to the palace. The fountain, whose form is similar to the one built in 1594 in Campo de Santana, was removed in 1723 and nothing more is known about it and its iconographic program. It is possible that, in its position in front of the episcopal palace, it celebrated the archbishops of Braga. As for the double stair, which was a single one in the early 16th century, one has again here the use of duplication in order to enhance prestige.

To finish this chapter, I am going to discuss the most ambitious work of this Archbishop: the reconfiguration of Campo da Vinha. What he did there was nothing more, nothing less, than to emulate the contemporary *Piazza del Popolo* in Rome. This *Piazza* was constructed between 1516-1586, with the objective of affording prestige and grandeur to the northern entrance of Rome through the construction of new façades and by the placement there (in 1589) of an Egyptian obelisk, brought to the city originally by the emperor Augustus in 10 B.C. This stood in the precise intersection of the three avenues that led from the *Piazza* towards the city (Burke 1975: 80, 81). This was one of the four Egyptian obelisks that the popes ordered to be re-erected in Rome, with the purpose of embodying a symbolic connection between the Roman antiquity and the Christian posterity, the two histories of Rome (Schama 1995: 284, 285). The reasons for my comparison between Braga and Rome are the following.

In 1595, the Archbishop acquired and donated a large parcel of land in the western part of Campo dos Touros to the religious order of St. Augustine in order to build a new convent there (whose construction started in 1596) and where a faculty of Theology was installed in order to provide a better formation for preachers (Ferreira 1932: 101). It is interesting to notice that this convent was called Nossa Senhora do Pópulo (our Lady of the People), which is the same name as one of the churches on the *Piazza del Popolo* and that lent its name to it. Since it is known that this Archbishop had a great devotion for the image of the Lady that was in the Roman church (Cunha 1634-35: 410), one can see here an intentional connection. Moreover, in both cases these buildings belonged to the Augustinians, although in the case of Braga one can also add that the Archbishop was favouring his own religious order since he too was an Augustinian.

Another important point of comparison is that an obelisk was also built on Campo da Vinha (although not with the exact shape of an Egyptian one), and this can be seen on the maps of both c. 1694 and c. 1757. The Roman obelisk had four fountains at its corners, and the Braga version too had four corner water-spouts in the form of dolphins (fig. 22). As with the Roman obelisk this too was built in the intersection of three important roads. One, to the south-west, R. Biscainhos, leads to the important commercial area in front of the Nova Gate, a place where the archbishops were also ceremonially received before entering the City. Another, to the south, R. Nova da Misericórdia, leads to the Mercy House and the Cathedral. Finally, the one to the south-east, R. Fonte Cárcova, leads to Campo de Santana. I couldn't find the date of the obelisk's initial construction; it is known that in 1603, the Archbishop had already given orders to start the works of water supply to Campo da Vinha (AMB, *Cartas dos Senhores Arcebispos e Cabidos*), although the oldest reference I found about the obelisk dates from 1633, though by then it was already built and pouring water (AMB, *Livro Actas Câmara* Cx.16, lv. 33, fl. 321). Another similarity is that both the Campo da Vinha and the *Piazza del Popolo* are on the northern side of, respectively, Braga and Rome.

Finally, there are also façades of great monumentality in Campo da Vinha, such as the Seminar, the nun convent of Salvador (Savior) and the Pópulo monastery, which are distributed in different parts of the Campo, respectively south, north and east, in order to make their presence more felt. One only needs to look at the maps of c. 1694 and c. 1757 to see how the mass of these buildings extended throughout a large extent of this area. So, all the Archbishop had to do was to take advantage of the prior existence of the Seminar on the southern side and of the planned nun convent in the northern side, and then add the Pópulo monastery to the western side, making sure that these two buildings were imposing enough.

But why would this Archbishop want to emulate the *Piazza de Popolo*? As I have mentioned in previous chapters, in religious societies spatial organisation is based in the emulation of sacred and prestigious models. In this case, the Archbishop by emulating one of the most prestigious squares of Rome, which was the capital of the Catholic world, is putting Braga at the same level, which can be seen as a way of reaffirming its trembling primatial status.

Finally, it is useful to note that there is also some influence from the Catholic Reformation in the reorganisation of this public space. After all, the dominant buildings in this area were all religious not secular. One only needs to compare the 1594 map (where only the seminar is visible) with the one from c. 1694 to see the difference. After the construction of these three buildings, wherever any person inside this area looked there was always a prominent religious building. This is interesting because this area had been, since the early 16th century, the main meeting point for the population of Braga to relax and chat. So, the presence of these buildings can be seen as a way of conditioning the interaction between individuals, constantly reminding them of the importance of the practice of Christian virtues.

Yet, despite the Archbishop's best efforts, the situation would only get worse for both Braga and the Mitre, as will be seen in the next chapter.

10

An identity crisis

The year 1619 was a turning point in the relationship between Portugal and Spain in the matter of the Hispanic Monarchy. Until then, there hadn't been any serious attempt to question this unity. Influential sectors of Portuguese society were still hoping that the king would eventually make Portugal the head of this monarchy and Lisbon its capital. In 1619, the king Philip II (III of Spain), after 36 years of royal absence in Portugal, went to Lisbon in order to obtain from the Portuguese Parliament a solemn oath recognising his son as his successor. The Portuguese didn't waste this unique opportunity and staged a grandiose reception in order to obtain from the king a confirmation of Portugal's autonomy (which was recently being eroded in some areas) and, above all, to convince him to make Lisbon the capital of the Hispanic Monarchy (Kubler 1988: 110-112). The Portuguese were quite explicit regarding their expectations by putting ambiguous messages along the triumphal arches of the royal route simultaneously praising and threatening the king (ibid.: 113, 114). However, the king was not impressed and after obtaining the oath returned quickly to Madrid. No Spanish king would then ever visit Portugal again during the era of the Hispanic Monarchy. It is easy to imagine the tremendous disappointment in Portugal after these events: all remaining hopes about Portugal having a prominent place in this monarchy were gone. Worse still, Portugal's autonomy as an independent kingdom was being gradually eroded, becoming more and more a province of Spain.

But for Braga, the events of 1619 were even worse. As if the king's attitude was not enough, there were two incidents during this meeting that revealed that Braga's primate status was already being openly contested. From the moment of his arrival in Lisbon, Archbishop D. André Furtado de Mendonça was openly displaying his primate cross (Cunha 1634-35: 458). Yet, the Spanish officers opposed this, thus contesting Braga's status; the Archbishop replied by walking with his cross through the roads of the city as well as entering the royal palace with it (ibid.). As if this incident wasn't worrying enough, the Archbishop was completely shocked when the king informed him that he was going to allow the archbishop of Lisbon to proclaim the solemn oath of the Parliament, under the pretext that his diocese was the most ancient (ibid.: 459). The Archbishop protested vehemently arguing that he was the primate and therefore he should be the one to proclaim the oath, threatening to leave Lisbon and declaring invalid the meeting of the

Parliament (ibid.). The king eventually accepted but the Archbishop was furious and, after the meeting, visited several places within the diocese of Lisbon showing his primate cross affirming, as such, his superiority over the archbishop of Lisbon (ibid.: 460) whose reaction was to issue an interdict forbidding D. André Furtado de Mendonça from processing through the city. The temperature between the two men rose and it ended in mutual recriminations (ibid.). The relationship between them eventually got calmer after the intervention of the apostolic nuncios, with the Archbishop returning to Braga (Cunha 1634-45: 460; Ferreira 1932: 135).

This challenge to Braga by Lisbon was, in a way, even more shocking than the attitude of the Spanish officers. After all, though there had always been a conflict between Braga and Toledo, at least within Portugal Braga's position had been previously undisputed. Now, as Braga seemed to be losing to Toledo it didn't even have the consolation of being the first in Portugal, since there were other dioceses, more precisely Lisbon, willing to take its place. So, it seems that, despite Fr. Agostinho da Cruz's best efforts to reaffirm Braga's primate status through all the works he patronised (v. chapter 9), these not only failed to impress and convince the king but also, and unexpectedly, the Portuguese diocese of Lisbon. Nonetheless, in the wake of what happened in Lisbon, Braga's elite still sought to reaffirm the city's status with the construction of a couple more celebratory monuments.

One of those monuments was the cross (fig. 23) that can be seen in the post-1594 maps in front of the Nova Gate[36]. This cross, whose construction started in 1621 (Oliveira 1999: 45; Araújo 2003: 23), substituted the early 16th century one in the same position. The new cross kept some of the elements of its predecessor: it had an *axis mundi* form with a quadrangular base, a column in the middle and a sphere on the top and continued to fulfil the roles of sacralizing the surrounding space and defending the City's gate. But there were also differences: it was more massive and higher than the previous one, being built on Classical lines. With such monumentality, it was hard for anyone passing to miss it. Frutuoso Basto mentions it 1627, comparing it to those that can be found in Rome (p. 10): again, the emulation of Rome. But there is more. Notice that the lower part of the column has on it a pattern of diamond shapes. These,

---

[36] Today, this cross is near the chapel of S. Sebastião.

46

within Western traditions symbolise universal sovereignty, incorruptibility, absolute reality (Chevalier and Gheerbrant 1994: 265). Notice also that this cross has two arms, unlike the previous one, which only had one. Thus this is not just any cross: it is that of the archbishops of Braga as primates, which is additionally supported by the values associated with the diamonds. In my view, the audience with whom this cross was communicating were royal and other officers coming from Lisbon. So the cross was placed at the point where the road from Lisbon to the south-west terminated at the Braga city wall. Thus, it was reminding those officers, and all other visitors from afar, precisely who was the primate in Portugal.

As for the second celebratory monument, it was built in Campo de Santiago. According to a document of the City Hall, in 1625 it was decided to build here a fountain since the surrounding area didn't have much water (AMB, *Cartas Arcebispos Cabido*: doc. 26). Yet, looking at its form[37] (fig. 13), one can see that there were also other reasons for its construction. After all, why would a fountain simply to provide water need an obelisk and a two-arm cross? As for the cross, it is important to remember that this monument substituted the cross that already existed in this area, which means that it continued to fulfil its role. Yet, because the cross was archiepiscopal, one can see here an intended association of the archbishops with the prestige of the obelisk. The choice of this area for another celebratory monument was, probably, because this was the entrance on one of the City's major axes – R. Santa Maria.

Despite this last effort, another fountain, built at the same time among a grove of trees (known as Carvalheiras) near the chapel of S. Sebastião[38] (ibid.), points, on the other hand, to a considerable scepticism by Braga's elite about the effectiveness of celebratory monuments. Again, as with the design of the other fountain, the main reason invoked for construction was the provision of water to the surrounding area (ibid.). Yet, looking at its size and setting, it is possible to infer another intention. This fountain was smaller than previous ones and is in an enclosed area, within the trees, as can be seen on the post-1594 maps, unlike the others which are always in open areas and visible to a wider audience. So, why these differences?

In my view, what Braga's elite was doing was transforming the area of Carvalheiras near the chapel of S. Sebastião into an Arcadian Garden. As I argued before in chapter 7, Braga had, since the early 16th century, been organised within a cosmological scheme with an interior City, an external Garden and beyond it, the Chaos. In

relation to the Garden, while the area closer to the City was cultivated, as one moved further away, Nature became less intensively touched by human hand, thus crossing into the archetypal landscape known as Arcadia, where a pastoral economy was practised (Cosgrove 1993: 293). There were two types of Arcadia described in Classical literature. In the first, of Greek origin, Arcadia is described as a harsh landscape, inhabited by brutish people that lived in caves or the rudest huts (Schama 1995: 526, 527); the second, developed later by the Roman Virgil, was, by contrast, an idyllic place, from which all savage things have been banished, and full of trees, fountains, brooks and an eternal Spring, and separated from other places by woodland (Schama 1995: 528, 529; Mulinacci 1999: 33). It was this latter type of Arcadia that was adopted by Europeans in the 16th century, particularly thanks to Sannazaro's book *Arcadia*, published in Venice in 1519 (Schama 1995: 531) and whose influence is also visible in Portuguese Arcadian literature (Mulinacci 1999). Looking to what was happening in Carvalheiras, in Braga, an isolated area covered with trees and with a fountain in the middle was created outside the City. Only the brook and the "Eternal Spring" were missing, but not too far away to the south flow the waters of river Deste about which the archbishop D. Rodrigo da Cunha would write a few years later that they "make the fields pleasant to the sight, turning them with the flowers (…) into a joyous and perpetual Spring" (1634-35: 27; my translation). So, it seems all elements of Arcadia were present. Why was Braga's elite adapting this space to an Arcadia?

The Eden-like character of Arcadia, with its own laws, independent from the problems of human society, was seen by people as an ideal shelter with therapeutic effects on the anxieties of the present (Cosgrove 1993: 296; Mulinacci 1999: 104, 105). So, with all the anxieties surrounding Braga's degrading status in the 1620's, one can understand better why the elite sought to create a place of temporary refuge and detached pastoral idyll. And its members certainly passed a considerable amount of time there enjoying the environment, seated on the benches which are known to have been placed around the fountain (AMB, *Tombo Bens Câmara* 1737: 101v). Moreover, it was even decided to open a new gate into this area through the City's wall just in front of the chapel of S. Sebastião (AMB, *Livro Actas Câmara*, Cx. 16, lv. 33, fl. 52). This more direct link between Arcadia and the interior of the City is another indication of an intention to make frequent use of it[39].

But there was also another reason for the construction of this Arcadia. On all maps of Braga, it is possible to see between the trees of Carvalheiras a quadrangular stone, which was used as table. This stone was already there

---

[37] Though there is a date – 1745 – engraved in this monument, its structure is already visible in the c. 1694 map. That date is probably related with some reconstruction that took place by then in the obelisk, since the stone where the date is, is different from the one of the rest of the fountain.
[38] Today, this fountain is inside Braga's Municipal Market. Its upper part, with a torch symbolising the fire of faith, is not the original one. According to the *Tombo Bens Câmara*, it had initially a pyramid and a two-arm cross (1737: 101).

---

[39] There was by then another gate in one of the towers of that area, as it can be seen in the 1594 map. This gate was built in 1581 (being smaller than the one represented, since it is referred as a *postigo*, that is, small gate) and it was used to support some privies that were built in that tower (Arquivo Municipal 1970: 400). Obviously, in such circumstances, this gate was not the most appropriate to make a connection between the City and Carvalheiras.

before the 16th century and it was used during the festivities of St. John to place little baskets of fruits which were later given to the horsemen that participated in the hunt of the black hog (Belino 1895: 134), in what seems to have been a sort of ritual of fertility and abundance. By the early 17th century, the ceremony of the fruit baskets had already been abandoned (ibid.: 134), perhaps because of the Catholic Reform, but the stone remained there. What is interesting about this stone is that it is of Roman origin and it was locally considered as the oldest insignia of Braga, since its inscription contained the Roman name of the city (Figueiredo, ms. [1723-24]: fl. 4; AMB, *Tombo Bens Câmara* 1737: 101v). I don't know if this tradition dated from the Middle Ages, or resulted from the intervention of 16th century humanists, nevertheless, what matters is that by the early 17th century the Roman stone was considered to be an insignia. According to D. Luís Figueiredo, in 1625, the City Hall, after taking the decision to build a fountain here, also decided to re-incise the letters of the inscription, since they were very worn (1723-24: fl. 4v). So, we can see here a connection between both actions. As for the inscription – BRACARA AUGUSTA FIDELIS ET ANTIQUA (which were Braga's titles in 1625) – it was "transferred" from the top of the stone to its four sides, with each of them having one of the principal words (ibid.: fls. 4, 4v). This inscription was not an authentic representation of the original – *Bracara Augusta* –, a fact that a member of the Portuguese Royal Academy of History, Jerónimo Contador de Argote, had already noticed in 1732 (p. 232), when he demonstrated that the two last adjectives – *Fidelis* and *Antiqua* – had been added centuries later. Nevertheless this serves to underline the intention by Braga's elite in 1625 to forge a link with the Roman past. What then was the purpose of inserting this stone into this new Arcadia?

Although we may argue that Braga's cosmology was organised around its archetypal landscapes of City, Garden and Chaos, nevertheless all three were inserted into a pattern of cyclical time within which the positive or negative value of each of them varied according to their position at an upward or downward phase of the cycle (Cosgrove 1993: 297). So the City can be seen at one point in time as the pinnacle of civil life or, at another, the seat of corruption, guile and violence, whereas the Chaos could be either the place of uncouth nature or the vibrant seedbed of social life (ibid.: 297, 298). So, every time that the cycle is descending and nearing its term, a certain dose of suffering is reserved to humanity, that is, the members of a certain group (Eliade 2000: 144), which in this case are the inhabitants of Braga. Since Braga's status was being down-graded, it was perceived by its inhabitants (particularly the elite, who had most to lose) that the City itself was decaying. In these circumstances, the Garden (particularly the Arcadia, which was symbolically the area of the Garden farthest away from the City) ends up being more virtuous than the City since it is not corrupted by humanity; therefore this area becomes the seedbed of a new social life, of a new City that will emerge once the cycle is completed. It is here that the Roman stone comes in. Being the insignia of the

Roman city it stands therefore as its representative. It is also in the area where, according to the 1594 map, the Forum of the Roman city, or more precisely its Centre, was. Finally, as I mentioned in chapter 7, the Roman city was associated with the beginnings of Braga, when the city was perceived as being closer to perfection, since it was at the beginning of the cycle. So, putting all this together, I argue that the Roman stone was *the seed* of a new City. Its square shape symbolises an idea of stability, of a created universe in opposition to Chaos. Its stone, through its hardness, makes reference to the idea of the absolute, of the sacred. As for its words, since it was through the Word that God created the world, they contain the essence of Braga as a potency waiting to be recreated. The integration of this stone into the Arcadia was therefore a way of ensuring the quick and healthy recreation of a new City. The inhabitants of Braga that went to the fountain to get some water or just sat around it could also contribute to this process. Notice that on the more detailed c. 1757 map, the Roman stone was on a ledge above the fountain, which would make it, as well as its inscription, visible to anyone near it. Anyone approaching the Roman stone from the fountain, curious to read the inscription that was written along its four sides, would be forced to walk in a circle around it. In this way a circum-ambulatory ritual would be performed, sanctifying and assuring the potential harmony of this World.

To sum up, this Arcadian program can be seen the as the result of a crisis of identity concerning Braga and Portugal's role within a monarchy that was suppressing their identities and becoming more Spanish. There is in this program a desire to break with the present and return to an idealised past, as part of a reaction that emerges in the 1620's and 1630's that would eventually lead to a break with Spain in 1640. This reaction can also be seen in other events that took place in Braga in those decades.

The beginning of the construction of a new church in Braga in 1625 on the western side of Campo dos Remédios by one of the confraternities dedicated to the Passion of Christ, the Confraternity of Santa Cruz (Costa 1993: 16), is another sign of this reaction against the current political situation. The documents from that time mention that the reasons for its construction were related to the desire of the Confraternity to have its own house as well as the need to accommodate the growing numbers of members (ibid.: 14, 72). Yet, looking at the façade of the church[40] that was built (fig. 24), there are elements there that also point to other motivations. The façade is quite monumental, being built along the lines of the Doric Order, with Doric columns on the ground floor and Ionic columns on the first floor, thus following the canons of Classical architecture treatises. According to these treatises the Doric Order was to be used in churches dedicated to Christ as well as brave and courageous saints (Serlio 1982 [1611]: 262). Yet, since only a minority of

---

[40] Still intact today, except the pediment which is from the 18th century, as well as the towers (Oliveira 1999: 131, 132).

the population was familiar with these subtleties, there is also in the façade a number of elements that make more explicit reference to the Passion of Christ. So, the instruments of the Passion are visible, as well as the Holy Cross, a Tree of Life and a palm-tree, the latter making reference to the Resurrection of Christ after the Calvary. On top of the pediment there are three statues, representing the Roman emperor Constantine, his mother the empress St. Helen and finally Portugal's first king Afonso Henriques (Costa 1993: 19, 70). The statue of Constantine is a clear allusion to the battle of the Milvian Bridge against the forces of the Roman tyrant Maxentius. On the eve of the battle, Constantine, whose army was outnumbered, saw a cross in the sky with the words *In Hoc Signo Vinces* (Latin for "In This Sign (the Cross) You Shall Conquer") written on it. And thanks to the power of the Cross, his army defeated the numerically superior enemy's army. In the aftermath of the battle he issued the famous Edict of Milan, in 313, which put an end to the persecution of Christians and gave them the legal right to worship publicly. As for St. Helen, a devout Christian, she found the Cross of the Lord on a visit to Jerusalem. The statue of Afonso Henriques can be explained by reference to the miracle of the battle of Ourique in Southern Portugal, in 1139. In this battle, the Portuguese forces fought a numerically superior Muslim army and, just as happened to Constantine, the same miracle of the Cross took place before the battle, which ended with a Portuguese victory. That miracle was eventually seen as a sign of divine protection over Portugal and in its aftermath Afonso Henriques declared himself king of Portugal (until then a county of the kingdom of Leon) (Mattoso 1993: 70). This episode is associated with one of the founding myths of Portugal: Portugal's creation resulted from a political act of its first king, under divine sanction (Buescu 1991; Nogueira Silva and Hespanha 1993: 30). It is this message that, in my view, the façade of the church of Santa Cruz is transmitting to a large audience, through its association with the meaning of the statues and the cosmic symbols of life (the cross and the trees). There is an appeal to the return of a king that would guarantee Portugal's autonomy (life); an autonomy that resulted from divine sanction, which meant that Spanish attempts to dissolve that autonomy went against God's wish. And an independent Portugal would obviously serve Braga's pretensions much better.

There are also other elements that suggest that the purpose of this confraternity was more than simply the devotion to Christ, having also this political agenda of resistance against Spain. We should also remember that this confraternity was founded in 1581 through the actions of several members of Braga's elite, particularly clergymen (Costa 1993: 13, 14). Considering that Portugal was incorporated into the Hispanic Monarchy in the previous year, it is possible that the foundation of this confraternity at that time was not casual. The elevation of this confraternity to Royal Fellowship in 1822, something celebrated by the royal shield of arms visible on the pediment (ibid.: 20, 21), is another element that shows the close connection between this confraternity and Portugal's royalty.

The publication in 1634-35 of a history of the archbishops of Braga, written by the archbishop D. Rodrigo da Cunha, constitutes another sign of strong dissatisfaction. This history was written because of the request made by Braga's inhabitants to this archbishop in the form of an allegorical play performed during his entrance into the city in 1627; something that was accepted by him with a smile (Basto 1627: 74-76). This history begins by mentioning the antiquity of the city, particularly pointing out the existence of several Roman remains. The inscriptions that were in Campo de Santana and on some of the buildings of the city were all mentioned and the images of some of them even printed (Cunha 1634-35: 12-19). The history also referred to the remains of buildings with large dimensions, such as an amphitheatre and an aqueduct, that were still visible among the ruins of the Roman city between Braga and Rio Deste (ibid.: 11). Yet, despite Braga having antiquities that few cities could boast, the Archbishop theatrically put them aside by saying that the greatest glory of this city was not in its antiquities but in being the first Hispanic city to receive the faith of Christ (ibid.: 27, 28). According to the Archbishop, it was near Braga that the Apostle Santiago (St. James) first disembarked when he came to Hispania, and it was in that city that he began to preach (ibid.: 29, 67). St. James chose S. Pedro de Rates as the first Hispanic bishop and, as such, this made Braga the primate see (ibid.: 30, 69). In this way, the Archbishop explicitly asserted through history the primate rights of Braga within Hispania. After asserting this in the first chapter of the book, the Archbishop began a long and uninterrupted genealogy of all the archbishops of Braga, who acted as the heirs and keepers of the original pact between the Apostle and the first bishop of Braga; a pact, whose persistence ensured the primate status of the city and the prestige of its inhabitants and, of course, the archbishops. In order to make this genealogy even more illustrious, the Archbishop decided to accept as true some apocryphal chronicles written in 1594 and considered ten more of his predecessors to be saints, over and above the four already officially accepted by the Church (Senna Freitas 1890, vol. 1: 170; vol. 2: 412, 413).

In 1635, D. Rodrigo da Cunha was removed and a new archbishop, D. Sebastião de Matos, who was faithful to the Spanish king, was imposed on Braga (Araújo Oliveira 1991: 187, 189). The publication by D. Rodrigo da Cunha of the history of the archbishops of Braga shortly before this was almost certainly one of the reasons for his removal, since it questioned Spanish attempts to degrade Braga's status. On the other hand, the financial difficulties that the Hispanic Monarchy was then facing due to its several failed ventures, forced it to raise multiple and heavy taxes in Portugal affecting all social strata, without respecting existing privileges (ibid.: 187). The king was expecting these measures to be strongly resisted, thus the nomination of a new archbishop who would, he hoped, put them into effect without raising objections (ibid.). In this respect, D. Rodrigo da Cunha had already shown, through his actions, that he could not be trusted to do this. The reaction was fast. In 1636 there were disturbances in some cities of the archdiocese – Viana and Vila Real – and in 1637 in Braga itself, with members of all social groups taking part , though without success (ibid.: 188, 191, 192). Similar disturbances also happened in several other cities of Portugal.

But the political situation by then in Braga was even tenser since there were also other factors disturbing social peace. Since the 1620's there was some civil agitation caused by the common people, who wanted to have a greater participation in Braga's political life, and a serious disturbance taking place in 1640 (ibid.: 193, 200). So, as we can see, the measures taken in the late 16th century to stop the social rise and political participation of the common people were not having the desired result.

In 1640, a coup removed the Spanish king from the Portuguese throne, with a new dynasty – the Bragança – declaring Portugal's independence from the Hispanic Monarchy. However, any expectation in Braga that this event would mark the beginning of a new era more favourable to Braga's interests was short-lived since the political situation deteriorated even further. A long war between the two kingdoms followed lasting 28 years, which brought severe problems to Braga. Further disturbances took place in the 1640's and 1650's, due to the persistence of high taxes caused by the war effort, as well as several abuses involving the recruitment of soldiers (ibid.: 194, 197, 202). All of this was happening in addition to the open conflict between Braga's aristocracy and its merchant and other classes with the latter trying to take advantage of the unstable situation to have a more active participation in the city's political life (ibid.: 193-195, 199-201). Obviously, this conjuncture of social conflict and political instability, as well as its long duration, considerably weakened the feeling of community among Braga's inhabitants.

But shouldn't the archbishops, in their role as lords of the city, have acted as a moderating influence in order to diffuse social tension? The answer is yes; the problem is that since 1641 Braga had had no archbishops. At the time of the 1640 coup, the archbishop was D. Sebastião de Matos, who, as I mentioned before, was faithful to the king of Spain. This archbishop organised in 1641 a conspiracy to murder the new Portuguese king, which was discovered before being attempted, and D. Sebastião de Matos was arrested (Ferreira 1932: 165, 166). One can easily imagine the shock and shame that Braga's inhabitants felt after knowing that their lord had conspired against the life of Portugal's king. Even worse, due to Spanish pressure, the Holy See refused to recognise Portugal's new dynasty, which meant that the Portuguese king could not nominate a new archbishop for Braga (ibid.: 179, 180). Only in 1671, after the end of the war with Spain, was it possible for the archbishops to return to Braga. So, during thirty long years and in the middle of a war and social instability, Braga was without archbishops, who had been, since the days of D. Diogo de

Sousa, the mainstays of the city's Catholic identity. This series of events would have serious consequences, since the figure on whom Braga's identity was centred was not there, thus making it difficult for a common Catholic identity to persist as a means of uniting its inhabitants.

Obviously, with so many members of the clergy living in Braga and with a Chapter substituting for the archbishops in their absence, one would assume that they would be able to hold the situation together. Not quite. The problem was that since the early 16th century authority in Braga had been strongly personalised in the figure of the archbishop, an authority further enhanced after the Council of Trent which had imposed on the bishops a more vigilant role over the spiritual and moral well-being of the people. In other words, there was too much power concentrated in a single figure. And with the head absent for such a long time, the corporate body of the Church in Braga started to have problems, with a significant number of the clergy simply not having the capability to do what was expected of them. This is clear from the constant complaints of the common people, not only in Braga, but also elsewhere in Portugal. For example, it was common for men to avoid military service by claiming themselves to be clergy with the connivance of the Chapters (IAN/TT, *Capítulos Gerais Estados Povos*, vol. 15: 188v-189). This resulted in an incompetent, ill-educated clergy and this had damaging consequences for its reputation (ibid.). Also of concern was that many members of the clergy were engaged in commercial activities, something that was forbidden, again harming their status as well as damaging the interests of the townspeople (ibid.: 189, 189v). Finally, it became more common for nuns to disregard their vows and leave their convents, and this resulted in many scandals (ibid.: 190, 190v). This is understandable, however, if one remembers that many nuns were forced into that status against their will. It was the bishops who, after the Council of Trent, had been given the main responsibility for the discipline of convents and since they were absent throughout Portugal for about 30 years, one can better understand the actions of many of those nuns.

So, the clergy, supposedly models of Christian virtues, had lost during this period, much of its prestige among the people, something that would have important consequences for Braga's identity, as we shall see in the next chapter.

11 – A fragmented identity

In 1671, after the end of the war with Spain and with the resumption of diplomatic relations with the Holy See, a new archbishop – D. Veríssino Lencastre – was elevated to the see of Braga. Apparently there was a return to the *status quo ante*: Braga's primate status was no longer threatened due to Portugal's independence and the presence of an archbishop would consolidate Braga's Catholic identity and community feeling. However, expectations regarding the second point were too optimistic.

It is important to remember here that Braga had been without an archbishop for 30 years. Thirty years is a long time, particularly in the societies of the *Ancien Regime* where the majority of the population would have been young. What this meant was that by 1671 most of the inhabitants of Braga were not aware of the role of the archbishops as guarantors of the city's identity, since they had not even been born by 1641 or were too young at this time to remember this role. As for the older generation, the memory of the archbishops was certainly considerably tarnished by the actions of D. Sebastião de Matos. So, the arrival of a new archbishop in 1671 was, for most of the population, the arrival of a stranger.

The archbishops' position was even more fragile due to the political conflict between the common people and the elite. The end of the war meant the consolidation of the new dynasty and consequently of elite authority as well. The archbishops belonged to and protected the elite, and, therefore, the resumption of their power over Braga meant that it would be more difficult for the common people to press for greater political participation in the city's political life, something that wouldn't make the archbishops particularly popular.

D. Veríssimo Lencastre was aware of these threats to his authority and made some effort to reaffirm the episcopal role. It is known that he tried to curb some abuses committed by the clergy. For example, he forced convents in Braga to have grated windows in order to enforce the seclusion of the nuns (AMB, *Index das couzas mais memoraveis*: fl. 124v). He was also careful to make several public appearances in order to make his presence visible, so that people would know that there was once again an archbishop in charge. So, for example, he made extensive visitations within the archdiocese and confirmed several of the faithful (Ferreira 1932: 187), thus performing his good shepherd role.

Yet, any positive impact caused by his actions quickly evaporated, since after his return to Lisbon in 1677 to direct the Inquisition, Braga remained without an archbishop for another six years. The reason for this was that his successor – D. Luís de Sousa – was the Portuguese ambassador in Rome, having only left that post in 1683. Obviously, this long absence did not help the archbishops' fragile position in Braga.

Nevertheless, after his arrival in Braga, D. Luís de Sousa, supported the construction of two churches – Congregados and S. Vítor –, which, in my view, reveal an attempt to reduce the gap between the people and the archbishops in particular and the clergy in general.

In relation to the first church, in 1686, one of the most influential members of the Chapter, João Meira Carrilho, took the initiative in helping the Congregation of the Oratory to establish itself in Braga, something that had the strong support of D. Luís de Sousa (ibid.: 194-196). Unlike religious Orders, this was a congregation of secular priests that didn't take religious vows and whose main concern was the improvement of Catholic life through a series of spiritual and practical exercises that they sought to disseminate through the performance of public ceremonies involving a wide audience (Santos 1997: 226, 227). This Congregation was also quite young in Portugal, with its first establishment being founded in Lisbon in 1668 (ibid.: 224).

Since the mid-17th century the prestige and effectiveness of the clergy had considerably deteriorated, and so the support for the establishment of the Oratory in Braga is understandable: it was a recent foundation and therefore the prejudice among the people towards its members was minimised. In this way, it was expected that members of the clergy would again play a more effective role, according to the precepts of the Catholic Reformation.

By 1687 the Oratory had a small church built in Campo de Santana, with its upper part visible on the c.1694 map. It lay in the southern part of this open space in front of the chapel of Santana (Oliveira 1994: 38). This choice of location wasn't accidental: after all, this was the area of Braga where there was a greater circulation of people and where its inhabitants and outsiders met and exchanged products, ideas and news. In this way, the members of the Oratory were able to engage more actively with the people and reaffirm the ideas of the Catholic Reformation as well as combating heresies that could develop in that place where people from different backgrounds would meet.

As for the church of S. Vítor, situated on the eastern edge of the out-wall area (fig. 25), the Archbishop promoted its reconstruction also in the year of 1686 (Smith 1972. 5; Oliveira 1993: 47). There are a number of interesting aspects about this church. One of them is the iconographic program inside the building. All the walls of the church are filled with panels of decorated tiles with episodes of the lives of 22 local saints, 16 male and 6 female (Smith 1972: 12) (fig. 33), with particular emphasis being given to S. Vítor, the first martyr of the Church of Braga. This iconographic program was based on D. Rodrigo da Cunha's history of the archbishops of Braga, since there are panels on which specific reference is made to the part of the book from which the episodes were taken (ibid.: 8). What was the purpose of this program?

In my view, the Archbishop was reaffirming the antique and illustrious pantheon of heroes responsible for the Catholic identity of Braga. Through this church, he was therefore promoting their cult and reasserting their importance in order to boost his prestige and authority since he was, after all, the heir of those heroes. There is nothing new here, since D. Diogo de Sousa had already done the same at the entrance of Braga's Cathedral in the early 16th century with the statues of four local saints (v. chapter 6). What is interesting is to compare the numbers of saints that are represented in both churches: 4 in one case and 22 in the other. This seems to underline D. Luís de Sousa's feelings of insecurity since he felt the need to represent so many saints to support him…

There were also a number of elements inside and outside this church that helped to enhance this program. The filling of the walls with panels, for example, whose scenes are made within a geometrical design that gives the illusion that one is looking into a three dimensional space akin to a theatrical stage (fig. 26). The resulting realism not only makes the actions of the saints more believable to the viewer, facilitating therefore the process of identification and reflection, but also gives the illusion that the wall does not exist, since space seems to extend beyond it. In this way, the interior of the church no longer seems to be a closed space. This effect is further reinforced by the opening of several large windows in the side walls of the building, with a resulting explosion of light not only helping the panels to be seen, but also giving the interior of the church the impression of being a celestial and infinite space, therefore closer to God, instead of a closed and earthly space, closer to Mother Earth. The blue and white colours of the decorated tiles also contribute to giving the interior a more celestial character. These changes inside the church also find their correspondence outside it, on the façade. Here, if one looks at its embrasures, not as isolated elements as in empiricist analysis, but rather as articulated ones, they seem to give the façade the form of a human face: the two side niches in the upper half are the eyes and the door is the mouth. And the human face, let's not forget, is the face of God (Duby 1993: 290). The typical façade of the previous era had the form of a cave entrance and this was now gone. So, all these characteristics not only contributed to the Church's efforts since the Catholic Reformation to give a more transcendent character to the divine, but also they provided a more celestial, humanised and less abstract setting to the iconographic

program: they helped to make it more "authentic" and closer to the faithful.

There were also other, topographic elements that helped to enhance the church of S. Vítor. The building is on top of a small elevation, placing it in a higher, and therefore more heavenly, position in relation to the surrounding area. The connection between the church's entrance and the road was made through a large and monumental stairway, symbolically connecting Heaven and Earth, in order to emphasise the importance of the church.

Another interesting point about this church is that the Archbishop ordered the enlargement of R. Régoa, the road connecting it with Campo de Santana (Oliveira 1993: 126). In this way the church became perfectly visible from Campo de Santana, the area where there were two buildings – the chapel of Santana and the church of Senhora a Branca – that also celebrated the origins of Braga. In this way, a visual link binds this prestigious area to the new celebratory church, one specifically associated with the saints of Braga.

Yet, despite these efforts, the Archbishop fell ill in 1687, remaining in bed until his death in 1690 (Ferreira 1932: 196), something that hindered his attempts to reaffirm his role as the focus of Braga's Catholic identity.

Braga remained without an archbishop for a couple more years until 1692 when a successor was nominated: D. José de Meneses. However, he suffered from gout and he only arrived in Braga in 1694. His government didn't start well. A couple of days after his arrival there was a disturbance by the common people demanding a representative in the City Hall as well as complaining about the lack of bread (Senna Freitas 1890, vol. III: 280, 281; Ferreira 1932: 201). It is possible that the complaint about the bread was just a way to soften the main complaint, which was about the political representation. The Archbishop resisted this show of force by ordering the opening of the barns and declaring that he would be the representative of the common people (ibid.; ibid.). Nevertheless, the situation must have been quite serious since royal troops were sent to the city, remaining there for two and a half months until everything cooled down (ibid.; ibid.). What this disturbance reveals is that the efforts made by the previous archbishops to return to the *status quo ante* were not having the desired result, with the divorce between the archbishops and the people continuing. As for D. José de Meneses, he was incapable of doing anything to change this situation. Suffering from gout, he simply remained in his room in the palace from the first day of his arrival until his death early in 1696 (ibid; ibid).

With D. José de Meneses inaction, the archbishops' standing in Braga reached its lowest point since the early 16th century. This is quite visible, for example, in an episode that took place after his death, when his body was displayed in the palace for people to pay him their last respects. Since his body was starting to decompose, people were shocked and started to shout obscenities, following a tumult inside the palace during which one of the servants ended up being stabbed (ibid.: 281; ibid.: 204). What this episode reveals is that the archbishops had lost their aura. In religious societies, the bodies of people with aura do not decompose. Since the archbishops since the 16th century had striven hard to surround themselves with this aura, this episode is quite revealing of how degraded their standing in Braga had become. As for the tumults inside the palace, that was something unheard of since the 1470's (v. chapter 5).

Another testimony of the degradation of the archbishops' standing in Braga is visible in a description of their palace in late 1696, written shortly before the arrival of the new archbishop, D. João de Sousa. According to this the palace had started to leak water, the glass in the windows was broken, and several tiles on the roof were missing (BNA, 54-VIII-20, n. 397). In other words, it was an abandoned house, something that can be seen as a metaphor of the failure of the archbishops to maintain their position as the symbolic core of Braga's Catholic identity.

The new archbishop, D. João de Sousa, despite a relatively short period of government – 1697 to 1703 –, instigated some measures in an attempt to change this state of affairs. He ordered the printing of the Constitutions of the Diocese of Braga (Ferreira 1932: 217), something important for the better regulation of the clergy, since the rules determining the fundamentals of religious life in this way became more familiar to the members of the clergy. This Archbishop was also responsible for the construction of a new sacristy in the Cathedral, with a treasure room for the display of its relics (ibid.: 214, 215). The new building (still visible) is large and built in the Classical style, thus providing a more grandiose setting for the relics. So, in my view, the Archbishop was expecting to promote their cult and, in this way, to reaffirm the Cathedral as the spiritual centre of Braga. The Archbishop also initiated the process for the beatification of Fr. Bartolomeu dos Mártires (ibid.: 218, 219), one of Braga's most popular archbishops, who had ruled the city between 1559 and 1582. It can be assumed that D. João de Sousa was attempting with this measure to "borrow" his prestige for the good of the Mitre. Yet, despite D. João de Sousa's efforts, his measures were not successful since his successor, D. Rodrigo Moura Teles, continued to face the same problems (v. chapter 12).

To sum up, in the late 17th century a combination of weak archbishops, short periods of government, periods without an archbishop and limited measures, contributed to the overall failure of the attempts to reaffirm the archbishops as the focus of Braga's Catholic identity.

Actually, the best evidence that the archbishops' efforts were failing can be seen in a parallel phenomenon that had been taking place since 1670: the gradual control by the common people of the direction of several religious confraternities. Until then, the direction of a confraternity belonged to a clergyman or a member of the nobility of the city (e.g. AISV, *Livro Termos S. Vicente* 1594-1609, 1669-1682). The only exception had been confraternities that were simultaneously professional and religious, in which case there was a clergyman occupying the strategic position of secretary, since everything had to pass through his hands (e.g. AISV, *Estatutos Irmandade Santo Homem Bom* 1688: 7). In both cases the control of the management activities of the confraternities was firmly under the control of the elite. After 1670, this situation changed radically.

In 1674, certain members of the Archconfraternity of the Cordon decided to break with it and found a Third Order of St. Francis (Proença 1998: 48). These sorts of institution were for laymen who wished to live more according to the spiritual life of the religious Orders. In its statutes of 1680 it is mentioned that the presence of members of the nobility and from religious Orders is not desirable (fl. 1v); however, priests continued to be accepted, since they could direct the Third Order as well as being secretaries (fl. 4). Even so, the relationship between priests and members of the common people was not very good, since in 1695 the statutes were reformed again and in the very first article it is explicitly stated that in no circumstance could any clergyman direct the Third Order. The control of the Third Order was now fully in the hands of members of the common people.

Another example is the confraternity of S. Vicente. According to the statutes of 1723, although nobles and clergymen could be part of the confraternity, they could not direct it (fl. 23). This measure was certainly established in a statutory reform of 1675 (although this document itself is lost), since after that date the Acts of the confraternity only mention members of the common people being in a directive role (AISV, *Livro Termos S. Vicente* 1669-1682, 1682-1700).

A third example is the confraternity of Passos, which was established in the convent of Pópulo. At least since 1695 there had been accounts of quarrels between the confraternity (whose members were mostly from the common people) and the monks, with the former ending up leaving the convent in 1724 (AISC, *Livro Segundo Termos Irmandade dos Passos* 1686-1740: 103, 447). Nobles had also not been popular since in 1707 the confraternity had obtained from archbishop D. Rodrigo Moura Teles the guarantee that they couldn't have any directive role (AICS, *Estatutos Irmandade dos Passos* 1707: 31).

Even in confraternities where the clergy presence was solely limited to the secretary, there were also changes. For example, the confraternity of Santo Homem Bom, which drew together the tailors of Braga, had reserved in its statutes of 1688 the place of secretary solely to a priest (fl. 7). Yet, when the statutes were reformed in 1725, there was no reference stipulating that the secretary should be a priest (fl. 15v). The place was, therefore, open to laymen.

In my view, these changes reveal an attempt from the common people to affirm themselves towards the clergy and the nobility in the laic sphere of the Church. Since 1670 the political affirmation of the common people had become notably difficult due to the stabilisation of Portugal's political life. That was clearly visible in the failed uprising of 1694 when the Crown intervened militarily to help the local elite. Challenges to the traditional political order were not acceptable. So, through the control of confraternities, the common people sought an alternative mode of self-expression and affirmation towards the elite. There are here echoes of the ideas of the Age of the Holy Ghost, with its ideal of a religion that is free, spiritual and without hierarchies. This link can be observable in a number of examples.

The new Third Order of Saint Francis was initially established in the church of the Holy Ghost (Proença 1998:48), something that I consider very interesting since, as I argued in chapter 7, this church was associated with the ideology of the Age of the Holy Ghost. So, the establishment in this church was intentional, showing the desire of its members to live more fully within those ideals.

In the statutes of several of these confraternities can be seen clearly a concern with the practice of a more religious and ethical life. For example, while the Church expected the faithful to confess at least once a year, the members of the confraternity of S. Vicente were expected to confess also in the (six) days of the confraternity's festivals (AISV, *Estatutos S. Vicente* 1723: 28). The confraternity of S. Crispim and S. Crispiniano, the confederation of the shoemakers, was even stricter, expecting its members to confess at least once a month and, if possible, every week (ASB, *Estatutos S. Crispim and S. Crispiniano* 1702: 6v). Its members were also expected on Sunday afternoons and on holidays to say their rosary with the family, read spiritual books and make a nightly examination of their conscience (ibid.: 5v, 6). It must be stressed, however, that these practices don't reveal a rebellion against Catholic dogmas and ethics, as happened in Northern European countries influenced by Protestantism. There was still a respect for Catholicism and priests continued to perform the Mass.

But this autonomy of confraternities was an even more complex phenomenon, since with the failure of the archbishops to reaffirm their role as the focus of Braga's Catholic identity, confraternities became alternative centres of that identity. In other words, Braga's previous identity imploded as a result of the conflict between the common people and the elite. Now, instead of a community living in Braga whose members were united by a set of common values, there was instead a multiplicity of communities living in Braga with different loyalties. A good example of this fragmentation of Braga's identity is the construction of the new churches of S. Vicente (fig. 27) and the Third Order of Saint Francis. The construction of the former began in 1689 and the latter in 1694 (Oliveira 1993: 47), a period that coincides with the presence of ailing archbishops in Braga.

Both churches are large and have structures similar in design to the church of S. Vítor. They were meant to be highly visible in the urban landscape, serving as a focus for its members as well as being a mode of assertion towards other groups in Braga. This is particularly notable in the location the church of the Third Order: to the north of the castle in Campo de Santana, near a new entrance to the City opened in the wall (more on this entrance later in this chapter), as can be seen on the map of c. 1757 (number 21). This church is therefore in the area of Braga where there was more circulation of people. As for the church of S. Vicente, it was rebuilt on its previous site.

There are also elements in these churches that indicate that their ultimate fidelity resided outside Braga, and thus not directed towards the archbishops. In the case of S. Vicente, on top of the pediment was erected a cross with three arms, none other than the symbol of the Pope. It could also be read in the inscriptions flanking the main door that this confraternity benefited from the indulgences (that is, remissions of the punishments of committed sins) given by the Lateran. What is interesting about this is that the Lateran was the cathedral of the diocese of Rome and thus of the Pope. The members of the confraternity of S. Vicente were therefore putting themselves under the auspices of an entity beyond Braga, that is, Rome. As for the Third Order of St. Francis, since 1695 the patron saint was the Immaculate Conception (Proença 1998: 77, 78). What is interesting here is that since 1646 the Immaculate Conception was the patron saint of the kingdom of Portugal.

Actually, this movement towards fragmentation was also extended to elite confraternities, something that reveals divisions within the elite itself. In 1693 one of these, the confraternity of Santa Cruz, decided to remove the tower at the back of its church and build two new towers on the façade (AISC, *Livro Termos Santa Cruz* 1589-1701: 504). Until then, the only church in Braga with two towers on its façade was the Cathedral, something that, as I mentioned in chapter 6, was a form of distinction. This confraternity by building these two towers was, therefore, consciously emulating the Cathedral. These towers were built at a time of weak and/or absent archbishops and so, in my view, their construction reveals disbelief by sectors of the elite about the capacity of the archbishops to regain their previous status. With this emulation (otherwise unthinkable if the archbishops had been stronger) the confraternity was thus making of its church the main focus of identity for its members in Braga. The good relations that this confraternity had with the Portuguese Crown are also a good indication of where its fidelity lay.

Going back to the churches of the Third Order and S. Vicente there are elements in their façade that indicate other aspects of the way these confraternities lived their religious lives. While they are structurally similar to the church of S. Vítor, there are differences in the organisation of the façades. The façade of S. Vítor, for example, is not much different of what became typical after the Catholic Reformation in the mid-16th century, with little realistic ornamentation making reference to a natural religion, being rather composed of geometrical lines. Yet, in the case of the other two churches, particularly S. Vicente (fig. 27), there is an abundant representation of such decoration, as spirals, wreaths and vegetation. This is very interesting, because what this reveals is that the common people never fully accepted the strongly intellectualised version of Catholicism that the clergy attempted to enforce. "Feeling" the sacred through the senses was also an important part of that experience, as the façade reveals, and only nature could provide the means for that experience. Yet, it must be noted that there isn't here a return to pagan practices and a total rejection of the more intellectualised version of religion. As discussed before, the latter was also increasingly part of the religious experience of the common people. What is found here, rather, is a synthesis of that experience. The façade says it all: it is structured within God's geometric design and is ornamented by natural motifs. Despite the return of nature, the core controlling plan is now that of the divine intellect.

Actually, it is interesting to note that between the 1730's and the 1760's (the period usually designated by art historians as late baroque, followed by rocaille), that is after the consolidation of the confraternities dominated by the common people, the façades of a number of churches (whether from confraternities or religious orders) and institutional buildings under the control of Braga's elite, underwent a reform that made them akin to the previous two churches, that is, a geometrical design and an (even more) abundant natural ornamentation. Examples include the new aisle in the archbishop's palace in the area turned to Campo dos Touros; the new building of the City Hall; the church of Santa Cruz; the church of the Mercy House; the church of the Oratory (fig. 28) (cf. Smith 1968, 1972, 1973 and Oliveira 1999 for more information about these works). The same sort of changes in ornamentation is also visible in the retables built by that time (cf. Alves 1989a; 468; 1989b: 408). In my view, what is happening with these changes is an attempt from the elite to regain the confidence of the common people by showing more tolerance towards nature as well and, therefore, to more sensorial forms of experiencing the sacred.

There is an interesting paradox going on here: while before the late 17th century the common people were closer to a more natural experience of the sacred, only afterwards adopting a more intellectual viewpoint in order to affirm itself towards their social superiors, the elite, on the other side, tended always to have a more intellectual view of the sacred, only showing later more tolerance towards an experience of the sacred through nature (as long as the core of religious life continued to be intellectual) with the political intention of keeping the common people under control.

The fragmentation of Braga's social identity in the late 17th century is also visible in other dimensions. Still considering the confraternities controlled by the common people, an interesting aspect is that anyone wishing to be part of them had to fulfil a number of social requirements to be accepted (cf. AVOTSF, *Estatutos Ordem Terceira S. Francisco* 1680: 3v; AISV, *Estatutos Santo Homem Bom* 1688: 4, 4v; ASB, *Estatutos S. Crispim e S. Crispiniano* 1702: 17v; AISV, *Estatutos S. Vicente* 1723: 23v, 24). The first requirement that is always mentioned is the need to have pure blood. It was a common belief in the society of the Modern Era that, to a large measure, the virtues and vices of human beings were determined by the qualities of the lineage of each person, that is, by blood (Cordeiro Pereira 1998: 278). Obviously, within this ideology, the lineages of nobles were the most pure, something that legitimated their superior position in society, while at the same time excluding their most direct adversaries – the Jews – because their blood was not pure (ibid.: 278, 279). The exclusion of Jews is something that was also present in the confraternities, with two other categories without pure blood also being commonly identified: Muslims and Black Africans (brought to Portugal to work as slaves). Another category of the excluded were those whose jobs were considered as low or vile, such as slaughterers (because of the taboo of blood), doorkeepers (seen as a sort of watch dog) and tax collectors (who were usually concessionaries of the Crown, having the right of retaining some of the money collected). Finally, day labourers not capable of fulfilling their financial obligations towards the confraternity were also not accepted. In my view, what these requirements reveal is that the common people, not having access to the nobility, were using the confraternities as a way of emulating the caste attitude of the elite, by demanding and displaying attributes such as pure blood and wealth that were asserted by the nobility as signs of superiority.

These requirements meant also that there were divisions within Braga's popular body, with some of its members remaining outside the mainstream movement of the confraternities. These members were part of more marginal groupings such as the tavern. This can be seen as a kind of 'counter church', with a dissolute life and where ideas were freely discussed, disputing to the priests the male clients on Mass days (Minois 2004: 408). And in Braga it is known that taverns had by that time their fair share of clients since not only did the archbishops have frequent problems with them, but also the confraternities. In the first case, the archbishop D. Rodrigo Moura Teles even forbade the taverns' activity in 1718 accusing them of being used by all sorts of troublemakers (AMB, *Index das couzas mais memoraveis*: fls. 92v, 146). It is also interesting to see that by then the taverns were located near the entrances of Braga, in places such as Real and Goladas (ibid.), which were already within the Chaos but close enough to make their presence tempting (or threatening) to the inhabitants of the city. As for the confraternities, it is known that the statutes of some of them specifically maintained that the clients of taverns should not be accepted (ASB, *Estatutos S. Crispim e S. Crispiniano* 1702: 17v).

But there was also another division visible among the popular body at that time: the formation of a group identity among its richest members, usually merchants and jewellers, constituting what would be known in the 19th century as the bourgeoisie. Its members, despite keeping their connection with the confraternities, attempted to split from the common people and to rival the elite, in a process that is apparent in residential patterns and architecture.

First, the case of residential patterns, the axis of R. Sousa/R. Souto is paradigmatic. Reading the list of its tenants in the *Index* it is notable that there was a gradual establishment of members of the "bourgeoisie" on this road axis throughout the 17th century, in a process that was consolidated by the early 18th century. By the time of the 1750 map almost all the houses that are shown on it belonged to members of this group in contrast to the 16th century when, as discussed above (v. chapter 6), its tenants were mostly from the elite. However, the latter, for reasons that will be analysed shortly, gradually lost interest in living there. It was the "bourgeoisie" who took advantage of this situation, and who moved massively into the central areas of Braga, particularly the R. Sousa/R. Souto axis, the most prestigious of them all. By moving here, the members of this newly formed "bourgeoisie" not only gained prestige, but also more awareness of themselves as members of a distinct group thanks to the proximity that resulted from their concentration into a single area. Also, by sticking together they felt more protection in an unstable world.

The consequent transformation of this axis into a mostly commercial area was probably behind a couple of changes that took place in its vicinity during the 17th century. One of them was the opening of a new entrance (not a gate) in the area of the wall to the north of the castle, somewhere during the 17th century but before the c. 1694 map[41] since it is already visible on this map. This opened a new exit from R. Souto and allowed, therefore, a larger volume of traffic. The other change was the removal of the pillory from its position in front of R. Souto in 1694, with its neighbours (mostly members of the "bourgeoisie") having paid for that change to be brought about (Thadim 1764: fl. 70). The pillory was moved no great distance, just a few metres to the north, remaining close to the fountain, as can be seen on the c. 1757 map. This change is understandable considering the growth of traffic along R. Souto, which meant that the pillory was causing an obstruction.

But why did a substantial numbers of the elite lose interest in living in this area, thus allowing the establishment of the "bourgeoisie" here? According to the genealogies of noble families, it is noticeable that many of them, such as the Fraga, Fonseca Coutinho, Leite Pereira, Pacheco Pereira, Paiva Brandão, Portocarreiro, Bravo, left their residences in the City and went live in the outskirts during the 17th century (cf. Afonso 1954, 1962, 1968, 1969, 1970, 1975). It is important to remember that after the 1620's/1630's Braga's elite was being affected by a strong social and political crisis: the attempts of the Hispanic Monarchy to degrade Braga's status, the long war with Spain, the constant conflicts with the common people and the lack of Episcopal authority, among others. While, spatially, this change was irrelevant – just a few metres beyond the wall - symbolically, it is full of meaning because what it reveals is that these families were leaving what they perceived to be a decadent City and moving into a therapeutic and uncorrupted Garden.

As for the houses built by the nobility in the Garden of Braga, many are visible on the c. 1757 map. Here, it is possible to see also geometric gardens of large dimensions attached to those houses. The most common design of these gardens is cruciform, a symbol of the Earth and of an organised World. In this way, through their gardens, where the order of the World is anchored to an orderly Nature, these members of the elite were also looking for solace in a period of constant threats to the traditional order. But providing solace was not the only reason behind the construction of these gardens. It is interesting to note that gardens, at this time, ceased to be closed to the outside as they used to be, and were displayed to a wider audience though the opening of windows (albeit with bars, lest anybody enter) in the walls surrounding the elite residences[42]. This is visible either in still surviving buildings (such as the palace of Biscaínhos on the road of the same name) or in some of those represented on the 1750 map (such as house 5 in R. S. João). Even in the archbishop's palace a huge garden following this cosmological scheme was built in the area close to the new opening in the wall to the north of the castle, as depicted on the c. 1757 map. On the 1750 map, in this area (on road 7, known as Loura) a large gate is shown flanked by two windows that allowed for those passing by a view of the garden. Through the public display of these gardens, the elite was showing to the common people its capacity to replicate and control the order of Nature (and therefore the World and social order), attempting in this way to legitimate its superior status in Braga (v. Leone 1984 for a similar study). Yet, the persistence of social instability is an indication of the limited success of these gardens.

Second, in relation the other point that I made about the rivalry between the elite and the "bourgeoisie"– that is, architecture –, there are a number of important changes that took place in house façades.

One of these is the appearance of symmetrical façades on the houses. During the 16th century there wasn't much concern about this, with the asymmetric distribution of openings. The appearance in the middle of that century of treatises on Classical architecture with drawings of symmetrical buildings did not immediately change the

---

[41] Also visible in the c. 1757 map.

[42] Notice that these "public" gardens is something that can also be found throughout Portugal in the 17th and 18th century, with relief being commonly used as a way of emphasising them (Carita and Cardoso 1987: 95, 225, 260), something that was not possible in Braga, due to its flat ground.

character of the overall composition of the façades in Braga; rather, what was more common was a selection of certain architectural details (Sousa Pereira 2000: 85). Yet, by the late 17th and early 18th centuries, it is notable that a considerable number of façades start to be organised along symmetrical lines (Soromenho 1991: 190; Sousa Pereira 2000: 138). This is something that is well represented on the 1750 map with houses whose façades are either fully symmetrical or, more commonly, only their upper floors (fig. 29). Why this change?

Most of the houses where this was happening belonged mostly to the elite or to the "bourgeoisie". By contrast, most of the common people's houses still had asymmetrical façades as shown on the 1750 map. So, in my view, in this context of fragmented identity and social rivalry, those adopting symmetry – mostly elite and "bourgeoisie" – are putting at their service the "purity" and prestige of the geometric lines of Classical architecture and consequently a social superiority in opposition to each other as well as towards the common people. Even so, despite all this motivation to change, it is interesting to notice that some members of the elite didn't feel the need to reaffirm their status through symmetric façades, opting instead to continue to live in houses associated with previous symbols of power, that is, large buildings with adjacent towers (fig. 16).

Another important change that starts to be visible at that time was the use of grated windows on house façades, in forms of design that would make the interior of the houses more discreet to anyone viewing from outside. Until then, their use did not seem to have been common in Braga. The earliest reference I have found for them dates from 1667 and it is from a house (number 38) in R. Souto that belonged to a member of the elite and where it is mentioned that two of its windows were grated[43] (ADB, Prazos do Cabido tome 64: fl. 104). The next reference I have found to these grated windows is in 1701, but this time on a merchant's house (ibid., tome 78: fl. 228v), again in R. Souto (number 40). After this date, their reference in documents became more regular.

The purpose of grated windows in houses was to protect the virtue of the families (i. e., women) living there (Rebelo da Costa 1788: 56). This is related to the dominant view among the elite about the main role of married women: that they should protect the "honour" of the husband, or, in other words, that they should not commit adultery, and the best way to achieve this was to keep women as much as possible inside houses (Nizza da Silva 2001: 443, 444), since they were the guarantors of family lineages.

Grated windows in Braga usually appeared on houses of the elite and the "bourgeoisie". Yet, looking carefully at the 1750 map, one can notice important differences in their use. In the case of the elite, only some houses have them and even so their use is usually restricted to one or

two windows. Obviously, this wasn't clearly enough to protect the interior of the houses from external view due to the large size of these houses. Yet, if we take into consideration the fact that there were, in noble houses, rooms reserved for the activities of women and their servants (ibid.), this lack of grated windows is more understandable. Even so, in some cases, it is possible that the grated windows that are visible on the 1750 map in elite houses were probably used as a way of "protecting" the portable oratory of the hall from less proper, external activities. After all, with the fragmentation of Braga's identity by then, roads were becoming less and less spaces of unity and ordered behaviour among its inhabitants. Since the oratory is a piece of furniture, it is never mentioned in the Prazos do Cabido, which only describes architectural features. However, in the neighbouring city of Porto, in a 1746 description of an elite house in R. Flores, there is reference to an oratory that was between two grated windows; as for the remaining windows of that house, it is evident that they were not grated (v. Ferrão Afonso 2000: 286).

On the other hand, in the houses of the "bourgeoisie", the use of grated windows is quite common. Indeed, they are one of the elements that make this group more distinctive, particularly along the axis of the R. Sousa/R. Souto (fig. 29), since all the windows of the "bourgeois" houses are covered with grates. Yet, what is interesting here is that the "bourgeoisie", through the emphatical use of grated windows, was adopting, around 1700, an elite ideology about women in order to distinguish themselves more markedly from the remaining members of the common people[44]. These lower class houses did not have grated windows (fig. 15), because, being poorer households, they were redundant since women had to participate more actively in economic activity in order to support the family. This meant that they had to be much more frequently outside houses.

One final point I want to point in this chapter about the weakening of the feeling of communal solidarity in Braga is about the external stairs in houses: they gradually disappear. By the turn of the century, quite noticeably, there was a change in access to stairs, from the roads to inside the houses (e. g. houses 20 and 21 in R. Alcaide). Even the stairs in the archbishop's palace didn't escape this change, and were transferred to its interior in 1709. By the time of the 1750 map only five external stairs remained: two in the in-wall area and three in the out-wall area. So, as roads became more and more places of competition between rival social groups who were using them for propaganda, such as for example the numerous processions of the confraternities or the different house

---

[43] And where it is also mentioned that they were oiled, allowing therefore a better preservation.

[44] Nonetheless, despite this concealment, there was a concern in letting light enter inside the divisions of the houses with grated windows. Notice that in many of those houses (fig. 29) there is a smaller white window on top of the grated one that allowed the entrance of light. Besides, this colour not only reflected light better, but also contributed to the white symbolism in the façades, already analysed in chapter 6. The position of that smaller window also guaranteed that nobody outside the house could see people inside it.

façades, the former link between halls and roads gradually eroded and stairs returned to the interior of houses, to increase the intimacy of these spaces.

It was, therefore, within this context of fragmented identity, that a new archbishop, D. Rodrigo Moura Teles, arrived in Braga in 1704.

12

The New Jerusalem

D. Rodrigo Moura Teles ruled Braga for a long period of time, from 1704 to 1728, during which he was responsible for a sustained effort to overcome the city's identitarian fragmentation; an endeavour that would culminate in a new identity for Braga.

However, in the beginning, the Archbishop's actions didn't differ from those of his predecessors. Shortly after his arrival, he spent the years of 1705 and 1706 in systematic pastoral visits to the archdiocese in order to inquire about the Catholic habits of its inhabitants and the clergy (Ferreira 1932: 230). The results were not very reassuring, since in late 1706 he published a pastoral letter with several instructions about the discipline of the clergy, popular customs, obligations of parish priests and the decency of cult practices (ibid.). In 1713, the Archbishop organised a synod in order to reinforce these measures (ibid.: 233), thus indicating that they were not having the desired effect. D. Rodrigo Moura Teles was, therefore, showing his concern for assuming and taking seriously his vigilant role over his flock, which was, as discussed in chapter 8, one of the most important measures of the Catholic Reformation.

The Archbishop also instigated the construction of religious and civilian buildings in several cities of the archdiocese. Examples include the female convent of S. Bento in Barcelos: the female convent of Nossa Senhora da Conceição in Chaves; the female convent of Madre de Deus in Guimarães; the male convent of S. Bento in Viana; and the jails of Valença and Moncorvo (ibid.: 230-233, 248-251, 268). In the case of the jails, the idea was to give more physical comfort to the inmates in order to avoid the moral degradation that could result from precarious conditions (Rocha 1996: 160). In this way, by assuming the role of good shepherd, he was attempting to assert his authority in other places of the archdiocese outside Braga, with the buildings acting as material markers.

Following the construction of a new sacristy and treasure room by his predecessor, the Archbishop also promoted a major program of works in the Cathedral in order to reaffirm it as the spiritual centre of Braga. So, between 1707 and 1712, several chapels in the Cathedral, including those of Braga's archbishops that were saints, were rebuilt, something that gave them a more monumental appearance (Rocha 1996: 76-80, 94-99). The Archbishop was in this way intending to promote their cult and to celebrate their importance for Braga's

inhabitants. In 1713 it was decided to open fourteen new windows in the nave walls as well as building a new dome with windows at the centre of the building in order to provide more light to the interior of the church; the walls of the nave were also covered with decorated tiles (ibid.: 77, 78, 83-87). These changes are very interesting because they follow those that were seen in the previous period in the church of S. Vítor. Unfortunately, the decorated tiles are lost and it is not known what their iconographic program was, though one can assume that it celebrated the archbishops and/or the Blessed Mary.

D. Rodrigo Moura Teles also paid attention to the monuments that testified to the antiquity of Braga, although within an agenda that sought also to celebrate Braga's archbishops. So, in 1715, he was responsible for the reconstruction of the chapel of S. Sebastião, in the area of Carvalheiras, and made substantial financial contributions for that purpose (Ferreira 1932: 246, 247). The resultant building[45] was quite different from the previous one: it had a central plan with four equal arms (thus forming a perfect cross) and a central dome. There is again here a reuse of central-plan models that make reference to a Paleo-Christian past. Yet, this time the model that is being followed is not the octagon chapel built by D. Diogo de Sousa in Campo de Santana, but rather a cross. It is useful to notice that this cruciform plan was common in the region of Braga in the 6th and 7th centuries (Maciel 1995: 128-139). This type of plan first appeared in the West during 5th century, with the best preserved example being the mausoleum of Galla Placidia in Ravena. In the Iberian Peninsula, it was introduced by the Byzantines, who occupied its southern areas for some time (ibid.). This was the time when some of the most important sanctified archbishops of Braga (S. Martinho de Dume and S. Frutuoso) lived, who were also responsible for the construction of religious buildings with cruciform plans, some of which were still visible in the 18th century. There was clearly an awareness in the 18th century of how old these buildings were and who made them. One of them was the mausoleum turned church of S. Frutuoso (still intact today) (fig. 30). In this case, it is even known that when the Franciscans (to whom D. Diogo de Sousa had given the church; v. chapter 7), attempted to build a new church, D. Rodrigo Moura Teles forbade it for fear that the memory of the older church would be lost, only allowing the new construction so long as the previous one was kept intact

---

[45] Still there, although with some modifications: an extended main chapel and a tower.

(Soromenho 1991: 94). So, evidently, there was a strong connection between this kind of church and the first sanctified archbishops of Braga. This architectural scheme was also being assembled in the area where the Roman stone stood that since the 1620's had symbolised the birth of Braga. Thus, in my view, what the Archbishop was attempting to achieve, by building this church, was to remind everyone that the city's origins were also indissolubly connected with the Catholic archbishops.

It was also in 1715 that the Archbishop initiated some changes in Campo de Santana that would end up adding a new dimension to this space. In the area near the Souto Gate where, since the early 16th century, there had been a porch for merchant activity, the Archbishop promoted its substitution by an arcade (Thadim 1748-64: 88). The resulting structure continued to perform the same supporting role for commercial activity. What is interesting about it is its form. While today the arcade is substantially changed due to a late 18th century rebuilding, its original form is still visible on the frontispiece of the 1750 map where it is shown with fourteen monumental and classical arches (fig. 31). It is useful to remember that fourteen is twice the number seven, the sacred number, but why this strongly symbolic investment by the Archbishop in an area that was mostly connected with commercial activity?

An answer to this question can be found in the statue that was put on top of the arcade (fig. 32) in this schema (v. BNL, Figueiredo, ms. [1723-24]: fl. 61v). This statue (moved in the late 18th century to the top of Nova Gate, after this was rebuilt) represents a female figure that stands as an allegory of Braga. The figure holds a lance in one hand, a small image of the Cathedral in the other and has a shield by its side with the city's name written on it. The lance is another symbol of the *axis mundi*, usually being associated with contexts that tend to express the strength of the public authority (Chevalier and Gheerbrant 1994: 399). The Cathedral represents the archbishops, while the shield represents both the universe (that is, Braga and its inhabitants) as well as protection (ibid.: 296). So, this association is a way of reaffirming the Cathedral, i.e. the archbishops, as the *axis mundi* of Braga and consequently as the guarantor of the city's order.

This message was given further emphasis through an inscription in Latin below the statue, which, though it was discarded when the statue was moved, had the following words according to the Inácio José Peixoto (1992 [1790-1808]: 73):

NOBILIS AC ANTIQUA VOCOR SUM BRACARA FIDA/ TURRIBUS INDE POTENS, MENIBUS INDE SURGENS./ HESPERIA PRINCIPES PRIMATUM LITOR HABERA/ ORBIS AD INVIDIAN NUBILA CLARA PETO

(A noble and ancient force I am called, I am Braga, arising thence to minds, trustful in my towers whence [my] strength comes. As chief primate in the West, I shall be a shroud and protector shield to the envy of the World).

There is here a reference to the titles of Braga as well to the Cathedral's towers, that is, the archbishops, from which comes the city's strength and the protection of its inhabitants.

This reference to the Cathedral through the allegorical figure as being the *axis mundi* of Braga is very interesting. Until that time the Cathedral was physically situated in front of Praça do Pão at the centre of the City. So, why bring a representation of the Cathedral to the Garden space? Remember that until then, Braga was divided within a cosmological scheme having an inner City, with the Cathedral at its centre, and an external Garden that was not of the same status as the inner City due, among other things, to that very absence of the Cathedral. So, in my view, what the Archbishop was attempting to do was bring the Cathedral, symbolically, to this area outside the walls. That is why there is a monumental arcade with a reference to the sacred through the repetition of the number seven: it was a way of emulating the narthex that was at the entrance of the Cathedral's building in Praça do Pão. But, what was the purpose of this program? I argue that the Archbishop was attempting to make of Campo de Santana a stage to project the Cathedral's power. Notice that the arcade and the statue were in the area of Campo de Santana where all the commercial activity took place. This area was, after all, the most important meeting place in Braga, with members of all social groups being engaged there in their daily affairs, and hence a place also where an actor with difficulties of affirmation, that is the Archbishop, could cause a larger impact, unlike the limited space of Praça do Pão, which was also mostly associated with religious and political events. In this way, through this program, the Archbishop was attempting to convince Braga's inhabitants that the "normality" of their daily lives resulted from the protective presence of the Cathedral.

Also notice that this project of extending the Cathedral to the Garden was facilitated by the considerable blurring of the borders between the City and the Garden that took place during the 17th century: several aristocratic families moved to the Garden, while several merchant families moved to the axis of R. Sousa/R. Souto. So, through this program, the Archbishop was expanding the City into the Garden, making of Campo de Santana the radial focus of the out-wall area, with the same status as Praça do Pão in the in-wall area. Actually, this was something that was already planned since 1714. Reading the descriptions of houses in *Prazos do Cabido*, it is interesting to notice that since that year, the roads and public spaces outside the wall were no longer referred to as being on the outskirts of the City. Only a couple of the more distant roads – Chãos de Cima and Cruz da Pedra – were still mentioned, and even so not always, as being on the outskirts (e.g. tome 88, fls.: 17v, 184v).

This program also marks a subtle change in the Archbishop's attempts at reasserting his authority over Braga. While until then he was concerned to reaffirm the Cathedral as the "Centre of the World", now he was being more pragmatic and was taking the Cathedral *to* the World.

In 1719 and 1720, the Archbishop also took some measures to dignify Campo de Santana even more as well assuming his role as good shepherd by promoting the construction of two new religious houses. One was the female convent of Penha de França (Ferreira 1932: 251-253; Rocha 1996: 103-111). The other was the House of Rescue of Mary Magdalene, which was an institution that attempted to save prostitutes from their lives of sin and teach them Christian virtue along with some honest trade (Ferreira 1932: 254; Friedrichs 1995: 231).

Yet, despite the Archbishop's best efforts, his systematic attempts to reaffirm the Mitre as the focus of Braga's identity all but failed. The best indication of that failure is a major urbanising project that started in 1719-1720 where, I will argue, the Archbishop gave up being the sole focus of Braga and attempted to unite its inhabitants through a new identity.

This project took place at Mount S. Margarida, a barren and rocky hillock to the northeast of Braga. In 1719, the construction of a chapel named Senhora da Guadalupe (Lady of Guadalupe) began on its highest point (Oliveira 1993: 54) (fig. 33). In 1720, in the area below this chapel, the construction of a residential area was begun with four roads that formed a perfect cross and with a lozenge-shaped square at the intersection (ibid. 2001b: 159). Both the chapel and the residential area formed an indissoluble unity with one of the roads being a direct route to the chapel itself, which, in its turn, had oversight of the houses below (Soromenho 1991: 84). It is also known that the Archbishop was financially connected with both parts of these constructions (Rocha 1996: 148).

This project is usually associated with the need to accommodate a growing population (Oliveira 1999: 67). This is surely the case, but was not the only reason. It is useful to remember that this was a religious society and therefore any intervention in the space would tend to follow an ideal model based on the sacred world. In this case, I would argue that the elements associated with this project were based on the model of the sanctuary of the Lady of Guadalupe in Mexico City, built after an appearance of the Virgin on that place in 1531. First, the Mexican sanctuary is close to the city and to its north, just like Mount Santa Margarida in Braga. Then, the mountain where the Virgin appeared was barren and rocky (Saint-Joseph 1743: 144); and Mount Santa Margarida had the same characteristics prior to the new development. Finally, a miracle occurred as part of the appearance of the Virgin on the Mexican mountain in which several flowers appeared (ibid.: 152); in the case of Braga, after the construction of the chapel, the construction of the square, roads and houses brought

order and life to a piece of land whose characteristics made it closer to the Chaos.

What was the purpose of this analogy?

The Lady of Guadalupe was also represented as the Immaculate Conception, since she appeared on the day of its celebration (ibid.: 145, 149). What is interesting here is that after the coup of 1640, in which Portugal split from Spain, the new Bragança dynasty, in order to reinforce its legitimacy, declared in 1646 that the Immaculate Conception, which was the Bragança patron saint, would also be the patron saint of Portugal. In this way, the Bragança became sort of a protector of the kingdom and the Virgin became the Queen of Portugal; thus the kings and queens of Portugal henceforth were portrayed without a crown which was depicted rather on the images of the Virgin. This not only reinforced the position of the Bragança, but also by making of the Virgin the mother of all the Portuguese, the new dynasty managed to find a powerful symbol to unite them all.

All Portuguese cities, including Braga, had to swear an oath to the Virgin as the patron saint of Portugal as well as placing at their main gates a standard commemorative slab of the event (Ferreira 1932: 178, 179), thus giving a more material and durable presence to the oath. These slabs are still visible in cities near Braga such as Guimarães, Ponte de Lima, Barcelos, Caminha. There is no evidence for the existence of such a slab in Braga, though it is unlikely that there wasn't one since the city had vested interest in an independent Portugal as being more likely to preserve its primate status. It is possible that there had been a slab at the Nova Gate, but later removed when the gate was rebuilt in the late 18th century.

So, taking into consideration this re-assigning of the Immaculate Conception as a unifying symbol of the state, I would argue that the Archbishop, by building his new chapel, was attempting to associate his city and status with this change of circumstance. In effect he was seeking to create a new Centre of the World and thus to unite Braga's inhabitants around a common referent. Mount Santa Margarida assumed, therefore, the role of sacred mountain that until then had belonged to the Cathedral. The residential area built below it was, in its turn, the idealised World that resulted by association with this new Centre. Notice also that it assumed a form that until then was associated with the interior of the in-wall area: it has a cross shape, a geometrical square and rectilinear roads. The houses in the square all assumed the same geometrical and symmetrical design, as can still be seen today, thus affirming an image of harmony and unity. This set of characteristics was also possible because, since 1715, as I have argued above, the Archbishop had been enlarging the perimeter of the City to encompass most of the Garden. There was also intention of building a fountain, symbol of life, at the centre of the square (AMB, *Livro Actas Câmara* Cx. 20, lv. 41, fl. 50v), though for reasons I am unaware of only in 1772 was a fountain made there.

Despite the Archbishop's attempt at making the Immaculate Conception the new focus of Braga, it is interesting that he also attempted to associate it with the Mitre. This is visible in the shape that the chapel of Guadalupe assumes: a perfect cross, similar to the reconstructed chapel of S. Sebastião. As I mentioned before, this form is associated with the first archbishops of Braga. Also important is that the construction of one of the first churches dedicated to the Virgin in the world and the first in Hispania was attributed to its first archbishop, S. Pedro de Rates, (Santa Maria 1707: 18, 19). So, through this chapel, D. Rodrigo Moura Teles attempted to reaffirm Braga's association with the Virgin, through the See's pioneer role in promoting her cult, expecting thereby to retain some of the influence of the Mitre.

Even so, despite the notable changes that this project brought to Braga's identity and landscape, it soon became obvious to the Archbishop that it was actually not enough to reunite its inhabitants. So, a couple years later, in 1722, he embarked on an even more radical project: the sanctuary of Bom Jesus do Monte (Good Jesus of the Mount).

This sanctuary was built on a high hill about three kilometres to the east of Braga. Prior to that, there had been, since 1629, in that place a *via crucis*, that is, a reconstitution of the route of Christ to the Calvary in Jerusalem (Massara 1988: 25, 35, 36). By this time, this tradition was already old in Catholic Europe, with the first of these reconstituted calvaries on mountains dating back to 1224, when under the initiative of St. Francis, the first one was built in Mount Verna, just outside Varallo, in Piedmont (Schama 1995: 436). This route was used by pilgrims who, through the imitation of the last and painful moments of Christ's life, attempted to purify and regenerate themselves (Massara 1988: 86). It is also known that along the route there were small niches with images representing the episodes of the Passion, finishing in a small chapel on the upper part of the mount (ibid. 25, 35, 36).

In 1722, following a conflict between the Dean of the Chapter and the confraternity that administered this *via crucis*, the Archbishop nominated himself as the head of the confraternity and started the construction of the new sanctuary (ibid: 36). The works that followed (fig. 34) are usually represented by historians as a simple "upgrade" of the former *via crucis*, since they gave a monumental character to what was until then a space of seclusion and contemplation (Fernandes Pereira 1989: 93). An arched entrance to the stairway at the base of the mountain with the inscription "Sancta Jerusalem restaurada e reedificada" (Holy Jerusalem restored and rebuilt) was constructed; eight chapels were built in place of the previous niches; and a new church with a central plan instead of the previous chapel on the top of the mount. As the final approach to the church there was a monumental stairway in a pyramid shape, with allegorical fountains on each landing representing the human senses. The purpose of this stairway was to signify the frailty of the human body and the knowledge that emanated from

it; these were to seen as a contrast with the divine Truth that could only be reached by abandoning the material world (ibid.: 94). Thus at the beginning of the stairway there is the fountain of Sight while at the end there is Touch, an ascending journey from the least to the more sinful sense, which had the closest contact with the material world (ibid.).

While I don't disagree with these previous analyses of the Bom Jesus, I argue that the reasons behind the Archbishop's reconstruction were more complex. For a start, notice that this reconstruction gave to the upper part of the sanctuary – the monumental stairway – the form of a gigantic throne. Thrones were pyramid-shape structures that replicated the form of Solomon's throne that were deployed in the context of the Catholic Reformation with the purpose of showing the Blessed Sacrament and promoting its devotion in reaction to the Protestant critique of this dogma (Sancho Martins 1991: 20-31, 57). Such thrones were introduced in Portugal in 1608 and 1609, respectively by the Carmelites and Jesuits, as portable structures for the Lausperene, which was a continuous exposition of the Blessed Sacrament to the adoration of the faithful, normally for a period of 40 hours (ibid.: 25-29). In Braga, at least since 1660, there is information about its use in the Jesuit church of S. Paulo (ibid.: 30). By the late 17th century, this sort of structure started to be transferred to the retables of church altars and placed on permanent display (Alves 1989a: 468). In Braga, the first of this kind of retable appeared in the 1690's in the newly built church of S. Vítor (fig. 35) (Smith 1972: 6). But what was the purpose of this change? By that time, Europe's division between Catholic and Protestant areas was accepted by both sides and there was little danger of Protestant ideas spreading to Portugal. In my view, the answer is fragmented identity. The principal intent of the Blessed Sacrament is union with Christ through love, so that different people and groups would forget their differences and seek unity in their love for Christ. It is not a coincidence that the first throne in Braga appeared in the church of S. Vítor, whose intention was to promote the union of the local population (v. chapter 11). Now, with the Bom Jesus project the same phenomenon was being attempted but on a gigantic scale: from the limited space of a church to the entire landscape of the city, since the sanctuary overlooks Braga from its elevated position (fig. 36). Thus the pyramid shape of the stairs that leads to the church of the sanctuary and thus the circular shape of the latter, since this is the form of the Blessed Sacrament.

But there is more. In 1723 or 1724[46] it was written the *Notícias do Arcebispado de Braga* (Notices of the Archdiocese of Braga), which is a history of the archdiocese of Braga written by the auxiliary bishop of Braga D. Luís Figueiredo (Senna Freitas 1890, vol. 1:

---

[46] While this work is not dated, it can easily be dated to 1723 or 1724 taking in consideration the following elements: it mentions the new fountain in front of the archbishops' palace (fl.61v), which has an inscription mentioning that it was built in 1723, and also that the new towers of the Cathedral were being built (fls. 62, 62v), which were on their turn finished in November of 1724 (Thadim 1748-64: fl. 113).

97). This was on the same lines as the history written about a century before by D. Rodrigo da Cunha, although with some important differences as will be seen shortly. This history starts with the description of Braga, which is explicitly likened to a *paiz* (fl. 1). *Paiz* (land) and *paisagem* (landscape) were by then terms from painting that referred to panels with representations of trees, meadows, fountains as well as other "pleasant objects" from the fields (i.e., rural areas) (Bluteau 1720, vol. VI: 187). Braga is thus presented by D. Luís de Figueiredo in the following lyrical terms:

> To all it liberally offers a graceful view and green pomp with which its large and dilated fields are adorned, to which an infinity of crystalline fountains cuts and provides with liquid and exquisite silver. This display is adorned with leafy groves, fruitful orchards and scented gardens, which embellish this pleasant *Paiz*. Everything is born from the kindness of its climate, where neither the tough inclemency of the Winter nor the ardour of the Summer perform their customary tasks (fl. 1; my translation and emphasis).

Another important element is the description of the limits of this *paiz*. According to the author, Braga is "defended with the wall of the liquid currents of several rivers" (fls. 1, 1v; my translation). The author mentions river Cávado to the north, river Deste to the south and the waters of the Ocean to the west. This reveals an important transformation of Braga's Cosmos. Whereas since the early 16th century there was a City limited by its walls and a Garden beyond it, now, the former Garden was absorbed by the City (a phenomenon that started in 1715) and the area up to these named bodies of water became Braga's new Garden. Actually, another indication that Braga's old walls were having less and less importance in defining its limits is also visible in a petition sent some decades later, in 1796, by the City Hall to the Crown, requesting permission to demolish the towers and walls in order to use the stone to make drainage systems and other public works (Belino 1895: 125-128). It was even mentioned in the petition that the walls were made by Barbarians (ibid.), something that can be seen as a way of degrading their standing and so facilitate their demolition.

What is interesting about these two descriptions of Braga – the *paiz* and its limits – is that they only become meaningful when one stands on the top of the Bom Jesus. It is only from there that one can visualise a large green valley with the city in the middle as well as the boundary bodies of water, since the sanctuary is on the hills to the east of Braga[47]. Also, it must be noted that the description of the *paiz* is not realistic and quantitative but rather is abstract and qualitative, that is, it only pinpoints the elements that conform to the painting of a *paiz*. So, from the top of the Bom Jesus, Braga becomes the landscape painting of a *paiz*. Why?

I think it is important that the characteristics of the *paiz* as identified in this text are essentially a description of Paradise, of the Christian garden, and of an harmonious nature. Taking into consideration the role of nature as model of a legality and of a truth independent of social and even religious contingencies (Lenoble 1990: 264), I would argue that this correlation between Braga and the *paiz* in which it is the Garden and not the City that has predominance, constitutes an attempt to refashion Braga's identity. In other words, with the previous unity of Braga around the archbishops lost, now, Braga's identity is being refashioned around nature. Whereas until then, the Garden resulted from the actions of the inhabitants of the City that converted Chaos into a Christian nature, now there is, instead, a pre-existing Christian nature – the *paiz* of Braga – that makes possible the existence of the City. Now the centre of Braga, the Centre of the World, the sacred mountain connecting Heaven and Earth is not the Cathedral, but instead the sanctuary of Bom Jesus, outside the City and in the Garden, and therefore more pure, from whose top one can discern an harmonious nature of which the City forms a part. Actually, it is useful to notice that the throne, within Catholic liturgy, is expressively associated with Mount Zion, the cosmic mountain, with its steps being the virtues that the faithful had to practice in order to reach salvation (Sancho Martins 1991: 58). It was the same thing in Braga, where the monumental stairway imitated the form of the cosmic mountain. Also, as its inhabitants climbed to the top of the sanctuary, that was constantly beckoning them with its physical presence, in a movement towards union with Christ, they also had to make a gradual scourging of the body and the soul in order to be pure by the time they reached the top. And from here – the equivalent of the Blessed Sacrament and therefore the purest place – they would be presented with a view of the *paiz* of Braga. Braga's catholic identity instead of being based in an illustrious lineage of holy men was now based on a holy land of which all were sons and daughters.

The centrality of the sanctuary of Bom Jesus in the creation of a new identity for Braga can also be seen in the inscription at its entrance where this space is called Jerusalem. Jerusalem was a vision of peace, justice and union for all the tribes of Israel and later, within Christianity, became the symbol of the messianic kingdom and of the Church opened to all peoples (Chevalier and Gheerbrant 1994: 385). In this respect it is also important that the church of Bom Jesus has a central plan just like the Holy Sepulchre in Jerusalem. This sanctuary heralded, therefore, the beginning of a new era of union for Braga's inhabitants, of a New Jerusalem, a visionary Utopia, and where belonging to a certain confraternity or social group became of secondary importance.

This constructed notion of Braga as a *paiz* was a success, and this can be seen in several instances.

While, for example, in the history written by D. Rodrigo da Cunha, the archbishops are the only local actors that are named, in D. Luís Figueiredo's the situation is

---

[47] Though this visual effect is today mostly lost, due to the enormous expansion of the city in the last decades.

different since besides the archbishops there are also several chapters with references to other local players. Thus, there are also catalogues of the auxiliary bishops of Braga (chapter XX); of the parochial churches (chapter XXI); of the confraternity churches (chapter XXII); of the convents (chapter XXIII); of the ecclesiastical officers (chapter XXIV); of secular officers (chapter XXV); and of military officers (chapter XXVI). Also interesting is that this later history was written by an auxiliary bishop and not by the Archbishop. So, by this process, other actors that until then were in the shadows now passed to the centre stage and became also part of the history of Braga. The archbishops were no longer alone.

History texts written after the 1720's explicitly refer to Braga as a *paiz*. For example, Contador Argote in the dedication to his ecclesiastic history of Braga mentions Braga as a *paiz* (1732) and Manoel Silva Thadim writes in the late 18th century a history of Braga with the suggestive title *História Eclesiástica e Política do Paiz Bracarense da Época do Século XVIII* (Ecclesiastical and Political History of the "Pays" of Braga in the 18th Century).

In 1729, it was decided that a new map of Braga should be made, though nothing more is known about it (Oliveira 1994: 37). The intention of making a new map of Braga is quite interesting because it reveals that the former official representation of the city – the map of 1594 – was no longer adequate and that a new one was needed. Nevertheless, it took about a quarter of century before such map was made, in c.1757, but one can see clearly on it the result of the changes that took place in the 1720's. This map, unlike the 1594 one, was made within an accurate mathematical projection of scale and thus a rationalist perception of space, but that doesn't mean that it was more "objective" since it was similarly made in such a way as to transmit certain messages. For a start, it is important to notice that the roads in the southern limits of Braga, in the area close to River Deste, are not represented on the map[48]. This allowed the centre of the map to be manipulated. Yet, this time it is not the Cathedral that occupied that position but instead the area of the castle and the arcade. The choice of this place is more understandable if one stands personally in that area. This is the place in Braga which has the best view of the sanctuary of Bom Jesus, which is in a straight line exactly to the east (fig. 36), the symbolic direction of Jerusalem for all Christianity. So, in this way the sanctuary of the Bom Jesus, although not depicted, is indirectly present on this map presiding over the most important public space in Braga, visible to everyone who would go there in their daily affairs. It is also interesting to see on this map that all religious buildings are carefully numbered and listed, all of them together contributing to the holiness and glory of the *paiz* of Braga, instead of rivalling each other. Ample green spaces are also visible in this map, giving to Braga the illusion of being an Utopian Eden and thus an harmonious *paiz*. Another important aspect of this map is

that, unlike the 1594 one, residential houses are not just mere stereotypes being there just to fill the space, but instead they are all individualised. This is very important because it allowed those living in Braga to identify their own houses, something that would make them feel part of the city. So, Braga's population became an integral part in the public representation of the city. The elements that were privileged in the 1594 map, such as religious buildings, the wall, the city hall, the archbishop's palace and the antiquities, were no longer enough in themselves to fully represent the city. One of the major ideas of Enlightenment thinkers, the use of the grid as a figure of human equality that could level social hierarchies (Taylor 2001: 30), had a practical application in Braga.

One last example is the Jubilee of 1774. Jubilees were full indulgences conceded by the pope in certain circumstances, and were based on a Hebrew festival that took place in periods of seven times seven years, the Great Year (Bluteau 1713: 212, 213). In the case of Braga, 1774 was year of the Jubilee of the Bom Jesus and its confraternity asked the archbishop in 1773 to obtain from the pope a Jubilee for their own sanctuary (Ferreira 1932: 374, 375). The archbishop was successful and the pope conceded ample privileges comparable to the sanctuary of Santiago of Compostela, in Spain, and to the holy places of Jerusalem, something that the city prepared to celebrate in 1774 with extraordinary festivities (ibid.) Compostela and Jerusalem were, of course, the two most important pilgrimage places of the Catholic world at that time. The placing of the Bom Jesus at the same level was an enormous honour and something that obviously filled all Braga's inhabitants with pride, making an important contribution to the corporate feeling of solidarity and union. Yet, when the festivities were about to begin the Crown blocked them (ibid.). This is very interesting because it shows again how important the Bom Jesus was. By then, the Portuguese government, under the leadership of the Marquis of Pombal, was a strongly centralising one, based on Lisbon and this statement by Braga of its autonomy and status wasn't welcome. So, by blocking the Jubilee, the Portuguese government was implicitly recognising the importance that the Bom Jesus had at that time for the political validation of Braga.

Though the Bom Jesus had contributed to provide Braga's inhabitants with a sense of common identity, it is important to observe that previous rivalries didn't fade away. For example, as I mentioned in the previous chapter, the "bourgeoisie" continued to fill its houses with grated windows and the elite refashioned the façades of some institutional and religious buildings, using abundant ornamentation. Nevertheless, the environment of strong social conflict, as happened in the 17th century, had vanished. Despite the rivalries, there was now a common identity in which all participated.

And what about the archbishop D. Rodrigo Moura Teles? Did he lose all his influence in Braga after the construction of the sanctuary of Bom Jesus? No, since he was careful to make himself (and his successors) *primus inter pares*, first among equals, the hero that through its

---

[48] For example, R. dos Pelames, which connected Campo de Santiago with River Deste, only had its upper half depicted on the map.

actions guaranteed Braga's identity, making him therefore an indispensable actor. There are some useful examples of this.

In the history of D. Luís Figueiredo, the archbishops are named before the other actors and their actions are fully described.

On the map of c. 1757, the first religious building in the list is the Cathedral. Actually, it is interesting to notice that in 1723-1724, the façade of the Cathedral was rebuilt. The main reason invoked for its reconstruction was that it was not properly proportioned (Rocha 1996: 90), in other words, it was not symmetrical. The resulting façade is still visible today (fig. 11), presenting a more Classical design. From the previous façade only the narthex remained, presumably due to the allusions it made to past archbishops. The reconstruction is more understandable if one takes into consideration that there were by then other churches with more Classical and monumental façades than the Cathedral. So, the purpose of the new façade was to reclaim the position of primacy for the Cathedral.

At the entrance to the sanctuary of Bom Jesus, there is, in addition to the inscription that identified the place as Jerusalem, another one where it is mentioned that D. Rodrigo Moura Teles was responsible for its construction. Also, at the beginning of the monumental stairway, there was a fountain with the coat of arms of the Archbishop (Massara 1988: 71) – seven castles –, again reminding the pilgrims who had made that reality possible.

This association between the Archbishop and the Bom Jesus is also visible in the fountain that was built in 1723 in the square in front of the Episcopal palace (fig. 27). Here it is possible to see a walled city with six towers and a seventh of large dimensions in the centre, with a child above it. Manuel Rocha gives some random explanations for this fountain: it could be related with Saint Theresa's allegory of the castle with seven levels of oration until reaching a mystical union with God, or alternatively, an apocalyptical dimension, since the tank of the fountain has twelve sides just like the foundations of Jerusalem (1996: 178). Eduardo Pires Oliveira, on the other hand, argues that since the castle was the heraldic symbol of the Archbishop, the fountain was made with the purpose of publicly exalting his personality (1999: 33). In my view, this fountain represents the city of Braga, which is likened to the New Jerusalem. One of the characteristics of the New Jerusalem is a central and gigantic tower that touches the sky and is visible to everyone (cf. Eliade 2000: 23); thus also the twelve foundations. The child on top of the tower lends its symbolism of youth and purity to this new city. As for the seven towers, I agree that they are connected with the Archbishop, though not to celebrate his ego, but more to associate himself with this New Jerusalem, which was only made possible through his actions.

Finally, the Archbishop also restored the Roman columns in Campo de Santana, which had fallen by that time, raising them and painting the letters with gold (Senna Freitas 1890, vol. 1: 139). Also, two of the columns had disappeared and the Archbishop offered two others that he had in the garden of his palace, having also made and added a thirteenth with an inscription celebrating him (ibid.). This inscription made reference to the restoration he did as well as listing his numerous titles, the first words being *Bracara Augusta Dynastes et Ampliator* (ruler and developer of Braga) (Belino 1895: iv). Besides the propaganda, the addition of a thirteenth column by the Archbishop is interesting for another reason. Thirteen is usually seen as a number of bad omen, yet, when in a group with twelve others, it can also be seen as the most powerful and sublime of those numbers (Chevalier and Gheerbrant 1994: 657). So, allowing that the twelve stones symbolised the people of God and the Apostles (v. chapter 7), the Archbishop, by associating himself with the thirteenth, thus legitimated an exceptional place, Christ's own, within that people.

Yet, despite the success of the actions of D. Rodrigo Moura Teles, the archbishops' strong influence in Braga would not last forever. The blow that would diminish it came in 1790. In this year the Portuguese Crown, under the influence of Benevolent Despotism, attempted to eliminate the remains of "regional powers", removing the archbishops' secular jurisdiction over the city, leaving them only with the religious one (Ferreira 1932: 395-401).

The more stable situation that the sacred mount of Bom Jesus had helped to create and symbolise, would only come again under stress in the 19th century during the Liberal Revolutions, in which the "bourgeoisie" gained the upper hand. Even so, the Bom Jesus has continued to be, up until the present day, an important landmark in Braga, not as an internal symbolic referent but rather as a Portuguese heritage icon. Its decline starts to become more visible in the second half of the 19th century, when the archbishops, in the new context of the Liberal Revolutions, with the clash between Republican ideas and religious faith, instigated a new sanctuary at Sameiro dedicated to the Immaculate Conception, which had been recently proclaimed as a dogma by the pope. In this way, through this new sacred mount, the archbishops sought to reaffirm Braga's Catholic identity against secular excesses.

13

Conclusion

With the *paiz* of Braga, I finish my analysis of Braga's identity and landscape during the Modern Era. Throughout this analysis I have attempted to put into practice the principles of the model that was outlined in the beginning of the book. This model is based on the metaphor of the network as an alternative to the more current metaphor of the machine as an organising principle to guide historical research of Portuguese cities during the Modern Era. So, instead of dividing cities into different components, I have argued that a better historical knowledge results from their articulation. Nothing exists isolated; instead, all things are connected through networks and as a result of this interaction they are constantly influencing each other and mutating into something new. I think that the best medium to observe and study these interactions and the changes that take place through time is the landscape. In order to give meaning to those changes I used the concept of identity, whereby they were seen as the result of affirmations, negotiations or negations of the identity of local inhabitants. In this way, it was possible to reach a better understanding of the persons living in Braga during the period under study.

The result of this alternative model can be seen in the following summary of Braga's identity and landscape during the Modern Era, where differences from empiricist models are notable.

First of all, it is important to notice that this was a society where there was a religious experience of the universe, which means that only spaces that followed sacred models could be considered as real. This idea was also valid for cities, including Braga, which sought to replicate on Earth the sacred models of Heaven. I have argued that in the late 15th century, Braga had a centre that connected both worlds, the Cathedral, and from which life flowed. The city was limited by a wall, beyond which there was the Chaos, that is, lands that in the perspective of the Braga's inhabitants were not organised along sacred models. It was a city with strong internal divisions, as can be seen from examples such as the closing of the houses to the outside, the appropriation of public space by private people and internal conflicts. The only thing that ended up uniting all the inhabitants was an even greater fear from the Dragon, that is, all sorts of dangers that came from beyond the walls, and against which there was an abundance of spiritual and physical defences.

This form of identity based in fear would be challenged in the early 16th century through the actions of the archbishop D. Diogo de Sousa who sought to develop a more positive identity among the inhabitants. This was mostly based on the affirmation of a strong Christian identity centred on the Cathedral and guaranteed by a prestigious lineage of holy men, of which the archbishops were the representatives. The Archbishop was therefore careful to put himself and his successors at the centre of this identity, something that would mark Braga's identity for the next two centuries. The Archbishop promoted profound changes in the city in order to give it a character closer to the evangelical origins of Christianity. The city assumed the form of the Cosmos, with the three continents and two perpendicular axes that formed a cross. At the centre, the Cathedral – symbol of the archbishops' power –, acting as Jerusalem, the navel of the world. In order to better emphasise its centrality, he rearranged the area around it to make the Cathedral even more patent. The roads were also rearranged in order to be larger and rectilinear allowing thereby an explosion of light – associated with God – inside the city, something that was extendable to the houses, which were now painted white and with larger and multiple openings to the roads, thus allowing the entry of light. Through light, all Braga's inhabitants participated in a common union with God. Also, in order to further diminish internal social tensions related with status, he promoted a general "social" upgrade of lower class houses through the widespread construction of upper floors and the use of stone (both noble symbols), making the common people an active participant in the ennoblement of the city.

The Archbishop also promoted the organisation of an intermediate space between the city walls and the Chaos: the Garden. This space was organised around large public spaces outside the city's gates, the Campos, and was associated with Nature, being thereby closer to the material world, in contrast with the city, whose model was Heaven. With this division, the Archbishop put in the Garden those activities considered less spiritual but nonetheless necessary for life, making more relevant in this way the spiritual character of the city. Among the activities that were practised in the Campos were leisure, physical healing, commercial activity and propaganda (particularly through the emulation of Rome's Classical and Marian past).

By the mid-16th century, Braga's Catholic identity started to be challenged by a number of factors – the Protestant

Reform, a crypto-Judaism as well as a crypto-paganism – that forced the city's elite to take a number of measures during the next decades in order to reinforce the official Catholic identity. Several religious buildings, such as convents, churches and even a seminar, were built in the city, which conveyed several messages. For example, the church of the Mercy House reaffirmed the importance of the practice of good works that was criticised by Protestants; all these buildings assumed more geometrical lines, putting aside the realistic representation of Nature that was common in previous buildings and that could be used for covert pagan devotions. There was also a care in placing these buildings in large public spaces in order to make them and the messages they conveyed more visible.

In 1580, with the union of the Portuguese and Spanish Crowns, Braga entered a period of uncertainty over its primate status, which was in risk of being lost to Toledo. This was something that worried more than anyone the archbishops because such status contributed to their strong position in Braga. So, in the late 16th and early 17th centuries a number of important works were undertaken in order to reaffirm Braga's primate status. For example, in order to impress an external audience the map of Braga of 1594 was drawn; the area of Campo da Vinha was transformed in order to emulate the prestigious *Piazza del Popolo* in Rome. In order to impress internal audiences and give an image of power and confidence, the Mitre organised an area of the city for bullfights, which had a strong cosmological importance for the common people.

Yet, despite these measures, by the 1620's and 1630's, Braga had lost considerable status within the Hispanic Monarchy. This caused introspection and a desire to return to a political situation more favourable to the city. The best example of this attitude is the transformation of the area around the chapel of S. Sebastião into an Arcadian Garden (a place of shelter from the difficulties of the present) and the symbolic siting there of the Roman insignia of Braga in the expectation that in such a pure environment a new city could flourish. Despite Portugal regaining its independence in 1640, the situation in Braga actually got worse, because the political circumstances of that event caused the absence of archbishops for a period of thirty years. The absence of Braga's strongest symbol caused the collapse of the city's identity. As a consequence, social conflicts between the elite and the common people, which the archbishops had managed until then to keep under control, were exacerbated.

In 1671, the archbishops returned to Braga and took a number of measures in order to bring the city to the *status quo ante*. Examples include the rearrangement of the Cathedral and the construction of the church of S. Vítor with the purpose of promoting the cult of several saints associated with the Mitre; the introduction of new convents, which were not connected to others whose previous behaviour was less than exemplary. However, these measures didn't achieve the desired result. Instead, during the late 17th and early 18th centuries, there was a notable fragmentation of the city's identity with the common people affirming themselves towards the elite through the control of several religious confraternities. This fragmentation was also visible in the formation at that time of a "bourgeoisie" that also attempted to assert its independence from the elite and other sectors of the common people through modifications in their houses' façades. These included the adoption of symmetrical forms, modelled on the pure intellectual geometry of Classical architecture and thus more prestigious, as well as the use of grated windows to conceal women, which was a form, in this society, of affirming the honour of the family.

In the 1720's, once the failure of the archbishops to return the city to the *status quo ante* became very apparent, D. Rodrigo Moura Teles, decided to recreate Braga's identity through the sanctuary of Bom Jesus do Monte, from whose summit the city was visible as a harmonious *paiz*. This sanctuary allowed the formation of a new identity that was based on the concept of a holy territory, in which all were equals since they were its sons and daughters, instead of the old identity of the illustrious lineage of holy men. This was something that was remarkably visible on the maps of 1750 and c. 1757, on which all the houses are carefully drawn. Nonetheless, the Archbishop attempted to recreate himself as *primus inter pares* in order to keep its influence in the city, something that his successors managed to keep until the late 18th century.

One final word: this summary of Braga must not be seen as something that can be fitted automatically to other Portuguese cities of the Modern Era. That's the kind of reasoning that one can expect from empiricism, where the purpose is to find laws to which everything is subordinated. In this work, because the guiding metaphor is the network and not the machine, each city has its own history: there are similarities but there are also differences. For example, some years after the construction of the sanctuary of Bom Jesus, similar sanctuaries were also built in the cities of Porto and Lamego. So, one can assume that there were similar problems in those cities and that Braga's model was being copied. On the other hand, in some coastal cities, such as Setúbal and Caminha, in the second half of the 17th century, the Crown promoted the construction of new walls that encompassed the former cities incorporating their fishing neighbourhoods, something that did not happen in Braga. These are glimpses of more complex examples awaiting further study. Even the account that I have given for Braga is by no means definitive, since that is just the result of the lines of research that I followed. Different lines will tell different things.

Bibliography

MANUSCRIPT SOURCES

I – Instituto do Arquivo Nacional/Torre do Tombo
'Capítulos Gerais dos Estados dos Povos' in *Cortes*, volume 15

II – Biblioteca Nacional de Lisboa
FIGUEIREDO, D. Luís (1723-24) *Notícias do Arcebispado de Braga*, cod. 143
THADIM, Manoel Joze da Silva (late 18th century) *História Ecclesiástica e Política do Paiz Bracarense da Época do Século XVIII*, cod. 682

III – Biblioteca Nacional da Ajuda
54-VIII-20, 397
54-VIII-24, 72

IV – Arquivo Distrital de Braga
Estatutos S. Crispim e S. Crispiniano (1731)
Índice dos Prazos das Casas do Cabido (1750), volumes I-IV
Memorial das Obras que D. Diogo de Sousa mandou fazer (1532-1565), Registo Geral, lv. 330, fls. 329-334
Prazos do Cabido, tomes 1-88
S. JOSÉ, Madre Dona Maria Luiza de (1759) *Fundação dos Remédios*, Fundo Monástico Conventual, Franciscanos, Convento dos Remédios, ms. 607
THADIM, Manoel Joze da Silva (1764) *Diário Bracarense das epocas, fastos, e annaes mais memoráveis desde o princípio do século XVI athe o meyo do século XVIII*, ms. 1054
Tombo do Cabido, volumes 1-2

V – Arquivo Municipal de Braga
Cartas dos Senhores Arcebispos e Cabidos, docs. 26
'Index das couzas mais memoraveis que se achão registradas nos livros do Senado da Camara desta cidade de Braga' in *Index de alguns livros de registo e memórias de receita e despesa*, pp. 103-153
Livro das Actas da Câmara *Cx. 16, lv. 33; Cx. 19, lv. 39; Cx. 20, lv. 41; Cx. 21, lv. 42*
Livro das Vereações (1500 (?)-1816)
Tombo dos Bens da Câmara (1737)

VI – Arquivo da Sé de Braga
Estatutos da Irmandade de S. Crispim e S. Crispiniano (1702)

VII – Arquivo da Irmandade de S. Vicente (Braga)

Estatutos da Irmandade de S. Vicente (1723)

Estatutos da Irmandade do Santo Homem Bom (1688)

Estatutos da Irmandade do Santo Homem Bom (1725)

Livro dos Termos da Mesa da Irmandade de S. Vicente (1594-1609)

Livro dos Termos da Mesa da Irmandade de S. Vicente (1669-1682)

Livro dos Termos da Mesa da Irmandade de S. Vicente (1682-1700)

VIII – Arquivo da Irmandade de Santa Cruz (Braga)

Estatutos da Irmandade dos Passos (1707)

Livro dos Termos da Mesa da Irmandade de Santa Cruz (1589-1701)

Livro Segundo dos Termos da Mesa da Irmandade dos Passos (1686-1740)

IX – Arquivo da Venerável Ordem Terceira de S. Francisco (Braga)

Estatutos da Arquiconfraria do Cordão (1615)

Estatutos da V.O.T. S. Francisco (1680)

Estatutos da V.O.T. S. Francisco (1695)

PRINTED SOURCES

ARGOTE, Jerónimo Contador de (1732) *Memórias para a História Ecclesiástica do Arcebispado de Braga*, tome 1, Lisboa Occidental: Of. de Joseph António da Sylva

BASTO, Frutuoso Lourenço de (1627) *Relação do recebimento, e festas que se fizerão, na augusta cidade de Braga, á entrada do Senhor Dom Rodrigo da Cunha*, [s.l.]: [s.n.]

BLUTEAU, Rafael (1713) *Vocabulario Portuguez e Latino*, vol. IV, Coimbra: Colegio de Artes da C. Jesus

BLUTEAU, Rafael (1720) *Vocabulario Portuguez e Latino*, vol. VI, Coimbra: Colegio de Artes da C. Jesus

CARVALHO DA COSTA, António (1706) *Corografia Portuguesa*, volume I, Lisboa: Of. de Valentim da Costa Deslandes

CUNHA, D. Rodrigo da (1634-35) *História Eclesiástica dos Arcebispos de Braga*, Braga: [s.n.], fac-simile edition of 1989

REBELO DA COSTA, Agostinho (1788) *Descrição Topográfica e Histórica da Cidade do Porto*, Porto: Of. de Antonio Alvarez Ribeiro

RODRIGUES, João (1627) *Relaçam verdadeira das Festas que fez a Augusta Cidade de Braga, no recebimento do Il.mo Sr. D. Rodrigo da Cunha*, Lisboa: [s.n.]

SAINT-JOSEPH, Francisco de (1743) *Historia Universal de la Primitiva y Milagrosa Imagen de N.ra Señora de Guadalupe*, Madrid: Antonio Marin

SANTA MARIA, Frei Agostinho de (1707) *Santuário Mariano*, tome 1, Lisboa: Of. Antóno Pedrozo Galvão

SANTA MARIA, Frei Agostinho de (1712) *Santuário Mariano*, tome 4, Lisboa: Of. Antóno Pedrozo Galvão

ICONOGRAPHIC SOURCES

Braga (c. 1694) in *Forum*, **15/16**, p. 23, Braga: Universidade do Minho

Ebora Colonia Romana (1501), Arquivo Distrital de Évora

Livro das Fortalezas (1509-1510), facsimile edition of 1997 by Arquivo Nacional da Torre do Tombo and Edições Inapa

Livro de Horas de D. Manuel (c. 1517-1530), Museu Nacional de Arte Antiga, Lisboa

Mappa da Cidade de Braga Primas (c. 1757), Biblioteca Nacional da Ajuda, Lisboa

Mapa das Ruas de Braga (1750), fac-simile edition of 1991 by Arquivo Distrital de Braga

Nova Bracarae Augusta Descriptio (1594) in Georg Braun, *Civitatis Orbis Terrarum*, volume V, fl. 3

Etymologiarum sive originum, Saint Isidorus, libri XX

MONOGRAPHS

ABREU, Leonídeo de (1983) *Braga: coisas de outros tempos*, preface by Eduardo Pires de Oliveira, Braga: Soares dos Reis Editor

AFONSO, Domingos de Araújo (1954) 'Da verdadeira origem de algumas famílias ilustres de Braga e seu termo' in *Bracara Augusta*, volume V, pp. 134-155, Braga: Câmara Municipal de Braga

AFONSO, Domingos de Araújo (1962) 'Da verdadeira origem de algumas famílias ilustres de Braga e seu termo' in *Bracara Augusta*, volume XIII, pp. 383-394, Braga: Câmara Municipal de Braga

AFONSO, Domingos de Araújo (1968) 'Da verdadeira origem de algumas famílias ilustres de Braga e seu termo' in *O Distrito de Braga*, volume 4, fasc. I-II, pp. 133-152, Braga: Imp. Livr. Ed. Pax

AFONSO, Domingos de Araújo (1969) 'Da verdadeira origem de algumas famílias ilustres de Braga e seu termo' in *Bracara Augusta*, volume XXIII, pp. 132-147, Braga: Câmara Municipal de Braga

AFONSO, Domingos de Araújo (1970) 'Da verdadeira origem de algumas famílias ilustres de Braga e seu termo' in *O Distrito de Braga*, volume 4, fasc. III-IV, pp. 682-708, Braga: Imp. Livr. Ed. Pax

AFONSO, Domingos de Araújo (1975) 'Da verdadeira origem de algumas famílias ilustres de Braga e seu termo' in *Bracara Augusta*, volume XXIX, pp. 279-363, Braga: Câmara Municipal de Braga

ALEXANDRE RODRIGUES, Luís (1995) *Bragança no Século XVIII*, MA dissertation presented to Faculdade de Letras da Universidade do Porto

ALMEIDA, André Ferrand de (1993) 'As Misericórdias' in José Mattoso (ed.), *História de Portugal*, volume 3, pp. 185-193, Lisboa: Editorial Estampa

ALVES, Natália Marinho Ferreira (1989a) 'Talha' in José Fernandes Pereira and Paulo Pereira (eds.), *Dicionário da Arte Barroca em Portugal*, pp. 466-470, Lisboa: Editorial Presença

ALVES, Natália Marinho Ferreira (1989b) 'Retábulo in José Fernandes Pereira and Paulo Pereira (eds.), *Dicionário da Arte Barroca em Portugal*, pp. 405-408, Lisboa: Editorial Presença

ARAÚJO, Domingos (2003) *Braga. Símbolos da Fé*, Braga: APPACDM

ARAÚJO OLIVEIRA, Aurélio (1990) 'A mitra e o clero bracarense na crise do século XVII' in *Actas do IX Centenário da dedicação da Sé de Braga*, volume II/2, pp. 181-207, Braga: Fac. de Teologia da Universidade Católica Portuguesa and Cabido Metropolitano e Primarcial de Braga

'Arquivo Municipal' (1970) in *Bracara Augusta*, volume XXIV, pp. 284-435, Braga: Câmara Municipal de Braga

'Arquivo Municipal' (1975) in *Bracara Augusta*, volume XXIX, pp. 377-426, Braga: Câmara Municipal de Braga

'Arquivo Municipal' (1976) in *Bracara Augusta*, volume XXX, tome 2, pp. 681-792, Braga: Câmara Municipal de Braga

'Arquivo Municipal' (1978) in *Bracara Augusta*, volume XXXII, pp. 415-474, Braga: Câmara Municipal de Braga

'Arquivo Municipal' (1980) in *Bracara Augusta*, volume XXXIV, pp. 937-992, Braga: Câmara Municipal de Braga

'Arquivo Municipal' (1982) in *Bracara Augusta*, volume XXXVI, pp. 545-601, Braga: Câmara Municipal de Braga

'Arquivo Municipal' (1983) in *Bracara Augusta*, volume XXXVII, pp. 393-448, Braga: Câmara Municipal de Braga

'Arquivo Municipal' (1984) in *Bracara Augusta*, volume XXXVIII, pp. 393-448, Braga: Câmara Municipal de Braga

'Arquivo Municipal' (1985) in *Bracara Augusta*, volume XXXIX, pp. 577-614, Braga: Câmara Municipal de Braga

AUSTIN, David (1998) 'Private and public: an archaeological consideration of things' in H. Hundsbichler et al. *Die Vielfalt der Dinge: Neue Wege zur Analyse mittelalterlicher Sachkultur*, pp. 163-206, Vienna: The Austrian Academy of Arts

BANDEIRA, Miguel Sopas de Melo (1994) 'Uma Panorâmica Seiscentista de Braga' in *Forum*, **15/16**, pp. 25-36, Braga: Universidade do Minho

BANDEIRA, Miguel Sopas de Melo (2000a) *O espaço urbano de Braga em meados do século XVIII*, Porto: Edições Afrontamento

BANDEIRA, Miguel Sopas de Melo (2000b) 'D. Diogo de Sousa, o urbanista' in *Bracara Augusta*, volume XLIX, pp. 19-58, Braga: Câmara Municipal de Braga

BAPTISTA PEREIRA, Fernando António (1994) 'A vida e a mentalidade. Do espaço, do tempo e da morte' in Irisalva Moita (ed.), *O Livro de Lisboa*, pp. 343-362, Lisboa: Livros Horizonte

BAPTISTA PEREIRA, Fernando António (2001) *Imagens e Histórias de Devoção. Espaço, Tempo e Narrativa na Pintura Portuguesa do Renascimento (1450-1550)*, Ph.D Dissertation presented to Faculdade de Belas-Artes da Universidade de Lisboa

BELINO, Albano (1895) *Letreiros e Inscripções da Cidade de Braga*, Porto: Typographia Occidental

BETHENCOURT, Francisco e Diogo Ramada Curto (eds.) (1991) *A Memória da Nação*, Lisboa: Livraria Sá da Costa Editora

BELINO, Albano (1900) *Archeologia Christã*, Lisboa: Empreza da História de Portugal

BOIVIN, N. (2004) 'Landscape and cosmology in the south Indian Neolithic: new perspectives on the Deccan ashmounds', *Cambridge Archaeological Journal*, **14.2**, pp. 235-257

BOORSTIN, Daniel J. (1987) *Os Descobridores*, Lisboa: Gradiva

BRADLEY, Richard (2000) *An Archaeology of Natural Places*, London: Routledge

BUESCU, Ana Isabel (1991) 'Um mito das origens da nacionalidade: o milagre de Ourique' in Francisco Bethencourt and Diogo Ramada Curto (eds.), *A Memória da Nação*, pp. 49-69, Lisboa: Livraria Sá da Costa Editora

BURKE, Gerald (1975) *Towns in the making*, London: Edward Arnold

CÂMARA, Teresa Bettencourt da (1989) *Óbidos: Arquitectura e Urbanismo*, Câmara Municipal de Lisboa and Imprensa Nacional/Casa da Moeda

CARITA, Helder and Homem Cardoso (1987) *Tratado da Grandeza dos Jardins em Portugal, ou da originalidade e desaires desta Arte*, Lisboa: Authors Edition

CARMICHAEL, D.L., J. Hubert, B. Reeves, and A. Schanche (eds) (1994) *Sacred sites, sacred places*, London: Routledge

CARREIRA, Adília Maria Caldas (1989) *Leiria, cidade episcopal. O urbanismo leiriense do século XVI ao século XVIII*, MA dissertation presented to Faculdade de Ciências Sociais e Humanas da Universidade Nova de Lisboa

CASTELO-BRANCO, Fernando (1990 [1956]) *Lisboa Seiscentista*, Lisboa: Livros Horizonte

CHEVALIER, Jean and Alain Gheerbrant (1994) *Dicionário dos Símbolos*, Lisboa: Teorema

COELHO, Constantino Ribeiro (1992) *Braga antiga, velharias bracarenses... memórias do velho tempo e outros textos*, gathering, selection, introduction and notes by Eduardo Pires de Oliveira, Braga: [s.n.]

COGGINS, C. (1982) 'The zenith, the mountain, the centre and the sea', in A.F. Aveni and G. Urton, *Ethnoastronomy and archaeoastronomy in the American tropics: Annals of the New York Academy of Sciences*, **385**, pp. 111-123

CONCEIÇÃO, Maria Margarida da (1997) *Formação do espaço urbano de Almeida*, dissertação de mestrado apresentada à Faculdade de Ciências Sociais e Humanas da Universidade Nova de Lisboa

CONDE, Sílvio (1997) 'Sobre a casa urbana do Centro e Sul de Portugal nos fins da Idade Média' in *Arqueologia Medieval*, **5**, Porto: Edições Afrontamento

CONZEN, M.R.G. (1960) *Alnwick, Northumberland: a Study in Town Plan Analysis*, London: Inst. Brit. Geographers

CORDEIRO PEREIRA, João (1998) 'A Estrutura Social e o seu Devir' in Joel Serrão and A. H. de Oliveira Marques (eds.), *Nova História de Portugal*, volume V, pp. 277-336, Lisboa: Editorial Presença

CORREIA, José Eduardo Horta (1984) *Vila Real de Santo António. Urbanismo e Poder na Política Pombalina*, PhD thesis presented to Faculdade de Ciências Sociais e Humanas da Universidade Nova de Lisboa

CORREIA, José Eduardo Horta (1989) 'Urbanismo' in José Fernandes Pereira and Paulo Pereira (eds.), *Dicionário da Arte Barroca em Portugal*, pp. 507-513, Lisboa: Editorial Presença

COSGROVE, Dennis (1993) 'Landscapes and Myths, Gods and Humans' in Barbara Bender (ed.), *Landscape. Politics and Perspectives*, pp. 281-306, Oxford: Berg

COSGROVE, Dennis (1994) *The Palladian Landscape: geographical change and its cultural representation in sixteenth-century Italy*, Leicester: Leicester University Press

COSTA, Luís (1991) *Igreja Paroquial de S. Vicente*, Braga: APPACDM

COSTA, Luís (1993) *O Templo de Santa Cruz*, Braga: Irmandade de Santa Cruz

COSTA, Luís (1998) *Braga – Roteiro Monumental e Artístico*, Braga: APPACDM

DANIELS, Stephen and Dennis Cosgrove (1988) 'Introduction: iconography and landscape' in Denis Cosgrove and Stephen Daniels (eds.), *The Iconography of Landscape*, pp. 1-10, Cambridge: Cambridge University Press

DELUMEAU, Jean (1994) *A Civilização do Renascimento*, volume II, Lisboa: Editorial Estampa

DIAS, João José Alves (1985) 'Lisboa Medieval na Iconografia do século XVI', offprint from *Actas das Jornadas de História Medieval (1383-1385 e a crise geral dos séculos XIV e XV)*, pp. 239-250

DIAS, João José Alves (1998) 'A População in Joel Serrão and A. H. de Oliveira Marques (eds.), *Nova História de Portugal*, volume V, pp. 11-52, Lisboa: Editorial Presença

DOUGLAS, Mary (1991) *Pureza e Perigo*, Lisboa: Edições 70

DUARTE, Luís Miguel (1998) 'A Propriedade Urbana' in Joel Serrão and A. H. de Oliveira Marques (eds.), *Nova História de Portugal*, volume V, pp. 114-160, Lisboa: Editorial Presença

DUBY, Georges (1993) O Tempo das Catedrais. A arte e a sociedade. 980-1420, Lisboa: Editorial Estampa

ELIADE, Mircea (1989) Aspectos do Mito, Lisboa: Edições 70

ELIADE, Mircea (2000) O Mito do Eterno Retorno, Lisboa: Edições 70

ELIADE, Mircea (2002) O Sagrado e o Profano. A essência da religiões, Lisboa: Livros do Brasil

ESPANCA, Túlio (1993) Évora, Lisboa: Editorial Presença

FEIO, Alberto (1954) *O brasão de Braga. Origem e evolução*, Braga: [s.n.]

FEIO, Alberto (1984) *Coisas Memoráveis de Braga*, Braga: Universidade do Minho/Biblioteca Pública de Braga

FERGUSON, George (1966) *Signs and symbols in Christian art*, Oxford University Press

FERNANDES PEREIRA, José (1989) 'Bom Jesus do Monte, Santuário do' in José Fernandes Pereira and Paulo Pereira (eds.), *Dicionário da Arte Barroca em Portugal*, pp. 93-96, Lisboa: Editorial Presença

FERRÃO AFONSO, José (2000) *A Rua das Flores no Século XVI. Elementos para História Urbana do Porto Quinhentista*, Porto: FAUP Publicações

FERREIRA, José Augusto (1932) *Fastos Episcopaes da Igreja Primacial de Braga*, tome III, Braga: Mitra Bracarense

FERREIRA ALVES, Joaquim Jaime (1988) *O Porto na época dos Almadas*, Porto: [s.n.]

FLEURE, H. J. (1931) 'City morphology in Europe' in *Proceedings of the Royal Institution of Great Britain*, 27, pp. 145-55

FONTES, Luís, Francisco Sande Lemos and Mário Cruz (1997/98) '"Mais Velho" que a Sé de Braga Intervenção arqueológica na catedral bracarense: notícia preliminar" in Cadernos de Arqueologia, **14-15**, pp. 137-164

FRANÇA, José-Augusto (1962) *Lisboa Pombalina e o Iluminismo*, Lisboa: Bertrand

FRIEDRICHS, Christopher R. (1995) *The Early Modern City. 1450-1750*, Harlow: Pearson Education

GOITIA, Fernando Chueca (1982) *Breve História do Urbanismo*, Lisboa: Editorial Presença

HARLEY, J. B. (1988) 'Maps, knowledge and power' in Denis Cosgrove and Stephen Daniels (eds.), *The Iconography of Landscape*, pp. 277-302, Cambridge: Cambridge University Press

HORTA CORREIA, José Eduardo (1986) 'A Arquitectura – Maneirismo e Estilo Chão' in *História da Arte em Portugal*, vol. 7, pp. 93-135, Lisboa: Ed. Alfa

INSOLL, Timothy (2004) *Archaeology, Ritual, Religion*, London: Routledge

JOHNSON, Matthew (1999) *Archaeological Theory. An Introduction*, Oxford: Blackwell

KNAPP, A. Bernard and Wendy ASHMORE (eds.) (1999) *Archaeologies of Landscape: contemporary perspectives*, pp. 83-100, Oxford: Blackwell

KUBLER, George (1988) *A Arquitectura Portuguesa Chã. Entre as Especiarias e os Diamantes. 1521-1706*, Lisboa: Vega

LAHIRI, N. (1996) 'Archaeological landscapes and textual images: a study of the sacred geography of medieval Ballabargh', *World Archaeology*, **28.2**, pp. 244-264

LENOBLE, Robert (1990) *História da Ideia de Natureza*, Lisboa: Edições 70

LEONE, Mark P. (1984) 'Interpreting ideology in historical archaeology: using the rules of perspective in the William Paca Garden in Annapolis', Maryland in Daniel Miller and Cristopher Tilley (eds.) *Ideology, Power and Prehistory*, pp. 25-25, Cambridge: Cambridge University Press

LOURENÇO PEREIRA, Maria João (1998) 'O Afecto' in Joel Serrão and A. H. de Oliveira Marques (eds.), *Nova História de Portugal*, volume VII, pp. 657-665, Lisboa: Editorial Presença

MACIEL, M. Justino (1995) 'A Arte da Antiguidade Tardia' in Paulo Pereira (ed.), *História da Arte Portuguesa*, volume 1, pp. 103-149, Círculo de Leitores

MAGALHÃES, Joaquim Romero (1993a) 'As estruturas da produção agrícola e pastoril' in José Mattoso (ed.), *História de Portugal*, volume 3, pp. 243-281, Lisboa: Editorial Estampa

MAGALHÃES, Joaquim Romero (1993b) 'Os Cristãos-Novos: da integração à segregação' in José Mattoso (ed.), *História de Portugal*, volume 3, pp. 475-480, Lisboa: Editorial Estampa

MAGALHÃES, Joaquim Romero (1993c) 'Filipe II (I de Portugal)' in José Mattoso (ed.), *História de Portugal*, volume 3, pp. 563-570, Lisboa: Editorial Estampa

MARKL, Dagoberto (1995) 'O humanismo e os Descobrimentos: o impacto nas artes' in Paulo Pereira (ed.), *História da Arte Portuguesa*, volume 2, pp. 405-425, Círculo de Leitores

MARQUES, José (1993) 'As confrarias da Paixão na antiga arquidiocese de Braga' in Theologica, II serie, volume XXVIII, pp. 447-480, Braga

MARTINS, Fausto Sancho (1991) 'Trono Eucarístico do Retábulo Barroco Português: origem, função, forma e simbolismo' in *Actas do I Congresso Internacional do Barroco*, volume II, pp. 17-58, Porto: Reitoria da UP e Governo Civil do Porto

MARTINS, Manuela (2000) *Bracara Augusta. Cidade Romana*, Braga: Unidade de Arqueologia da Universidade do Minho

MASSARA, Mónica (1988) *Santuário do Bom Jesus do Monte: fenómeno tardo barroco em Portugal*, Braga: Confraria do Bom Jesus do Monte

MATTOSO. José (1993) 'Dois Séculos de Vicissitudes Políticas' in José Mattoso (ed.), *História de Portugal*, volume 2, pp. 23-163, Lisboa: Editorial Estampa

MAURÍCIO, Rui (2000) *O Mecenato de D. Diogo de Sousa Arcebispo de Braga (1505-1532). Urbanismo e Arquitectura*, Leiria: Magno Edições

MEA, Elvira (1990) 'O processo inquisitorial garante de depuração das visitas pastorais de Braga (século XVI)' in *Actas do IX Centenário da dedicação da Sé de Braga*, Volume II/2, pp. 67-95, Braga: Fac. de Teologia da Universidade Católica Portuguesa e Cabido Metropolitano e Primarcial de Braga

MEA, Elvira (1998) 'A Igreja em Reforma' in Joel Serrão and A. H. de Oliveira Marques (eds.), *Nova História de Portugal*, volume V, pp. 413-446, Lisboa: Editorial Presença

MECO, José (1986) *O Azulejo em Portugal*, Lisboa: Publicações Alfa

MENDES, António Rosa (1993) 'A Vida Cultural' in José Mattoso (ed.), *História de Portugal*, volume 3, pp. 375-421, Lisboa: Editorial Estampa

MINOIS, Georges (2000) *História do Futuro*, Lisboa: Teorema

MINOIS, Georges (2004) *História do Ateísmo*, Lisboa: Teorema

MOITA, Irisalva (ed) (1994) *O Livro de Lisboa*, Lisboa: Livros Horizonte

MONTEIRO, Nuno G. (1993) 'Sistemas Familiares' in José Mattoso (ed.), *História de Portugal*, volume 4, pp. 279-282, Lisboa: Editorial Estampa

MOREIRA, Rafael (1995a) 'Formulação e Crise da Nova Linguagem: o Serlianismo de Diogo de Torralva' in Paulo Pereira (ed.), *História da Arte Portuguesa*, volume 2, pp. 350-356, Círculo de Leitores

MOREIRA, Rafael (1995b) 'A Resistência Nacional e o Problema do Estilo Chão' in Paulo Pereira (ed.), *História da Arte Portuguesa*, volume 2, pp. 356-362, Círculo de Leitores

MUIR, Richard (1999) *Approaches to Landscape*, London: MacMillan

MULINACCI, Roberto (1999) *Do Palimpsesto ao Texto. A Novela Pastoril Portuguesa*, Lisboa: Edições Colibri

MURTEIRA, Maria Helena da Cunha (1994) *Lisboa da Resauração às Luzes. Uma análise da evolução urbana*, MA dissertation presented to Faculdade de Ciências Sociais e Humanas da Universidade Nova de Lisboa

NOGUEIRA SILVA, Ana Cristina and António Manuel Hespanha (1993) 'A identidade portuguesa' in José Mattoso (ed.), *História de Portugal*, volume 4, pp. 19-37, Lisboa: Editorial Estampa

NUNES, Henrique Barreto (1994) 'Uma imagem inédita de Braga no século XVII' in *Forum*, **15/16**, p. 21-23, Braga: Universidade do Minho

OLIVEIRA, Eduardo Pires (1993) *Estudos sobre o século XVIII em Braga*, Braga: APPACDM

OLIVEIRA, Eduardo Pires (1994) 'Um Novo Mapa de Braga de Finais do Século XVII' in *Forum*, **15/16**, pp. 37-53, Braga: Universidade do Minho

OLIVEIRA, Eduardo Pires (1999) *Braga. Percursos e memórias de granito e oiro*, Porto: Campo de Letras

OLIVEIRA, Eduardo Pires (2001a) *Riscar, em Braga, no século XVIII e outros ensaios*, Braga: APPACDM

OLIVEIRA, Eduardo Pires (2001b) *A Freguesia de S. Victor (Braga)*, Braga: Junta de Freguesia de S. Victor

OLIVEIRA, Jorge de, Panagiotis Sarantopoulos and Carmen Balesteros (1997) *Antas-Capelas e Capelas junto a Antas no Território Português*, Lisboa: Edições Colibri

PARCERO OUBINA, C., F. C. Criado Boado and M. S. Santos Estevez (1998) 'Rewriting landscape: incorporating sacred landscapes into cultural traditions', *World Archaeology*, **30.1**, pp. 159-176

PEIXOTO, Inácio José (1992 [1790-1808]) *Memórias Particulares*, Braga: Arquivo Distrital/Universidade do Minho

PIRES, Maria Lucília Gonçalves (1991) 'Imagens quinhentistas do Brasil – retórica da descrição' in *Mare Liberum*, **3**, pp. 225-233, Lisboa: CNCDP

PREUCEL, Robert W. and Ian Hodder (1996) *Contemporary Archaeology in Theory. A Reader*, Oxford: Blackwell

PROENÇA, Maria José (1998) *A Ordem Terceira Franciscana em Braga e a sua igreja*, Braga: VOT S. Francisco

RÉAU, Louis (1955) *Iconographie de l'Art Chrétien*, Paris: Presses Universitaires de France

REIS, António Matos (1990) 'A Arte na Arquidiocese de Braga, sob a égide de arcebispo D. Rodrigo de Moura Teles (1704-1728): o estilo, as obras e os artistas' in *Actas do IX Centenário da dedicação da Sé de Braga*, volume II/2, pp. 373-394, Braga: Fac. de Teologia da Universidade Católica Portuguesa e Cabido Metropolitano e Primarcial de Braga

REIS, António Matos (1995) 'Caminhos da História da Arte no Noroeste de Portugal no Primeiro Quartel do Séc. XVIII' in *Cadernos Vianenses*, **19**, pp. 155-200, Viana do Castelo: Câmara Municipal de Viana de Castelo

RIBEIRO DA SILVA, Francisco (1994) 'Tempos Modernos' in Luís Oliveira Ramos (ed.), *História da Cidade do Porto*, pp. 254-375, Porto: Porto Editora

ROCHA, Manuel Joaquim Moreira da (1994) *Arquitectura Civil e Religiosa de Braga nos séculos XVII e XVIII. Os homens e as obras*, Braga: Centro de Estudos D. Domingos Pinho Brandão

ROCHA, Manuel Joaquim Moreira da (1996) *Manuel Fernandes da Silva: mestre e arquitecto de Braga: 1693-1751*, Porto: Centro de Estudos D. Domingos de Pinho Brandão

RODRIGUES, Jorge (1995) 'A Escultura Românica' in Paulo Pereira (ed.), *História da Arte Portuguesa*, volume 1, pp. 265-331, Círculo de Leitores

ROSA ARAÚJO, José (1990) 'Feitiçarias nos tempos de D. Frei Bartolomeu dos Mártires' in *Actas do IX Centenário da dedicação da Sé de Braga*, volume II/2, pp. 111-118, Braga: Fac. de Teologia da Universidade Católica Portuguesa and Cabido Metropolitano e Primarcial de Braga

ROSSA, Walter (1995) 'A cidade portuguesa' in Paulo Pereira (ed.), *História da Arte Portuguesa*, volume III, pp, 233-323, Círculo de Leitores

RUSSEL, Josiah Cox (1972) *Medieval Regions and their Cities*, Newton Abbot: David & Charles

SANTOS, Eugénio Francisco dos (1997) "Beneditinos e Oratorianos: vizinhos, contemporâneos…, diferentes" in *Comemorações do 4º Centenário da Fundação do Mosteiro de S. Bento da Vitória. Actas do Ciclo de Conferências*, pp. 221-237, Porto: Arquivo Distrital do Porto

SCHOFIELD John and Alan Vince (2003) *Medieval Towns*, 2nd ed., London: Continuum

SENNA FREITAS, Bernardino José (1890) *Memórias de Braga*, vols. I-V, Braga : Imprensa Católica

SERLIO, Sebastiano (1982 [1611]) *The five books of architecture*, New York: Dover Publications

SCHAMA, Simon (1995) *Landscape and Memory,* London: HarperCollins

SIMÕES, João Miguel dos Santos (1971) *Azulejaria em Portugal no século XVII*, Lisboa: Fundação Gulbenkian

SMAILES Arthur Eltringham (1953) *The Geography of Towns*, London: Hutchinson

SMITH, Robert (1968) 'A Casa da Câmara de Braga (1753-1756)' in *Bracara Augusta*, volume XXII, pp. 283-320, Braga: Câmara Municipal de Braga

SMITH, Robert (1972) *Três Estudos Bracarenses*, Braga: Livraria Cruz

SMITH, Robert (1973) *André Soares. Arquitecto do Minho*, Lisboa: Livros Horizonte

SMITH, A. and A. Brookes (eds) 2001, Holy Ground: theoretical issues relating to the landscape and material culture of ritual space objects: papers from a session held at the Theoretical Archaeology Group conference, Cardiff, 1999, BAR **956**, Oxford: BAR Publishing

SOARES, Franquelim Neiva (1983) *Visitações de Dom Frei Baltazar Limpo na Arquidiocese de Braga*, Braga : [s.n.]

SOARES, Franquelim Neiva (1997) *A Arquidiocese de Braga no Século XVII. Sociedade e Mentalidades pelas Visitações Pastorais (1550 – 1700)*, Braga: A.F.S.N.S

SOROMENHO, Miguel (1991) *Manuel Pinto de Vilalobos: da engenharia militar à arquitectura*, MA dissertation presented to Faculdade de Ciências Sociais e Humanas da Universidade Nova de Lisboa

SOUSA, Armindo de (1993) 'Realizações' in José Mattoso (ed.), *História de Portugal*, volume 2, pp. 483-547, Lisboa: Editorial Estampa

SOUSA PEREIRA, Ana Maria Magalhães (n/d) 'Do Campo de Santana ao Caminho Novo para o Bom Jesus do Monte Carvalho. A Casa Térrea no Século XVIII em Braga' in *Carlos Alberto Ferreira de Almeida. In memoriam*, pp. 187-201, Porto: Faculdade de Letras da Universidade do Porto

SOUSA PEREIRA, Ana Maria Magalhães (2000), *Da Casa Grande da Rua dos Pelames à Casa Nova da Rua de Dom Gualdim. Braga, Séculos XVII-XVIII*, Braga: APPACDM

TAYLOR, Mark C. (2001) *The Moment of Complexity. Emerging Network Culture*, Chicago: University of Chicago Press

TEIXEIRA, Manuel C. and Margarida Valla (1999) *O Urbanismo Português. Séculos XIII-XVIII. Portugal – Brasil*, Lisboa: Livros Horizonte

THOMAS, Julian (2001) 'Archaeologies of Place and Landscape' in Ian Hodder (ed.), *Archaeological Theory Today*, pp. 165-186. Cambridge: Polity Press, Blackwell

TILLEY, Christopher (1994) *A Phenomenology of Landscape*, Oxford: Berg

TOSH, John (2002) *The Pursuit of History*, Harlow: Pearson Education

TOURAULT, Philippe (1998) *História Concisa da Igreja*, Mem Martins: Europa-América

TOWNSEND, R.F. (1982) 'Pyramid and sacred mountain' in A.F. Aveni & G. Urton, *Ethnoastronomy and archaeoastronomy in the American tropics: Annals of the New York Academy of Sciences*, **385**, pp. 37-62

TRENS, Manuel (1946) *María. Iconografía de la Virgen en el arte español*, Madrid: Editorial Plus-Ultra

VEIGA DE OLIVEIRA, Ernesto (1984) *Festividades Cíclicas em Portugal*, Lisboa: Publicações Dom Quixote

VEIGA DE OLIVEIRA, Ernesto and Fernando Galhano (1992) *Arquitectura Tradicional Portuguesa*, Lisboa: Publicações Dom Quixote

VERÍSSIMO SERRÃO, Joaquim (1958) *Un itineraire Portugais à la fin du XVIIe. siécle*, Lisboa: Bertrand

VIEIRA DA SILVA, José Custódio (2002) *Paços Medievais Portugueses*, Lisboa: IPPAR

WHEATLEY, Paul (1971) *The Pivot of the Four Quarters: a preliminary enquiry into the origins and character of the ancient Chinese city*, Edinburgh: Edinburgh University Press

WOODWARD, Kathryn (1997) 'Concepts of Identity and Difference' in Kathryn Woodward (ed.), *Identity and Difference*, pp. 7-61, London: Sage

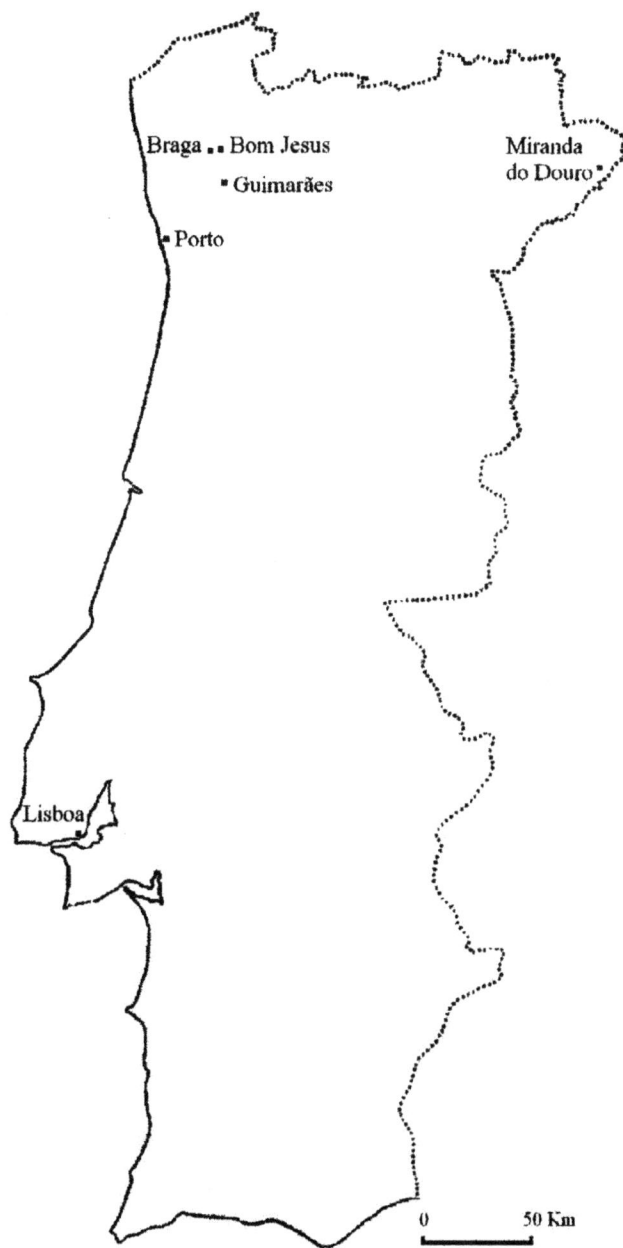

Fig. 1 – Map of Portugal.

Fig. 2 – Braga c. 1500 (map adapted from Teixeira and Valla 1999: 114).

A - R. Souto
B - R. Santa Maria
C - R. S. António
D - Market

1 - Cathedral
2 - Church of S. João do Souto
3 - Church of Cividade
4 - Church of S. Pedro
5 - Church of S. Vitor
6 - Chapel of S. Miguel
7 - Chapel of S. Sebastião
8 - Chapel of S. Vicente
9 - Episcopal palace
10 - Castle
11 - City Hall
12 - Maximinos Gate
13 - S. Francisco Gate
14 - Souto Gate
15 - S. Marcos Gate
16 - Santiago Gate
17 - Gallows

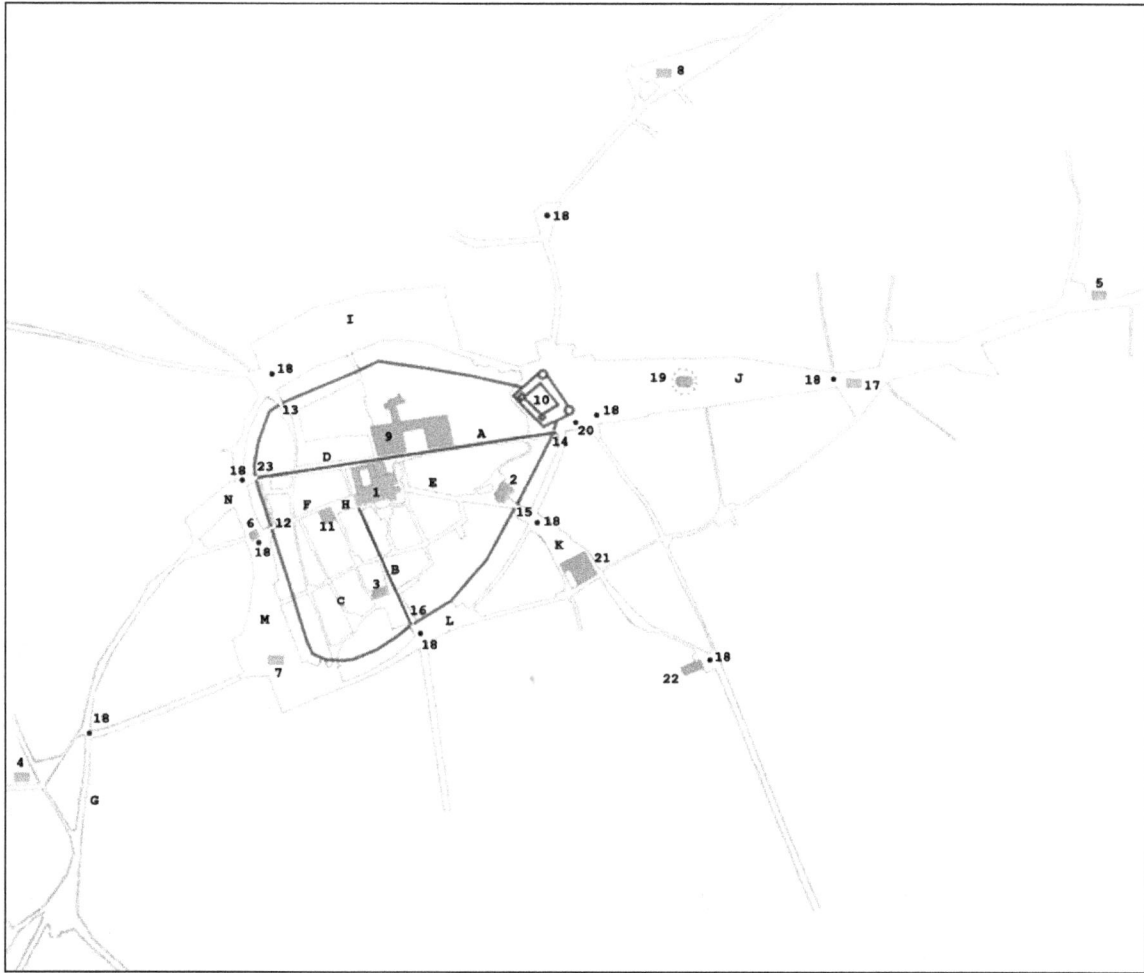

Fig. 3 – Braga in 1530 (map adapted from Teixeira and Valla 1999: 115).

──────── - T axis

A - R. Souto
B - R. Santa Maria
C - R. S. António
D - R. Sousa
E - R. S. Marcos
F - Praça do Pão
G - Campo da Vinha
H - Campo de Santana
I - Campo dos Remédios
J - Campo de Santiago
K - Campo de S. Sebastião
L - Campo das Hortas

1 - Cathedral
2 - Church of S. João do Souto
3 - Church of Cividade
4 - Church of S. Pedro
5 - Church of S. Vitor
6 - Chapel of S. Miguel

7 - Chapel of S. Sebastião
8 - Chapel of S. Vicente
9 - Episcopal palace
10 - Castle
11 - City Hall
12 - Maximinos Gate
13 - S. Francisco Gate
14 - Souto Gate
15 - S. Marcos Gate
16 - Santiago Gate
17 - Church of Nossa Senhora a Branca
18 - Chapel of Santana
19 - Chapel of Nossa Senhora do Amparo
20 - Pillory
21 - Hospital of S. Marcos
22 - Leper-house of S. Lázaro
23 - Nova Gate
24 - Cross

Fig. 4 – Braga in 1725 (map adapted from Teixeira and Valla 1999: 116).

———— - R. Misericórdia

A - R. Souto
B - R. Santa Maria
C - R. S. António
D - R. Sousa
E - R. S. Marcos
F - Praça do Pão
G - Campo da Vinha
H - Campo de Santana
I - Campo dos Remédios
J - Campo de Santiago
K - Campo de S. Sebastião
L - Campo das Hortas
M - R. Pelames
N - R. Misericórdia
O - Campo dos Touros
P - "Arcadia"
Q - Residential area on mount S. Margarida

1 - Cathedral
2 - Church of S. João do Souto
3 - Church of Cividade

4 - Church of S. Pedro
5 - Church of S. Vitor
6 - Chapel of S. Miguel
7 - Chapel of S. Sebastião
8 - Church of S. Vicente
9 - Episcopal palace
10 - Castle
11 - City Hall
12 - Maximinos Gate
13 - S. Francisco Gate
14 - Souto Gate
15 - S. Marcos Gate
16 - Santiago Gate
17 - Church of Nossa Senhora a Branca
18 - Chapel of Santana
19 - Chapel of Nossa Senhora do Amparo
20 - Pillory
21 - Hospital of S. Marcos
22 - Leper-house of S. Lázaro

23 - Nova Gate
24 - Cross
25 - Church of Mercy House
26 - Church of S. Paulo
27 - Church of Santa Cruz
28 - Church of the Third Order of St. Francis
29 - Chapel of Nossa Senhora da Guadalupe
30 - Convent of Remédios
31 - Convent of Salvador
32 - Convent of Pópulo
33 - Convent of Penha de França
34 - Congregation of the Oratory
35 - House of Rescue of Mary Magdalene
36 - Seminar
37 - College of Arts
38 - S. António Gate
39 - Gate to Campo de S. Sebastião
40 - Fountain
41 - Obelisk
42 - Arcade

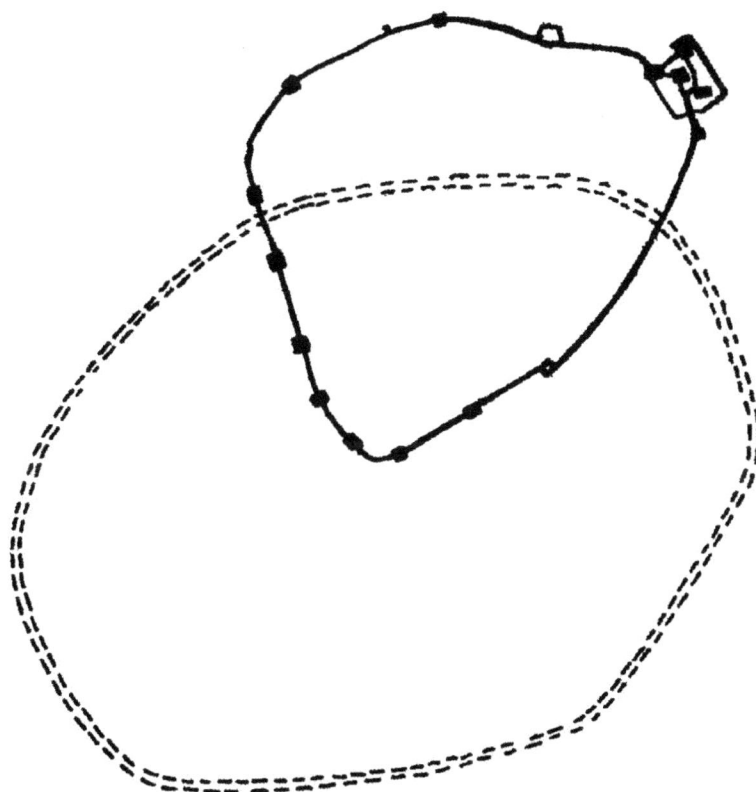

Fig. 5 – Area of Medieval Braga (single line) superimposed on the area of Roman Braga
(double line) (adapted from Bandeira 2000: 61).

Fig. 6 – Braga in an image of 1594
(source: Georg Braun, *Civitatis Orbis Terrarum*, volume V, fl. 3).

Fig. 7 – Medieval T/O map (source: St. Isidorus, *Etymologiarum*, libri XX).

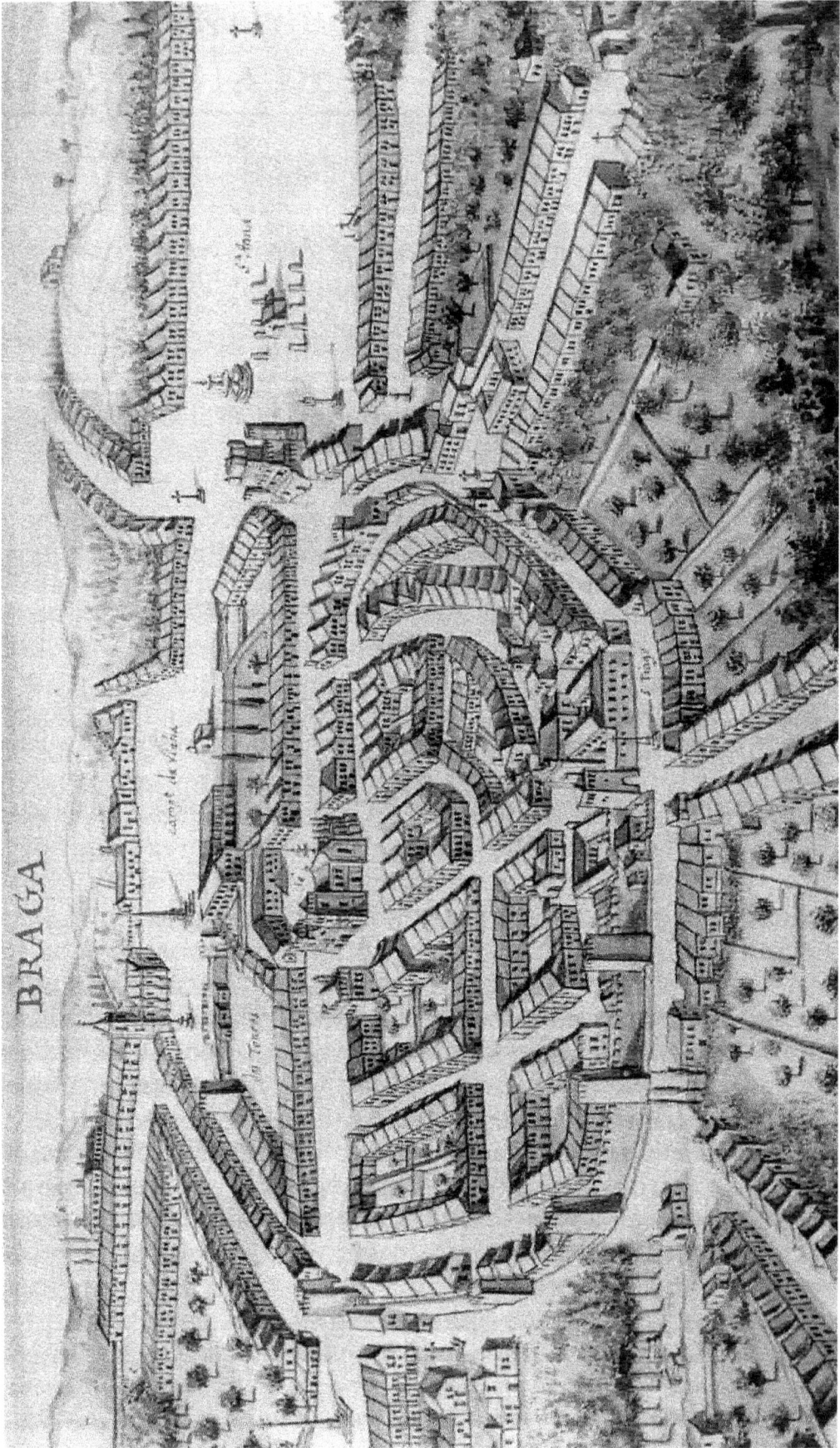

Fig. 8 – Braga in an image of c. 1694 (source: *Forum*, **15/16**, p. 23).

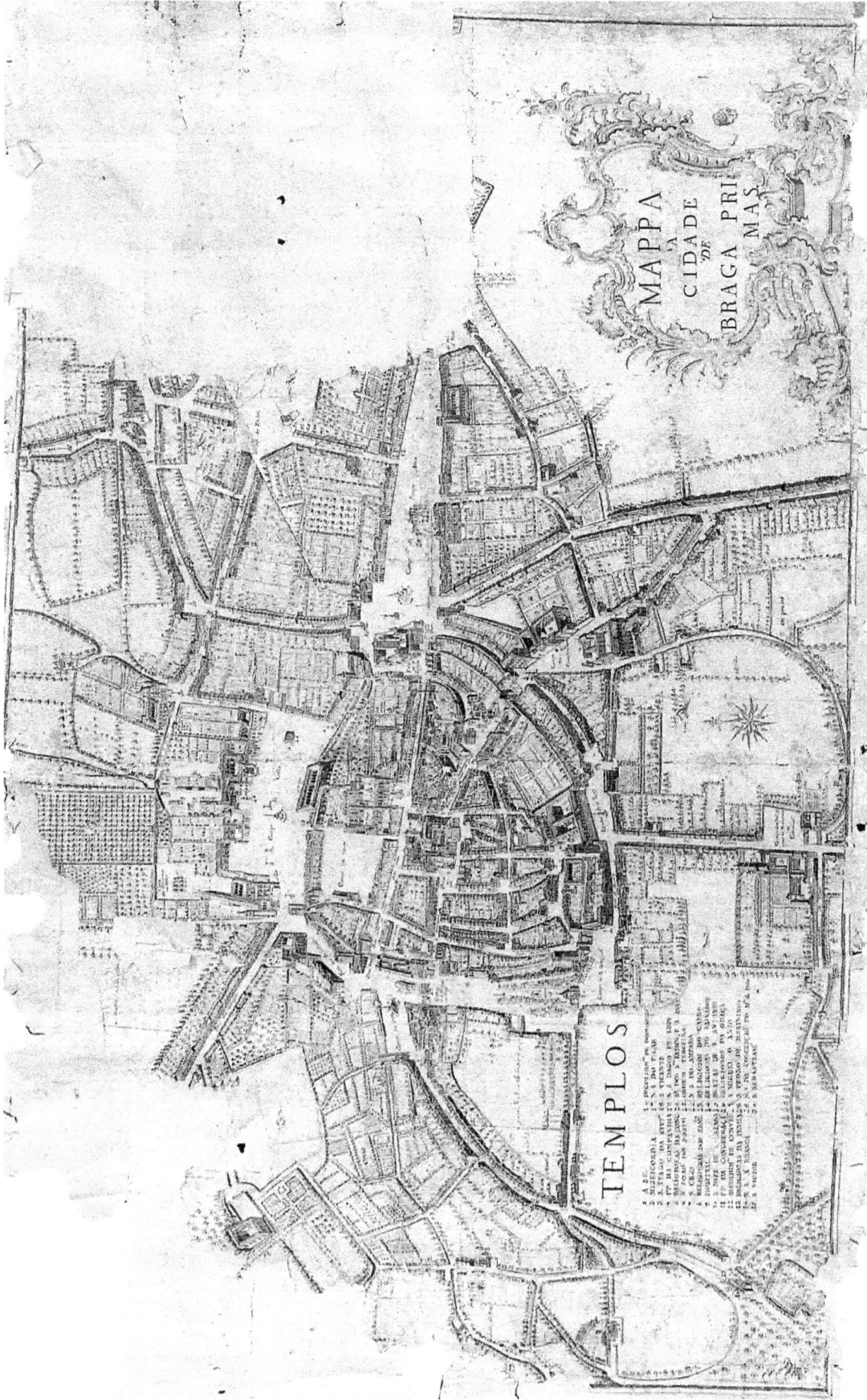

Fig. 9 – Braga in an image of c. 1757 (source: Biblioteca Nacional da Ajuda).

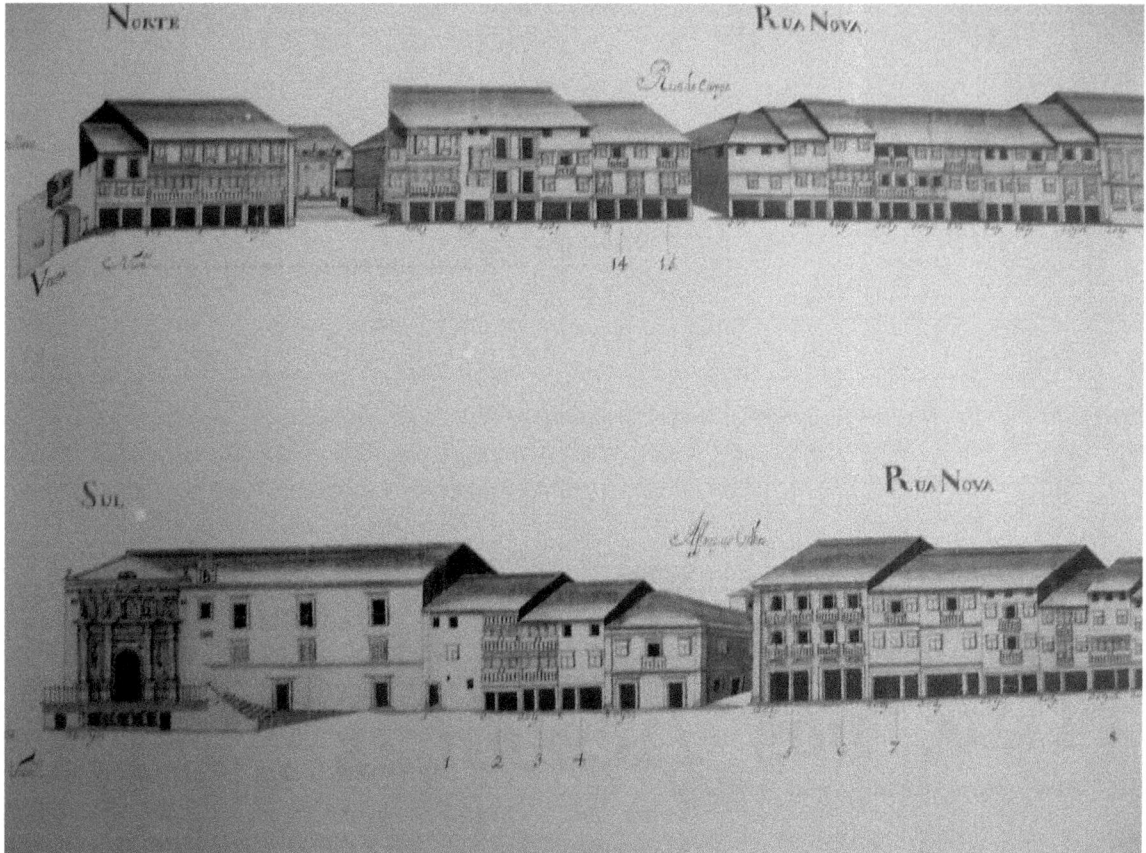

Fig. 10 – Section of R. Nova in the 1750 map. The Church of the Mercy House is on the lower left corner. (source: Mapa das Ruas de Braga).

Fig. 11 – The main façade of the Cathedral (author's collection).

Fig. 12 – A view of the main chapel of the Cathedral. Notice the statue of the Blessed Lady of the Milk below the window (author's collection).

Fig. 13 – Campo de Santiago: in the foreground, the 1625 fountain, in the background, the medieval tower (author's collection).

Fig. 14 – A view of the 15th century aisle of the Episcopal palace (author's collection).

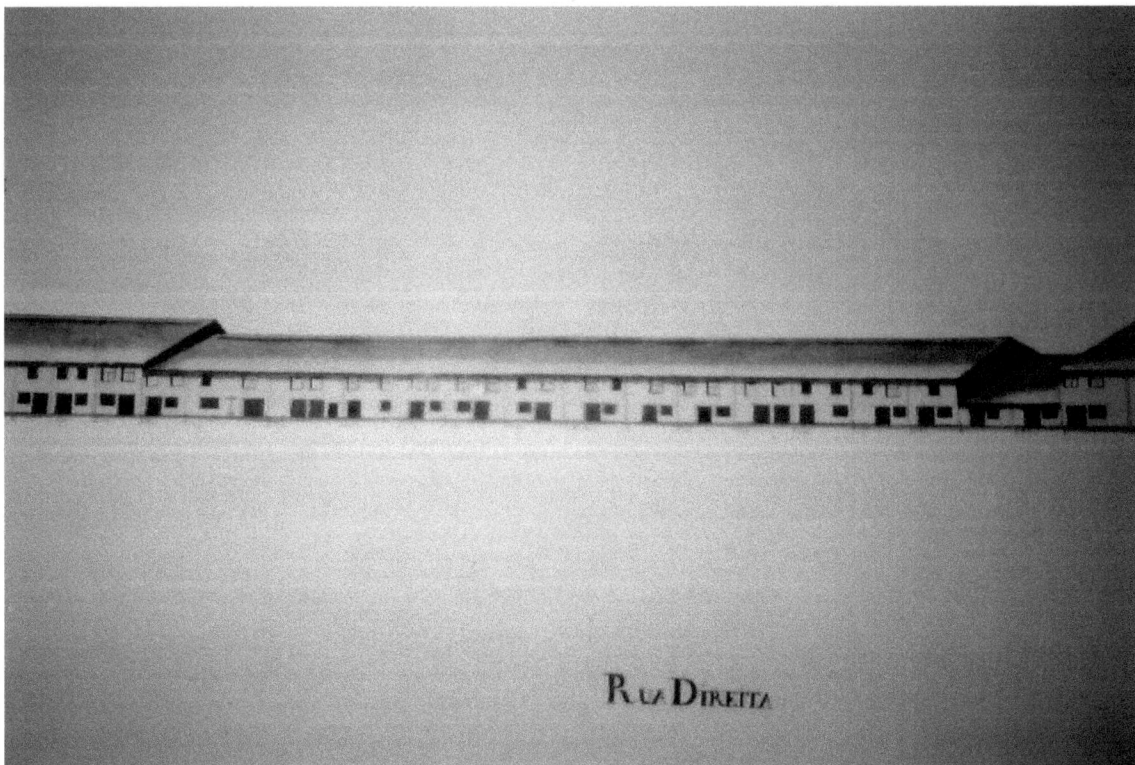

Fig. 15 – Partial view of R. Direita in the 1750 map (source: Mapa das Ruas de Braga).

Fig. 16 – Some noble houses in R. S. João in the 1750 map
(source: Mapa das Ruas de Braga).

Fig. 17 – The cross built by D. Diogo de Sousa in front of S. Marcos Gate (author's collection).

Fig. 18 – Church of S. Paulo (author's collection).

Fig. 19 – Decorated tiles of the early 17th century in the church of the convent of Salvador. The lower panel has abstract vegetation, while the upper one also has lozenges (source: author's collection).

Fig. 20 – The 1594 fountain that was built in Campo de Santana
(author's collection).

Fig. 21 – A view of the square in front of the entrance of the Episcopal palace: in the front the 1723 fountain in the back the late 16th century colonnade (author's collection).

Fig. 22 – The obelisk that was in Campo da Vinha
(author's collection).

Fig. 23 – The 1621 cross that was built in front of Gate Nova
(author's collection).

Fig. 24 – The main façade of the church of Santa Cruz
(author's collection).

Fig. 25 – The main façade of the church of S. Vítor
(author's collection).

Fig. 26 – Decorated tiles from the church of S. Vítor
(author's collection).

Fig. 27 – The main façade of church S. Vicente
(author's collection).

Fig. 28 – The main façade of the church of the Oratory
(author's collection).

Fig. 29 – Houses in R. Souto (source: Mapa das Ruas de Braga).

Fig. 30 – Church of S. Frutuoso (author's collection).

Fig. 31 – The arcade (to the right) in the 1750 map (source: Mapa das Ruas de Braga).

Fig. 32 – The 1715 statue representing Braga that was on top of the arcade (author's collection).

Fig. 33 – Chapel of Nossa Senhora da Guadalupe (author's collection).

Fig. 34 – Image of the Sanctuary of the Good Jesus in an 18th century image
(source: Luís Costa).

Fig. 35 – Pyramid-shape throne in the main altar of the church of S. Vítor
(author's collection)

Fig. 36 – The sanctuary of Good Jesus from the arcade in Campo de Santana. The two-towers church that presently is visible dates from the 19th century (author's collection)